CHIANG MAI

Photography and Text by

Luca Invernizzi Tettoni

ODYSSEY

Hong Kong

Published by The Guidebook Company Limited,
3/F, 20 Hollywood Road, Hong Kong

Grateful acknowledgement is made to the following authors and publishers for permissions granted:

Hodder & Stoughton Ltd for
Teak-Wallah by Reginald Campbell, © Hodder & Stoughton Ltd, 1935

Oxford University Press for
The Politician and Other Stories by Khamsing Srinawk, © Oxford University Press, 1973

Distribution in the United Kingdom, Ireland, Europe and certain Commonwealth countries by Hodder and Stoughton, Mill Road, Dunton Green, Sevenoaks, Kent TN13 2YA

Editor: Richard Lair
Series Editor: Claire Banham
Illustrations Editor: Caroline Robertson
Illustrations: Kittisak Nualvilai
Design: Christopher C Burt
Map Artwork: Bai Yiliang
Cover Concept: Raquel Jaramillo and Aubrey Tse

All photographs by Luca Invernizzi Tettoni
(except page 120 by Duangdao Suwannarangsi)

British Library Cataloguing in Publication Data has been applied for.

Production House: Twin Age Limited, Hong Kong
Printed in Hong Kong by Sing Cheong Printing Co. Ltd.

Contents

Special Topics

Maps

Excerpts

Introduction

Once known as the Kingdom of Lanna, northern Thailand with Chiang Mai as its major city is, in fact, the original seat of Thai culture and in many ways still the best place to see and understand the 'Thai Way'. A semi-autonomous region until the beginning of this century, northern Thailand retains a charm that is hard to express in words and indeed must be experienced first hand before one can understand the enthusiasm that the region engenders to its visitors. Is it the cool hazy air of sunny winter days or the happy countenance of its graceful people, or perhaps that special feeling that places of an old and enduring culture impart upon their landscapes that make it such a special place?

Part of the special appeal of northern Thailand is that it is so different from the rest of the country. Traditional art and architecture are distinctive with the styles of the ancient Lanna Kingdom characterising the indigenous temples and religious art. Cottage industries producing numerous types of handicrafts for long unique to the North are still flourishing while dances, cuisine, festivals and other cultural manifestations are distinct from those of other parts of the country.

The people, too, are different, with the northern Thais made more varied by influences from the neighboring countries of Burma, Laos and Yunnan province of China. Ultimately it is history that indelibly marks the region as different. It was here that the great Lanna kingdom was established in the thirteenth century with Chiang Mai as its capital. Despite mixed fortunes, including the 1558—1800 period of Burmese domination, the North retained a degree of independence until the early twentieth century. Such separate development has instilled in the people a very real belief in their own identity and a pride in their traditional way of life. There is a retention of basic values and gentle manners that justify Thailand's old sobriquet of the 'Land of Smiles'.

In recent years northern Thailand has been 'discovered' by the international tourist industry, first by the path–breaking budget travellers who came in the 1970s looking for adventure in the hills among the tribal people and their opium culture, and then the jet age tourists and their luxury hotel courtiers. However, like the legendary island of Bali, the people and culture of this region have remained strong enough to withstand the onslaught of foreign influences and have simply absorbed and adopted to change and the inevitable 'progress' of the now interdependent world of the 1980s.

The unprecedented economic boom of the past few years in Thailand is changing the physical landscape of northern Thailand and especially Chiang Mai. High–rise condominiums and new highways are being constructed at a feverish pace and the new rich of Bangkok have made it fashionable to have a summer home 'upcountry'. How this will affect the future of 'Lannaland' is hard to predict; perhaps the people will continue to adopt and absorb or maybe they will soon find themselves to be a minority in their own land. In any case, the sooner one visits northern Thailand the better, for the present is certainly more sure than the future.

Geography

Northern Thailand comprises roughly the area between the Shan Plateau of Burma and the Salween River to the west and the Mekong River and Laos to the east. Its present international borders are not defined by natural features but are rather the result of a series of treaties negotiated with England and France at the turn of the century and revised after World War II. The southern boundary of northern Thailand can be considered to be an imaginary line running from the town of Tak in the west to Uttaradit in the east. These boundaries approximate the limits of the ancient kingdom of Lanna, the whole area being governed from the capital of Chiang Mai, the city which is still the main commercial and administrative centre of the region.

In most people's minds 'the North' also includes the upper Central Plains, and therefore, for the purposes of this book, the ancient cities of Sukhothai and Sri Satchanalai have also been included. In fact these ruins had their origins in a different cultural milieu and have experienced a different history from Lanna.

The North is a mountainous region with an average altitude of 1,300 m (4,000 ft), the highest point being Doi Inthanon at 2,595 m (8,514 ft—*Doi* means 'high peak'). Most of the mountain chains are composed of limestone and schists from the Primary Period. Granitic outcrops from the Secondary Period occur in the Doi Khun Tan Range, at Doi Suthep, and at Doi Khun Bong. Several rivers traverse the mountain ranges from north to south, forming the flat and fertile alluvial plains that are the only areas of the region widely inhabited by Thai people, who are traditionally lowland cultivators. The mountains have always been the home of hilltribes and other minorities, peoples who have long enjoyed a special independence resulting from their isolation.

The main rivers of the North are the Ping (590 km long), the Wang (335 km), the Yom (555 km), and the Nan (627 km). The Mekong River, which for centuries played a major role in the history of Southeast Asia, now borders northern Thailand only for a short stretch and has lost much of its economic importance because, since the communist takeover in Laos, waterborne trade is no longer possible.

Before the advent of modern transportation, the convoluted geography of the region clearly dictated the path that social and economic development could take. A nearly impenetrable range of mountains—Doi Khun Kiat—separates the northern valleys from the Central Plains, and until the construction of a railway in the late 1920s, Lanna remained largely a world apart. The journey from Chiang Mai to Bangkok was made by boat, a hazardous trip because of the 16 cataracts that had to be negotiated along the upper reaches of the Ping River. Travelling upstream, the journey was made partly by river, poling the boat against the swift current, and partly on elephant back through the forest. The trip took several weeks. While contacts between Lanna and the Central Plains were always few, there was much trade and travel between Lanna, Burma, Laos and Yunnan province of China.

Ecology

Carl Bock, the Scandinavian explorer who travelled over the North one century ago, wrote in 1882, "Hardly a night passed without two or three heads of cattle being either wounded or carried off by marauding tigers ..." The mountains of Lanna were clearly once home to a rich fauna. Due to its location at the crossroads of three divergent faunal realms—the Indo–Burmese, the Malayan, and the Indo–Chinese—northern Thailand was populated by a large variety of species belonging to different worlds. This exceptionally interesting mix is still visible in the aviafauna, which has suffered less than the mammals from the assault of man. Within a radius of a few miles, one can find jays, rollers and hoopoes (belonging to the European and Indian realms), colorful sunbirds and sturdy hornbills (typical of the Malayan jungle), as well as Chinese egrets and Siberian robins (typical of regions further north).

Large mammals were to be found in great numbers. Wild elephants roamed the forests; captured and domesticated by numerous tribes, they were the most useful draught animal in the region. The now nearly extinct one–horned (Sumatran) rhinoceros and the two–horned (Indian) rhinoceros were also common. Several species of deer were quite common in the north: the sambar, the barking deer, the lesser mouse deer, and the hog deer—all very rare now—as well as the brow-antlered deer, now extinct in Thailand. Serow and goral, two species which are seemingly a primitive ancestor to both goats and antelopes, live on steep limestone mountains and have escaped extermination because of their peculiar habitat, nearly inaccessible to man. The tapir was also found in the North, along the Burmese border south of 18° of latitude. Large wild cattle included wild water buffalo; gaur, the enormous (weighing up to 900 kg) and aggressive bovine that feeds in open spaces of deciduous forest; and banteng, a somewhat less redoubtable but no less beautiful animal.

All large mammals are now extremely rare with only about 200 wild water buffalo left in all of Thailand. Tigers and leopards (which include the melanistic, or dark-pigmented, colour phase often mistakenly called 'black panthers') were once a menace to villagers but are now nearly extinct. Smaller cats (such as the marbled cat, jungle cat, leopard cat, Asian golden cat, and others) still survive in small numbers. The Tibetan black bear is now very rare, but the Malayan sun bear somehow survives and is often seen in cages at village fairs and temple zoos. Smaller mammals have better survived the encroachment of man. Still common are hog badgers, otters, mongooses, civets (including Indian civet, common palm civet, and masked palm civet), bush–tailed porcupine, weasels (Siberian weasel and black–striped weasel), many species of squirrels, rats (including the hairy bamboo rat) and bats.

Primates of northern Thailand include the aptly named slow loris, several species of macaque (rhesus, Assamese, stump–tailed, and pig–tailed macaque) and the white–handed gibbon. All are commonly hunted in order to steal newborn babies from the mother and sell them as pets. Few infants survive the fall from the trees when the mother is shot dead, and even fewer

Northern Thailand

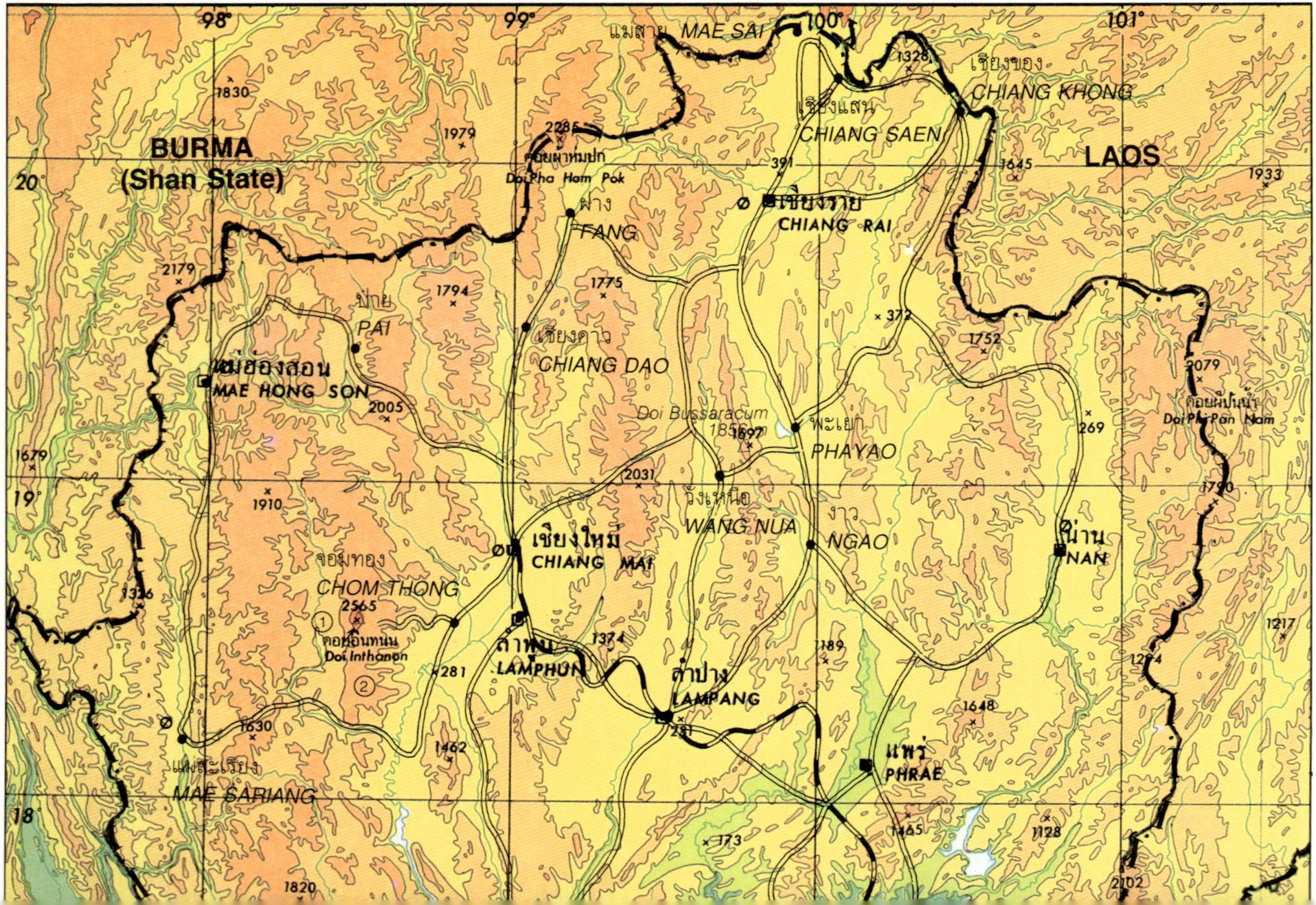

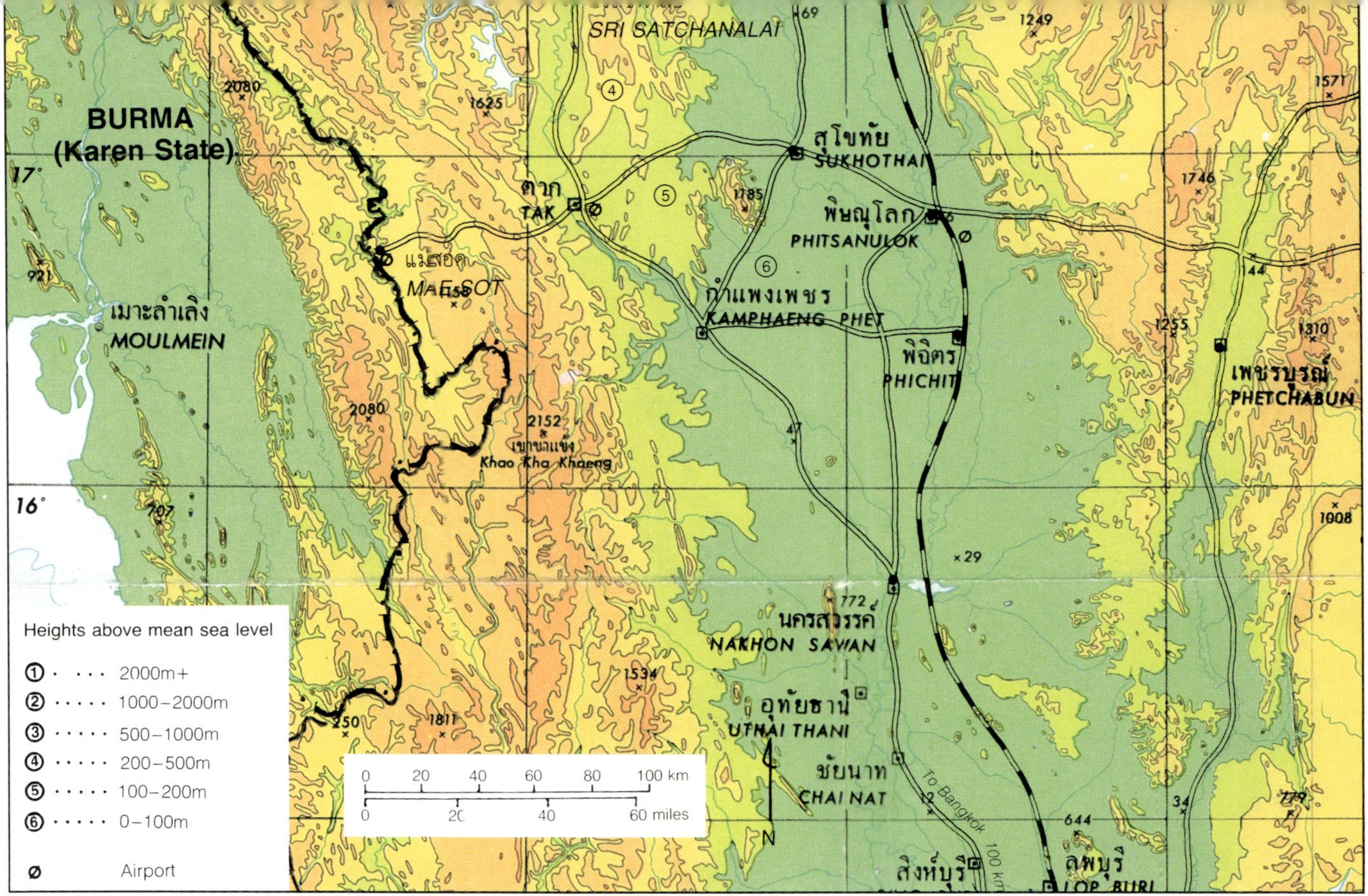

Royal Thai Survey Dept.

Climate

Thailand lies within the monsoon belt of the tropics and its climate is dictated by these seasonal winds and their interaction with local geographic features. The monsoons are generated by differences in temperature between the land mass of continental Asia and the oceanic bodies to the south and east. In Thailand, they blow alternatively from the southwest and the north-east. As a result there are three distinct seasons.

The southwest monsoon, normally blowing from May to October, carries moisture from the Indian Ocean which falls as rain over the whole country to produce what is always called—though somewhat misleadingly—the 'rainy season'. Precipitation varies from as much as 4,375 mm (175 inches) on the windward coasts of Phang Nga province in the South to only 875 mm (35 inches) on the leeward slopes of the mountain ranges paralleling the Burmese border. This season, with moderate temperatures of 23°C–33°C (75°F–90°F), is actually not a bad time to visit Thailand. Although the first thunderstorms of late April and May are sometimes violent enough to produce large hail-stones and high winds, the rains are not continuous but generally confined to short, sharp bursts that are more refreshing than tiresome. However, many unsurfaced roads become impassable during this time of year, so trekking in the hills may be difficult and unpleasant. September is the rainiest month of all.

The northeast monsoon draws cool, dry air from the Asian interior down over Thailand from November to February, resulting in mild and dry weather in all parts of the country north of Bangkok. The best time to visit northern Thailand is during this cool season when the average temperature ranges between 13°C–28°C (55°F–82°F) and sometimes much cooler at night; frost occurs occasionally above 1,856 meters (5,000 ft) in the mountains. The coolest months are December and January, when the mornings are crisp, the days warm and sunny, and the evenings chilly. This season coincides with the beautiful Loy Krathong Festival (November) and Chiang Mai's Flower Festival (early February); flowers are blooming and many temperate fruits, such as strawberries, are in fruition. During November and December the opium poppies are harvested.

The pre–monsoonal period, when the winds switch from northeast to southwest coincides with the sun moving northward across the equator and results in the so–called hot season of March to mid–May. During this season, which can be dusty and uncomfortable, the temperature ranges between 21°–40°C (73°F–104°F). The hottest month is April when temperatures exceed 38°C (100°F) every day and have been known to reach 45°C (113°F) in some parts of the North. Without a doubt this is the worst time of year to visit northern Thailand.

The following charts illustrate weather conditions at four representative locations in the North:

CHIANG MAI

314m (1,030 ft) 18° 47'N 98° 59' E 30 years

M	Temperature F° Highest recorded	Temperature F° Average daily max	Temperature F° Average daily min	Temperature F° Lowest recorded	Temperature C° Highest recorded	Temperature C° Average daily max	Temperature C° Average daily min	Temperature C° Lowest recorded	Precipitation Average monthly in	Precipitation Average monthly mm
J	97°	84°	56°	43°	*36*	*29*	*13*	*6*	.0	*0*
F	97°	89°	58°	49°	*36*	*32*	*14*	*9*	.4	*10*
M	102°	94°	63°	55°	*39*	*34*	*17*	*13*	.3	*8*
A	108°	97°	71°	59°	*43*	*36*	*22*	*15*	1.4	*36*
M	106°	94°	73°	67°	*41*	*34*	*23*	*19*	4.8	*122*
J	100°	90°	74°	69°	*38*	*32*	*23*	*19*	4.4	*112*
J	99°	88°	74°	66°	*37*	*31*	*23*	*19*	8.4	*213*
A	99°	94°	74°	70°	*37*	*31*	*23*	*21*	7.6	*193*
S	96°	88°	73°	65°	*36*	*31*	*23*	*18*	9.8	*249*
O	96°	87°	70°	60°	*36*	*31*	*21*	*16*	3.7	*94*
N	99°	86°	66°	54°	*37*	*30*	*19*	*12*	1.2	*31*
D	97°	83°	59°	43°	*36*	*28*	*15*	*6*	.5	*13*

MAE HONG SON

417 m (1,376 ft.) 19° 18' N 97° 50'E 30 years

M	Temperature F° Highest recorded	Temperature F° Average daily max	Temperature F° Average daily min	Temperature F° Lowest recorded	Temperature C° Highest recorded	Temperature C° Average daily max	Temperature C° Average daily min	Temperature C° Lowest recorded	Precipitation Average monthly in	Precipitation Average monthly mm
J	94°	86°	57°	43°	*34*	*30*	*14*	*6*	.5	*13*
F	99°	91°	57°	46°	*37*	*33*	*14*	*8*	.1	*2*
M	103°	97°	63°	51°	*39*	*36*	*17*	*11*	.3	*7*
A	107°	100°	72°	60°	*42*	*38*	*22*	*15*	1.8	*46*
M	106°	95°	75°	68°	*41*	*35*	*24*	*20*	6.9	*171*
J	103°	90°	75°	69°	*39*	*32*	*24*	*21*	7.3	*182*
J	97°	88°	73°	70°	*36*	*31*	*23*	*21*	8.5	*211*
A	94°	88°	73°	69°	*34*	*31*	*23*	*21*	10.4	*261*
S	95°	88°	73°	67°	*35*	*31*	*23*	*20*	9.8	*226*
O	95°	90°	72°	60°	*35*	*32*	*22*	*15*	4.1	*103*
N	95°	88°	66°	53°	*35*	*31*	*19*	*12*	1.0	*24*
D	93°	84°	61°	47°	*34*	*29*	*16*	*8*	.3	*8*

CHIANG RAI

394 m (1,300ft.) 19° 55' N 99° 50' E 30 years

M	Temperature F° Highest recorded	Temperature F° Average daily max	Temperature F° Average daily min	Temperature F° Lowest recorded	Temperature C° Highest recorded	Temperature C° Average daily max	Temperature C° Average daily min	Temperature C° Lowest recorded	Precipitation Average monthly in	Precipitation Average monthly mm
J	89°	81°	53°	35°	*32*	*27*	*12*	*2*	.7	*19*
F	94°	86°	55°	43°	*35*	*30*	*13*	*6*	.4	*9*
M	100°	91°	59°	49°	*38*	*33*	*15*	*10*	1.2	*28*
A	106°	95°	66°	52°	*41*	*35*	*19*	*11*	2.9	*72*
M	106°	91°	72°	63°	*41*	*33*	*32*	*17*	8.9	*224*
J	101°	90°	73°	65°	*38*	*32*	*23*	*18*	9.9	*249*
J	101°	88°	73°	67°	*38*	*31*	*23*	*19*	11.7	*292*
A	95°	88°	72°	65°	*35*	*31*	*22*	*18*	17.4	*436*
S	96°	88°	72°	65°	*36*	*31*	*22*	*18*	10.4	*260*
O	95°	86°	68°	55°	*35*	*30*	*20*	*13*	5.2	*130*
N	92°	84°	63°	42°	*33*	*29*	*17*	*6*	1.4	*35*
D	89°	81°	55°	40°	*32*	*27*	*13*	*4*	.9	*23*

TAK

115m (379 ft) 16° 51' N 99° 07' E 30 years

M	Temperature F° Highest recorded	Temperature F° Average daily max	Temperature F° Average daily min	Temperature F° Lowest recorded	Temperature C° Highest recorded	Temperature C° Average daily max	Temperature C° Average daily min	Temperature C° Lowest recorded	Precipitation Average monthly in	Precipitation Average monthly mm
J	98°	90°	59°	40°	*37*	*32*	*15*	*5*	.2	*4*
F	104°	95°	66°	52°	*40*	*35*	*19*	*11*	.2	*5*
M	107°	99°	73°	53°	*42*	*37*	*23*	*12*	[illegible]	[illegible]
A	110°	100°	79°	63°	*43*	*38*	*26*	*17*	1.8	*45*
M	109°	95°	77°	68°	*43*	*35*	*25*	*20*	7.6	*189*
J	101°	91°	77°	72°	*38*	*33*	*25*	*22*	3.6	*89*
J	101°	90°	77°	71°	*38*	*32*	*25*	*22*	4.0	*100*
A	99°	90°	77°	65°	*37*	*32*	*25*	*18*	4.0	*100*
S	97°	90°	75°	65°	*36*	*32*	*24*	*18*	9.7	*241*
O	95°	88°	73°	63°	*35*	*31*	*23*	*17*	6.5	*161*
N	95°	88°	68°	51°	*35*	*31*	*20*	*11*	1.6	*41*
D	97°	86°	61°	45°	*36*	*30*	*16*	*7*	.2	*4*

find their way to a cage. In the past, hilltribe people believed that the call of gibbons had a magical and beneficial effect on crops, and until very recently they protected this monkey; however, the increasing cash value of gibbons as pets coupled with a faltering of traditional values and beliefs have ensured that few gibbons are now seen around hilltribe settlements.

Today just about the only fearsome animals likely to be met in the jungles are leeches and the thirteen species of poisonous snakes which now thrive, thanks to the man–caused disappearance of the predatory eagles and hawks which used to regulate their numbers.

It is often believed that Buddhists are reluctant to take the life of animals, even the humblest, and therefore shun hunting. But if this was the case, the forests would still abound with wild animals. *The National Resources Profile*, published in 1987 by the National Research Institute of Thailand, admits quite frankly that today no large mammals survive outside the boundaries of National Parks.

Small mammals—such as civets, pangolins, and monkeys—are very easily seen, not in their forest habitat but rather in such depressing places as the 'jungle market' along the road from Chiang Mai to Lampang. Caged or tied with ropes or wire, they are lined up alongside wild honey combs and bamboo shoots, waiting to be butchered and eaten. The extermination of this rich fauna is not for the fur trade, as the Thais never learned to treat skins properly, but simply to add some protein to the diet without the nuisance of raising cattle or chickens. Numerous superstitions related to the supposed medicinal properties of various animals also play a role. A stellar example is the Chinese belief in the aphrodisiacal powers of rhinoceros horn, which has led to the imminent disappearance of two of the three Asian species of rhinoceros from the face of the earth.

Although hunting has been going on for centuries, wild animals were still relatively abundant as recently as thirty years ago. The factor that has greatly accelerated their extinction is the destruction of their habitat, largely stimulated by a dramatic increase in the human population coupled with an increased use of machinery. In Thailand, as in much of the world, an increase in food supply after World War II, augmented by greatly improved medical care and eradication of endemic diseases such as malaria, has allowed the human population to expand and utilize habitats that once sheltered large mammals.

The mountains of the North used to be covered by forests, both evergreen and deciduous. Evergreen forests are of many types, including tropical evergreen, hill evergreen, and coniferous forests. Typical tropical evergreen forest occurs from sea level to 1,000 metres (3,300 ft) in areas of at least 2,000 mm (80 inches) of rainfall and is quite rare in Thailand; it is found almost exclusively in the South. More common is the semi–evergreen and the dry evergreen forest, which is often mixed with bamboo and deciduous trees as well as grasslands. Hill evergreen forest, characterized by a low two–level canopy (true tropical evergreen forest has <u>four</u> layers of foliage reaching 60 m (200 ft) in height is found in the provinces of Chiang Mai, Chiang Rai, Tak, and Mae Hong Son. The dominant trees are oaks and chestnuts; orchids, mosses, ferns, and epiphytes are common in these moist, cloudy forests. Small areas of coniferous (pine) forests are also found in the North and, when they are not introduced species as a result of recent reforestation, they are a relic of a more widespread belt of pine forest existing since the cooler Pleistocene Epoch.

Deciduous forests are the most extensive type in Thailand, particularly in the North. They are found in areas with more pronounced seasons, and the bush and grass between and under the trees is easily burned during the dry season. In comparison with the evergreen forests, more light penetrates the lower levels of deciduous trees and consequently the undergrowth is much denser, providing a larger number and variety of animals with an ecological niche. The dominant trees are many kinds of dipterocarps, the most famous species of which is teak.

Virtually all forests in Thailand have been cyclically cleared for agriculture over the past ten thousand years, but in recent years the languid clearing-and-regrowth cycle has been disrupted. The pace of deforestation has accelerated rapidly since the first decade of the century, the tempo quickening since the 1960s. In 1961, 53% of the whole country was covered by forest, while in 1986 only 29% of the canopy forest cover was left—according to official figures. Conservationists are more pessimistic and put the figure for canopy forest as low as 20%, or even 15%, since official figures are based on satellite photographs which tend to count orchards and second growth as true forest.

The North, which in 1961 had 68.54% of the land still covered by forest, saw that figure reduced to 49.59% in 1985. The problem in the North is not merely a local problem since northern forests protect the watersheds of major rivers flowing into the Chao Phraya River, and the denudation of watersheds can cause heavy floods in vital areas of the nation.

Behind this catastrophic decline in forest cover there are three different factors: legal and illegal logging, slash-and-burn cultivation practised by the hilltribes, and encroachment by illegal settlers. While some effort is being exerted into checking the first two factors, encroachment by landless Thai farmers has now been accepted as inevitable since nobody wants to face the political consequences of displacing the ethnic Thai paupers. Since 1979 the Royal Forest Department has allowed illegal squatters in forest reserves to claim up to 50 rai (about 20 acres) of land each. As a result of this laisser-faire policy, during the years 1961–1985, 124,575 square kilometres of forest land were encroached, mainly in the North and the Northeast.

If little has been done to prevent deforestation, even less is being done to restore and replant lost areas. At the present pace of reforestation, making the unlikely assumption that existing forests are kept pristine, it would take 115 years to return to the same same degree of forest cover as existed twenty years ago.

At a time when there is worldwide concern about the destruction of the world's tropical forests, Thailand's forests continue to vanish at the horrifying pace of one million hectares per year. And vanishing with the forest is the rich fauna that lives within. The prognosis for a healthy ecological balance in

northern Thailand is bleak, but a gleam of hope is offered by an increasing concern on the part of Thai public opinion from all social classes. A good example is a proposed cable car going up Doi Suthep, planned in the early 1980s by a private development firm. Although the project made its way through a long bureaucratic process, the public perceived it as a desecration of a mountain that is not only a National Park but also the symbol of Chiang Mai and the site of a much revered temple. Polls revealed that most of the local population opposed the project, demonstrations were staged, and provincial authorities finally decided to shelve the project indefinitely.

Another positive case was the controversy over the proposed Nam Choan Dam, which would have cut into three sections the Thung Yai Wildlife Sanctuary; the project has now been cancelled, after a vehement campaign by conservation groups and concerned individuals, both in Thailand and abroad, which included the Thai press decrying the dam's irreversible effects. Even more importantly, in January 1989, all logging was banned in the country, following a disastrous flood in the southern provinces that killed more than 350 people in November of 1988. Aerial photographs of thousands of logs which washed down from the mountains and swept away entire villages were testimony eloquent enough to convince virtually everybody that conservation must become a national priority.

Besides logging, the forest faces one other very specific danger which is omnipresent in the mountains. Slash-and-burn cultivation, also called swidden or shifting agriculture, is the most primitive form of agriculture, a method practised since the early phases of civilization. In the Thailand of millennia ago, small communities used to farm in fertile pockets of upland areas and hunt in the periodically inundated lowlands. Only later did domestication of the water buffalo enable man to plough the fields and water management technology allow man to utilize lowland areas which were naturally irrigated, though only by periodic monsoon rains.

Slash-and-burn is the most efficient method for farming in the hills (at least so long as ecological factors are disregarded), and is based on cutting trees and bushes during the winter, letting them dry during the hot season, and then burning the logs and stumps in time to plant a crop early in the rainy season. The resultant ashes are sufficiently rich in nutrients to fertilize the soil for a short number of years, but cleared patches must be rotated continuously if erosion is to be avoided. If abandoned after only one year of growth, fields will return to forest within fifteen years, though full maturity will take longer.

The Karen practise slash-and-burn agriculture in this ecologically sound, short-cycle manner. When abused by shifting tribal groups that do not rotate the fields, such as the opium-growing hilltribes that have moved into northern Thailand in this century (the Hmong, Akha, etc.), slash-and-burn becomes very destructive. The forests degenerate into grasslands—or even bare hillsides—which can support almost no wildlife, and the barren slopes become prone to landslides and flash-floods which can bring disaster to the lowlands.

The People of Lanna

The origins of the Thai people have been an object of contentious academic debate for as long as Thai scholarship has existed. Conventional scholarship long had it that the Tai people originated in southern China and ultimately ruled a state called Nan Chao, from which they fled in the face of a Mongol invasion in the twelfth century. One contemporary school accepts the geographic origin but insists that the migration began many centuries earlier. An affiliation with the Chinese in the larger Sino–Tibetan group, formerly taken for granted, has been seriously questioned, and a new link with the Indonesian group, based primarily on certain linguistic similarities, has been proposed. Dr. Sumet Jumsai analyzing the amphibious habits of the Thai in his study, *Naga: Cultural Origins in Siam and the West Pacific*, postulates nothing less than a migration from Polynesia. At the same time, many Thai scholars insist that the Thai people are actually autochthonous, that is they originated in Thailand but then migrated north to Yunnan before subsequently descending to Thailand once again in the second millennium.

The debate promises to be never ending. While few serious studies have been undertaken, too many chauvinistic ideologies taint the results of what should be objective research. Under the Pibul Songram regime, which changed the country's old name of Siam into Thailand, 'Land of the Thai', a strong nationalism was felt necessary to nurture the young democracy. In order to modernize the country, attempts were made to minimize cultural and ethnic diversities and to present the history of Thailand as the progressive evolution of one single race in a quest for freedom. Although this ideology is no longer reflected in the official policy of the country, nationalistic feelings still surface in the work of many authors and certainly pervade much of the jingoistic writing that is likely to affect the man in the street.

Wherever their ultimate origin, however, at some point in history the Tai peoples were all in southern China, centered around what is now Yunnan province, and from there they moved southward and fanned out to settle in what is today Vietnam, Burma, Thailand, Laos, and Assam. Many people of Tai lineage and language are still living in Yunnan today. The Tai family includes several groups, each one speaking a different language within the larger linguistic family and each having individual cultural features. During the wanderings each ethno-linguistic group has assimilated local elements and evolved to different degrees of development.

The country that is today called Thailand has received several separate waves of migration or, perhaps more accurately, a continuous filtering in of people who gradually blended into the resident population. The Tai groups who established themselves in the valley of the Chao Phraya River found a well–cultivated and irrigated land inhabited by two highly civilized peoples, the Mons and the Khmers, which were overcome and eventually assimilated. The Tai groups which settled in the northern regions found a more difficult environment—a jungle-clad, mountainous land. Thus, the Tai of the Chao

Here Comes the Bride

When a king of Siam would take unto himself a wife, he chooses a maiden from a family of the highest rank, and of royal pedigree, and, inviting her into the guarded circle of his women, entertains her there in that peculiar state of probation which is his prerogative and her opportunity. Should she prove so fortunate as to engage his preference, it may be his pleasure to exalt her to the throne; in which event he appoints a day for the formal consummation of his gracious purpose, when the principal officers, male and female, of the court, with the priests, Brahmin as well as Buddhist, and the royal astrologers, attend to play their several parts in the important drama.

The princess, robed in pure white, is seated on a throne elevated on a high platform. Over this throne is spread a canopy of white muslin, decorated with white and fragrant flowers, and through this canopy are gently showered the typical waters of consecration, in which have been previously infused certain leaves and shrubs emblematic of purity, usefulness, and sweetness. While the princess is thus delicately sprinkled with compliments, the priests enumerate, with nice discrimination, the various graces of mind and person which henceforth she must study to acquire; and pray that she may prove a blessing to her lord, and herself be richly blessed. Then she is hailed queen, with a burst of exultant music.

Now the sisters of the king conduct her by a screened passage to a chamber regally appointed, where she is divested of her dripping apparel, and arrayed in robes becoming her queenly state,—robes of silk, heavy with gold, and sparkling with diamonds and rubies. Then the king is ushered into her presence by the ladies of the court; and at the moment of his entrance she rises to throw herself at his feet, according to the universal custom. But he prevents her; and taking her right hand, and embracing her, seats her beside him, on his right. There she receives the formal congratulations of the court, with which the ceremonies of the day terminate. The evening is devoted to feasting and merriment.

A Siamese king may have two queens at the same time; in which case the more favored lady is styled the "right hand," and the other the "left hand," of the throne. His late Majesty, Maha Mongkut, had two queens, but not "in conjunction." The first was of the right hand; the second, though chosen in the lifetime of the first, was not elevated to the throne until after the death of her predecessor.

When the bride is a foreign princess, the ceremonies are more public, being conducted in the Hall of Audience, instead of the Ladies' Temple, or private chapel.

The royal nuptial couch is consecrated with peculiar forms. The mystic thread of unspun cotton is wound around the bed seventy-seven times, and the ends held in the hands of priests, who, bowing over the sacred symbol, invoke blessings on the bridal pair. Then the nearest relatives of the bride are admitted, accompanied by a couple who, to use the obstetrical figure of the indispensable Mrs. Gamp, have their parental quiver "full of sich." These salute the bed, sprinkle it with the consecrated waters, festoon the crimson curtains with flowery garlands, and prepare the silken sheets, the pillows and cushions; which done, they lead in the bride, who has not presided at the entertainments, but waited with her ladies in a screened apartment.

On entering the awful chamber, she first falls on her knees, and thrice salutes the royal couch with folded hands, and then invokes protection for herself, that she may be preserved from every deadly sin. Finally, she is disrobed, and left praying on the floor before the bed, while the king is conducted to her by his courtiers, who immediately retire.

The same ceremony is observed in nearly all Siamese families of respectability, with, of course, certain omissions and variations adapted to the rank of the parties.

Anna Harriette Leonowens,
The English Governess at the Siamese Court *(1871)*

The Languages of the North

Over 80% of the people in Thailand speak related languages all belonging to the Tai or Daic language family, a language group that includes several tens of millions of speakers in northern Vietnam, southern China, Assam, Burma (especially the Shan States), Laos and Thailand. In this book, consistent with standard scholarly usage, 'Tai' refers to the larger linguistic group, while 'Thai' refers to citizens of Thailand, whatever language they speak. In Thailand today there are four major dialects of Thai: Southern Thai, Lao or *issan* (in the Northeast), Siamese or Central Thai (in the Central Plains), and *kham meuang* or Northern Thai (in the North). In northern Thailand there are also smaller groups of speakers of other distinctive Tai languages such as Shan (primarily by peoples who have come from northern Burma and Laos) and Tai Lüe (primarily people who have come from south China).

The spoken language of the North is most often called 'Northern Thai' in English; in the Thai of the Central Plains it is called simply *phasaa neua* or 'Northern Language', a name which indicates the extremely close relationship of the two languages. The Northerners themselves call their language *kham meuang* or 'Language of the Principalities'.

Although most often described as a dialect, Northern Thai has at least an equal stature with Central Thai as seen from a historical perspective—especially if we discount the last 50 or so years, which have brought a cultural invasion from the South. In fact, the two languages differ to about the same extent as, for example, Spanish and Portuguese.

Northern Thai is spoken by about 20% of the total Thai population; only 25% of the population speaks Central Thai as a first language, though some 97% of the population does speak reasonably fluent Central Thai. Central Thai (or the so–called 'Standard Thai') is the official language of government, schools and mass communications, and it is now clearly thought by all to be the lingua franca of the country. While there is absolutely no attempt to suppress the use of Northern Thai, this linguistic heritage is fast being eroded by modern influences (primarily state schools, television, and magazines) just as surely as dialectical differences are vanishing in America or Europe. It is not unusual to see a mother, for example, talk to her children in Northern Thai, while the children—understanding every word—answer in Central Thai. The dominance of Central Thai recalls Max Weinreich's aphorism, "A language is a dialect that has an army and a navy," though in fact "A language is a dialect that has a television station," might be more to the point.

Besides speakers of various branches of Northern Thai, the region also holds speakers of other Austroasiatic languages including pockets of Mon (especially around Lamphun), Lawa, Thin, and Khamu. There are also speakers of tribal languages not of Austroasiatic origin, including Karen (a people who have long inhabited the region) and the languages of such newcomers as the Hmong, Mien, Akha, Lahu and Lisu; these tribal groups collectively constitute perhaps slightly less than 1% of the total Thai population.

Northern Thai Food

Like its customs, language and architecture, northern Thailand has a cuisine that is largely distinct—one more aspect of everyday life that contributes to the flavour of an independent culture. It certainly contrasts with central Thai cooking and many of the really typical local dishes are impossible to find in Bangkok, but the influences of neighbouring regions are clearly felt. As in so many northern temples, the food has an overlay of much that is Laotian and Burmese.

The staple of the Lanna diet is not the soft, fragrant boiled rice of the Central Plains but is 'sticky rice', a different strain. Known locally as *khaaw niow*, cooking is by steaming, and eating is by fingers, each person kneading successive small handfuls into a small ball to scoop up food from communal dishes.

Sticky rice is essentially Laotian, as are also the special spicy dips of the North. Known generically as *nam phrik*, these are found all over Thailand, but the North has its unique varieties. *Nam phrik ong* is relatively mild, made with minced pork and tomatoes and sometimes unkindly referred to as 'Thai spaghetti sauce'; an essential accompaniment is crispy pork skin. *Nam phrik num* is more fiery, being principally a bowl of pounded young green chillies that are a few inches long. *Nam phrik tadaeng* ('Redeye Dip') is made from dried red chillies and should also be approached with caution. (Advice for sensitive palates: a mouthful of rice is a more effective emergency treatment for a chilli attack than a glass of water.)

Burmese influence can be tasted in two of the North's most famous dishes—*gaeng hang ley* and *khao soi*. The first is a thick pork curry, slightly sweetish, made with a distinctive combination of ginger, tamarind, turmeric, and curry. *Khao soi* is an egg-noodle luncheon dish with a lavish helping of thick curry broth and chicken, pork or beef as preferred. Its essential toppings are shallots, pickled vegetables (*phak dong*), and wedges of lime.

Northern food is not only regional cooking, but also country cooking—strong on flavours that are robust rather than delicate. Few edible sources are rejected, as a stroll around any market will reveal. Though not typical restaurant fare, the ubiquitous water buffalo makes a culinary appearance as *laab*. This chopped meat dish, garnished with pulverized rice, chillies, and other spices, including mint, is at its most traditional when eaten raw; the slightly bitter taste discernable in a genuine Northern *laab* is the animal's bile (the Akha favour dog prepared in this way, *à la tartare*). Insects also add to the exoticism of Lanna cuisine—witness the giant water beetles called *maengda* for sale in the markets with their legs neatly tied. When pounded in a mortar and put into dishes they impart an aromatic, perfumed flavour reminiscent of pear-drops, but they can also be eaten whole, as a crunchy snack (if your visit is out of season, look for the pickled *maengda*). There are even more localized specialities within the North—cow's placenta in Phayao, for example—but these are probably best left for the compulsive gastronome.

Phraya valley (the so–called Siamese) and the Tai of the North (called Thai Yuan or Lao Yuan) have had separate histories from ancient times. What they do share is an incredible capability to absorb and assimilate any useful element—ethnic or cultural—which crosses their path, and to make it their own in the span of a few generations.

In the thirteenth century, at the time of Mengrai and Sri Intaratit—the two kings who founded the first independent Thai principalities—the population of the Central Plains was mostly Mon-speaking people of the old Dvaravati realm, ruled by an upper class of Tais, while the Lanna kingdom of the North was populated by Mons and Lawas ruled by Tai chieftains. King Mengrai himself was the descendent of Lawa chiefs and had a Tai Lüe mother. The same pattern of inter-marriage and tolerant assimilation occurred in neighboring regions where other Tai people had migrated. In eastern Burma the Shan (Tai Yai) ruled over a Mon–Khmer population of various tribes of Austroasiatic origin, while in Laos the Tai people had completely subjugated the original Kha and Khamu and kept them working in their fields as slaves.

The single most important element that the Tais absorbed wherever and whenever they moved was Buddhism, the religion that was to be their unifying force for the next ten centuries. Although it is impossible to ascertain exactly when the Tais first came into contact with Buddhism—which was widespread in China long before it reached Southeast Asia—the Mons were undeniably instrumental in the total acceptance of Theravada Buddhism by the Tais. Mon religious art and architecture have left a permanent influence on every form of artistic expression.

The kingdom founded by Mengrai, called Lanna, covered more or less the whole of present day northern Thailand and was enriched through the centuries by the arrival of many new ethnic groups. Few of these groups have actually been totally assimilated, although today, given the intrinsic tolerance of Thai society and the unifying force of compulsory education, not to speak of the homogenizing power of modernization, such ethnic minorities may be difficult to spot at first glance.

Burmese invasions and two hundred years of Burmese rule must obviously have left some trace in the society; but it should be pointed out that much of the Burmese presence, which is still evident today in art and architecture, is of quite recent origin. At the end of the last century, British firms who received logging concessions often imported skilled Burmese carpenters to do their building. Burmese merchants made many a fortune in Lanna and often these merchants wanted to make merit by building or restoring temples. While these individual Burmese and their children have been completely assimilated, their religious zeal has left an enduring trace on the landscape of the North.

A more authentic migration is that of the Shan (the Tai Yai, called 'Ngiow' in Thai), who often encroached upon Lanna and finally moved east across the Salween river. Today they make up the majority of the population of Mae Sariang and Mae Hong Son, and groups of Shan people are found in Chiang Rai, Mae Sot and Mae Chaem as well.

Northern Thai Houses

Nearly all Thai houses are built on a raised platform that keeps the living quarters well above the ground and creates an open space below for working and for keeping animals and tools. This basic concept has remained unchanged over the centuries even while style and techniques of construction varied considerably.

The northern house is typified by outward-slanting walls and a more sturdy look than a central Thai house. It may be composed of two or three units but often these units open into a single large room which serves as sleeping quarters. The door to the inner part of the house is always guarded by a special lintel, called *ham yon* (literally 'magic testicles'-see illustration at bottom of p. 166) which has a magical power believed to protect the owner and his family from harm. The rooms open onto a verandah and a platform which serves for bathing and often for cooking, although the kitchen may be located in a separate building. Typical of Chiang Mai valley is a V-shaped decoration on the peak of the roof, called a *galae*, which probably once had a magical significance, the meaning of which is now lost. In recent years, *galae* have become fashionable decorations and a symbol of northern culture and are found on many types of buildings including the Chiang Mai airport terminal and even gas stations and shophouses.

The preferred material for house construction was teak wood, while the supporting pillars were made of single logs of even stronger wood. Even in the old days, however, wood was affordable only by the wealthy, and the majority of rural houses were simple cabins made of bamboo poles, split bamboo, straw mats, and whatever else was available.

By the turn of the century the classic design was supplanted by more modern techniques and designs introduced by Burmese carpenters; most of the old houses of Chiang Mai date from this period. These charming hybrid buildings show a mixture of Thai, Burmese and Western influences. Typically, their roofs are flatter than earlier houses, and the open verandah has been replaced by a closed room positioned across from the sleeping quarters.

Travellers interested in traditional northern Thai houses should visit the Kamtieng House on Asoke Road in Bangkok, on the grounds of the Siam Society; it is an authentic building of the classic northern type, originally built in Chiang Mai and then moved to the capital, where it was transformed into an interesting museum. In Chiang Mai there are traditional houses at the Lanna Cultural Centre and the Banyen Folk Art Museum, both on Wualai Road.

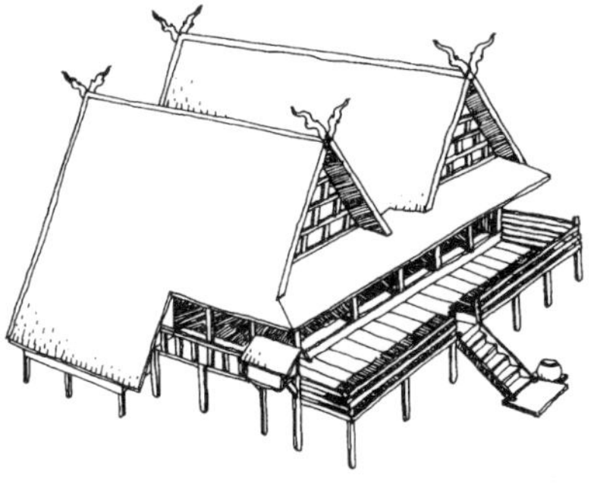

A *Galae* adorns the peak of traditional Lanna houses

Another group that settled in Lanna in comparatively recent times is the Tai Lüe, a race of peaceful farmers, the majority of whom still inhabit the Sipsong Panna region in Yunnan, where they once had a powerful kingdom. Apparently, only few Tai Lüe came to Lanna of their own free will; those in Lamphun province are the descendants of slaves captured during a raid early in the nineteenth century. Lampang province was similarly populated with Tai Lüe collected during a raid launched by the king of Nan—under pressure from the Bangkok government—at the end of the century.

The Tai Lüe had been resettled to repopulate vast areas that had been depleted by continuous wars. However, when the British claimed sovereignty over the area originally populated by the Tai Lüe, the Siamese government tried to send them back to Sipsong Panna to keep the colonial power at bay. Many groups never made it home and are now found in Phayao province.

Pockets of people from Laos are also found in Nan and Uttaradit provinces. These, however, are not of Lao race, but mostly Khamu (a people of Austronesian origin) who used to work in the forests as mahouts and woodcutters, and Tai Neua and Lao Puan who immigrated to Lanna during the last century. (The beautiful village of Laplae near Uttaradit is peopled by the descendents of immigrants from Laos.) The Tai Neua and Lao Puan are renown for their skill in weaving.

On the very brink of disappearance is the most primitive of Thailand's minorities, of which a few hundred can still be found in Nan province: the Phi Thong Luang or 'Spirit of the Yellow Leaves'. This is a nomadic tribe who still roam the forests, moving from camp to camp and sustaining themselves with whatever natural food they can gather. Their origin is unknown, but since their language seems related to the Khmer family it is possible that they were once a lowland people pushed by new settlers into wilderness where they subsequently regressed to a very primitive way of life.

The list of ethic groups living in the North also includes a sizeable number of Chinese. These immigrants belong to three quite distinct categories.

The 'Thai Chinese' (often called Sino–Thai in scholarly publications) are most often merchants, businessmen, or shopkeepers and constitute the largest portion of Thailand's thriving bourgeoisie; often intermarrying with the Thais, they are now completely assimilated and consider themselves Thai. They are a very recent addition to the Lanna ethnic pot, having moved northwards only after the Bangkok government had attained a firm grip on the northern regions. Most of them are found in Lampang, which appears to be one of the oldest Thai Chinese communities in the North. The cultural impact of these Chinese, however, is not very significant, unlike in the central region where they had a long influence dating from the early Ayutthaya period.

Various groups of the so–called 'Haw' consist of Chinese from Yunnan who immigrated from the north across land borders. They were usually of a much inferior cultural level than the overseas Chinese who arrived in Bangkok as official immigrants. Most were wandering traders and muleteers who

used to trade across the mountainous borders—and some occasionally still do. Many Haw eventually settled in Thailand. Another group of Haw are the descendents of the remnants of an army of bandits that roamed northern Thailand, Laos, and Vietnam in the 1890s. Many of these Haw are Muslims and have Muslim names. A typical village is Ban Tham near Chiang Rai.

The most recent Chinese entrants are remnants of the Kuomintang Army (KMT) who were left stranded in Thai territory—where they and their offspring live to this day—at the end of World War II. The KMT kept its military organization until the 1970s and actively pursued anti–communist operations that made their presence acceptable despite their involvement in the opium trade. Now they have abandoned all military activities and have been formally accepted as residents of Thailand. One of the largest KMT villages is on top of Doi Mae Salong.

Hilltribes

The Tai people, whichever group they belong to, are usually lowland farmers and seldom establish their villages on mountain slopes. Only very recently have overpopulation and scarcity of land forced poor and jobless families to settle on clearings opened up by the construction of new mountain roads. The rugged terrain of the forested hills was left practically unpopulated for centuries, and this factor accounted for the isolation and the conservative traditions of the little townships established in the valleys. Immigrations of non-Tai outsiders in the last century have filled this void, and today the mountains of northern Thailand are inhabited by half a million people belonging to several different tribes: the Hmong and the Mien (of the Sino–Tibetan group); and the Karen, Akha, Lisu, and Lahu (of the Tibeto-Burmese group). These tribes live in villages scattered across the mountains, each one preferring to settle at a certain level of altitude; the tribes do not possess definite territories but rather live interspersed in a mosaic of settlements. Each tribe upholds its own traditions, has a special style of dress, and speaks its own language. The Karen, by far the most numerous of the tribes, are the only group that has lived in the region from ancient times—probably even before the Tai arrived. The Lahu, Mien and Hmong started migrating into northern Thailand in the nineteenth century, while the Akha appeared as late as 1905, their second village being established only in 1925.

The largest waves of migration, however, happened in the 1960s and 70s. According to estimates presented by Paul and Elaine Lewis, in 1948 the hilltribes in northern Thailand numbered only 100,000, but by 1983 they totalled 416,000, an increase of 4 % a year —more than quadrupling in little more than one generation. The Indochina and Vietnam Wars were responsible for this exceptional migration; the Hmong, in particular, fought actively against the communists in Laos and were thus forced to flee to refuge in Thailand. Ironically, at the same time other Hmong groups in Thailand were fighting for communist causes, an involvement which did not endear the newly arriving Hmong to Thai officials.

The hilltribes of Thailand are probably the best studied of the world's tribal minorities—and among the best known to the general public. Their high visibility is due to their picturesque styles of dress and to their involvement in the cultivation and trade of opium. At the peak of the Vietnam War (which coincided with a communist insurgency in Thailand), political and narcotic agents swarmed all over the mountains; many anthropological studies were conducted to provide them with information. The exotic and flamboyant clothing and jewelry of the hilltribes has made them a prominent tourist attraction and a favourite theme for postcards and tourist brochures.

In contrast to their glamorous appearance, the hilltribes live a rather poor and unhealthy life. They view foreigners with diffidence and suspicion, and their confined and often impoverished environment means that they have little to offer to visitors—besides the occasional pipe of opium that tempts the adventurous traveller.

Recently there have been many projects attempting to integrate hilltribe communities into the mainstream of society and, particularly, to substitute opium farming with alternative crops. Such efforts have met with much success, and today Thailand is no longer a major producer, although it is still a conduit for opium caravans from Burma and Laos. A large part of the success is due to the efforts of King Bhumipol, who has dedicated much personal attention and much of his own funds to help the people of the mountains. Today, tribespeople make more frequent visits to town markets and are more confident in approaching the Thai authorities and the people of the valleys. Many children now receive a basic education (mostly from teachers provided by the Border Patrol Police) and nearly all speak a minimal amount of the Thai language. It will be a long while, however, before the mountains of northern Thailand are safe and healthy places to live; and the price to be paid for the development may well include the loss of cultural identity and many ancient traditions.

Hmong There are about 60,000 Hmong in northern Thailand, belonging to two distinct groups, the Blue Hmong, distinguishable by the knee-length pleated skirt worn by the women, and the White Hmong, distinguishable by a severe black costume. The Thai call them 'Meo', a name the Hmong dislike and consider derogatory. They are shrewd entrepreneurs and their wealth is publicly displayed, especially the heavy jewelry worn every day by the women.

Hmong villages are always built on the crest of hills at the highest possible altitude. Refugees resettled in valley bottom sites suffer enormously from the heat and are easily decimated by malaria and other lowland diseases. The Hmong are an independent and strong-willed people, always ready to fight back attempts to encroach upon their individualistic lifestyle; thus, they have been directly involved in virtually every recent conflict in Indochina. They were the first hilltribe to practice opium cultivation on a large scale in North Vietnam, at the instigation of the French colonial government. Until recently they have actively practiced opium cultivation in

Hilltribe Distribution of Settlements

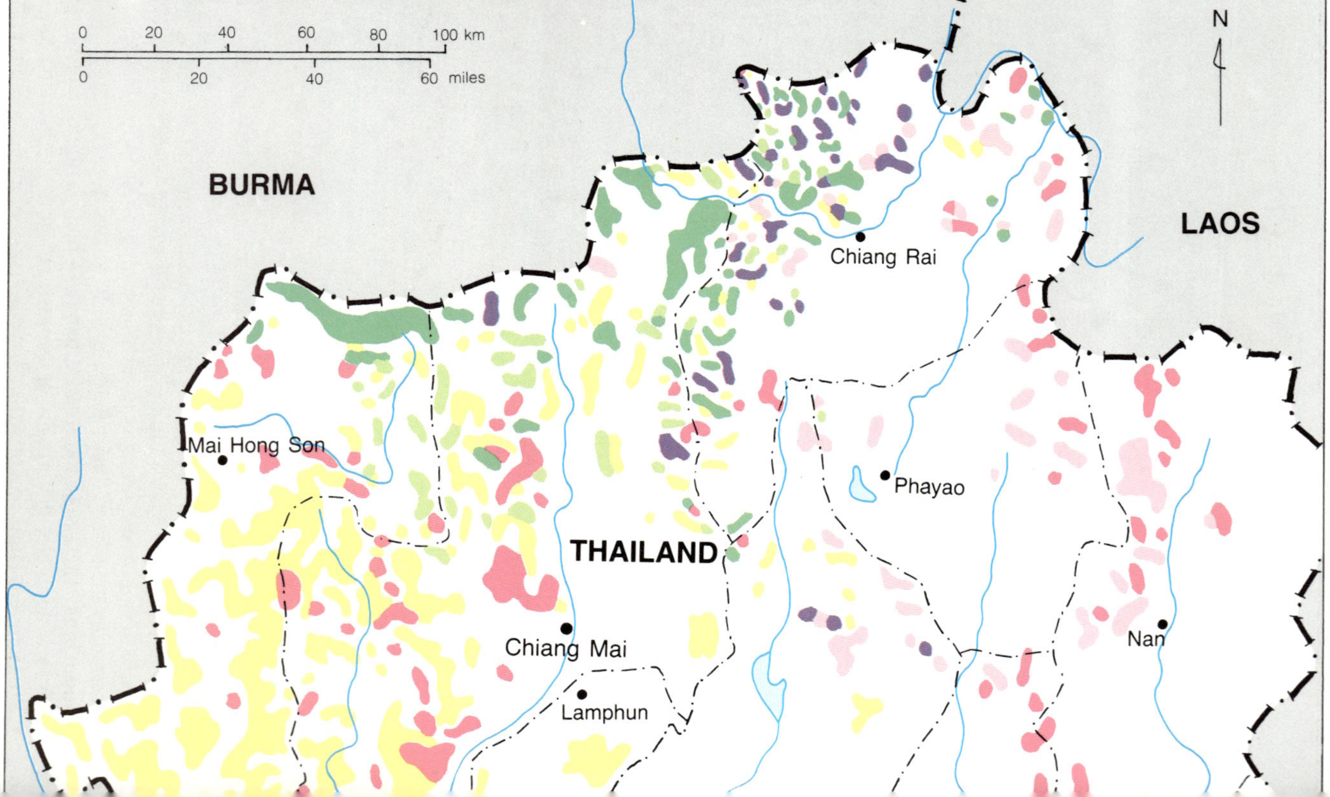

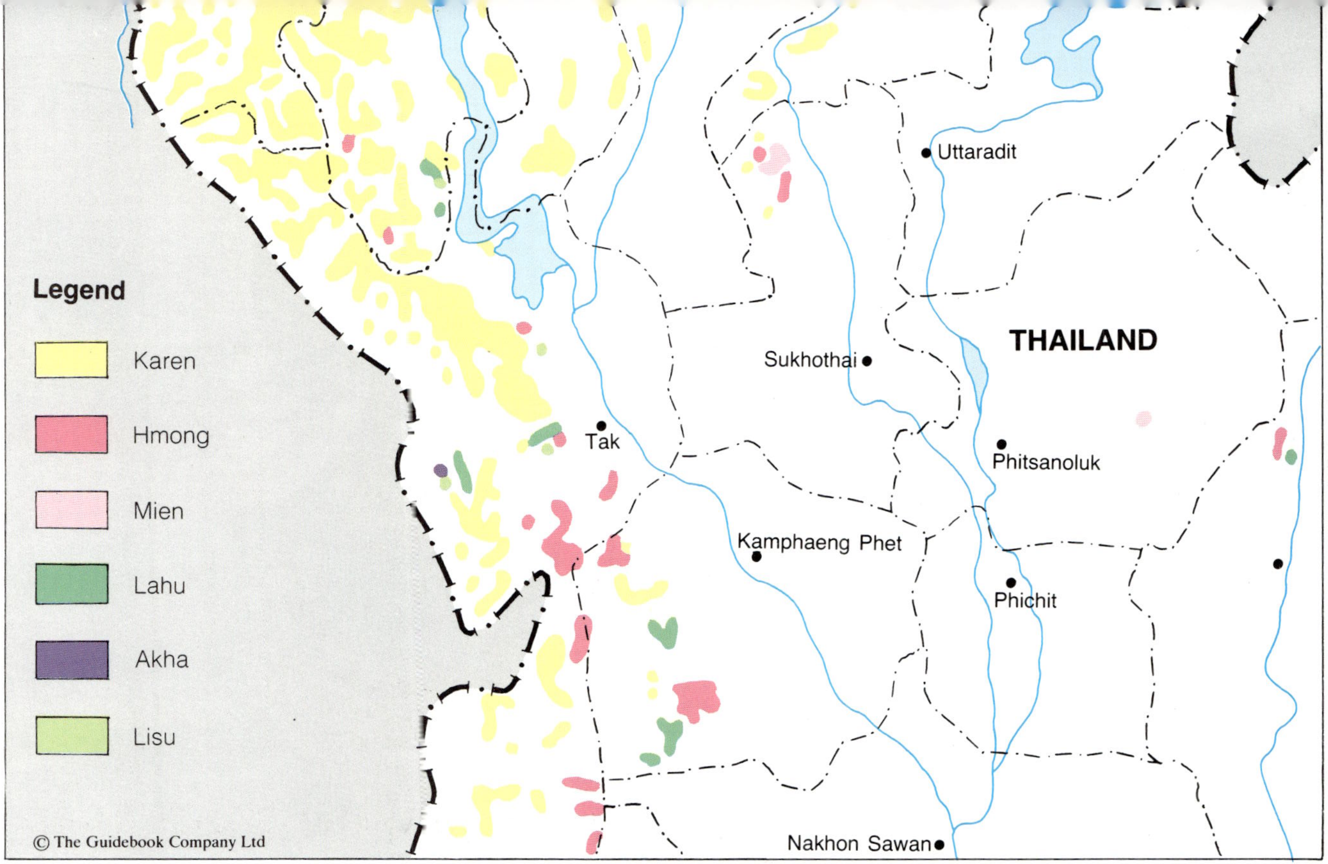

THAILAND
Uttaradit
Sukhothai
Phitsanoluk
Tak
Kamphaeng Phet
Phichit
Nakhon Sawan
Legend
Karen
Hmong
Mien
Lahu
Akha
Lisu

Thailand as well.

Yao The Mien, called 'Yao' by the Thai and generally known by that name, are the tribe that most clearly evidences a Chinese origin, both in appearance and in religious beliefs. There are approximately 30,000 Yao in northern Thailand, but they often seem far more numerous since they tend to be more adventurous than other tribes and are often seen in markets and towns.

The Yao follow Taoism much as it was practiced in China six centuries ago, and they have an elaborate ancestor cult, much like that commonly associated with the Chinese. They are the only hilltribe to have a tradition of literacy which dates back several centuries. The Yao utilize Chinese ideograms to write, in their own language, instructions for religious rituals, historical chronicles, and business documents. Taoist ritual as practised by the Yao employs large Chinese-style paintings (see photo on page 46) depicting the Tao Pantheon; these are often boldly expressionistic works of art, much sought after in the antique market.

Yao women are very skilled in the art of embroidery and wear elaborately embroidered loose pants. Other typical elements of the women's attire are a large indigo turban and a red puff, looking much like a feather boa, worn around the neck. Silver ornaments are usually worn only at ceremonies and festivals.

Karen There are nearly 250,000 Karen living in Thailand in 2,160 villages scattered along the western border, usually at low altitudes or even in

the lowlands. They are very skilled farmers, and although they employ the slash-and-burn method, the Karen seem to create far less damage than other tribes. Unlike the Hmong and the Yao, they build their houses on tall posts, in a fashion similar to the Tai.

The Karen are largely animists, though many groups have adopted either Buddhism or Christianity; many 'millennial' cults have emerged amongst them, cults promising happiness and freedom in a prosperous kingdom of the future—in this lifetime. Such spiritual answers to worldly problems reflect the frustration and the sense of oppression felt by the Karen, particularly by those living in Burma where they have been engaged in decades of armed struggle against the government.

Karen women are excellent weavers, producing a rough, homespun cotton fabric usually found in hues of red and orange; this cloth is fashioned into loose shirts and long caftan-like blouses and sarongs, and is often embroidered and decorated with seeds. Unmarried girls wear white. Jewelry consists mainly of long strings of beads worn in multiple strands around the neck. Bracelets are often made of such cheap metals as aluminium or brass. worn in great number so as to cover the forearm.

Lahu There are approximately 40,000 Lahu presently living in Thailand, most of them settled in the provinces of Chiang Mai and Chiang Rai. They belong to five different groups: Lahu Nyi (Red), Lahu Na (Black), Lahu Sheh Leh, Ba Lan, and the Ban Keo. The Thai call them "Musur", which means 'hunters', as the first Lahu to reach Lanna in the 1880s were

mainly professional hunters.

Lahu villages are usually situated at very high elevations, and the houses are built on stilts. Every village has a temple, a kind of unsheltered enclosure where rites to worship the supreme deity are held nearly every month. Many groups, however, have been converted to Christianity, while others follow new millennial cults. The dominant theme of Lahu culture, according to Paul and Elaine Lewis (who have worked as missionaries among them for nearly 40 years), is a desire for blessing, and their whole society is structured so as to maximize the receipt of blessings, which are sought after with the careful performance of rites and recitation of prayers.

Lisu There are about 20,000 Lisu in Thailand, mostly established here since the beginning of the century. All speak the same dialect but about half of them live in Chiang Mai province while the rest are scattered between Chiang Rai and Mae Hong Son. The women wear colorful red-and-turquoise dresses and, during New Year festivities, the girls are adorned with spectacular silver jewelry which covers the whole breast like a suit of armour.

The Lisu are animists and have a very independent lifestyle. They display a strong sense of pride and a desire for dominance that induces them to compete with each other in every field. Although they conservatively uphold their traditions, their shared desire for primacy has spurred them to obtain a better economic position than other tribes, and many Lisu are now living in good houses and enjoying affluent lifestyles. Lisu villages have changed considerably in recent years, and sometimes Thai techniques of construction have been adopted.

Akha The Akha began a long migration from eastern Tibet more than two thousand years ago. At some point in history they were settled permanently in Yunnan, where they had a fairly organized state and kept written chronicles of their history, but oppression by the Chinese—or perhaps natural disasters—pushed them into the highlands. Today they are a wandering people perpetually shifting across the mountains of Burma, China and Thailand, with no hope of ever again having an independent state.

The poorest and shyest of all the mountain tribes, the Akha number some 25,000 in Thailand, numbers that keep increasing as this is the only country where they are not harassed. They are found in the highest density in Mae Sai district on the slopes of Doi Mae Salong. Living in small villages located just below the crest of the hills, they build houses on stilts with a very low thatched roof that nearly reaches the floor near the walls. They are easily recognized by the astonishing amount of heavy silver jewelry they wear, even when working in the fields. Unfailingly accompanied by dogs (which are sometimes eaten) and usually sporting a pipe in her mouth, the Akha woman is a real character and conjures up an image of the kind that many people associate with northern Thailand.

The Akha presence in Thailand is not only quite recent but also quite insignificant in terms of either numbers or economics—with one exception. They are opium farmers and often opium (or even heroin) addicts as well; this makes them probably the least healthy and the most miserable of the

Yao mothers in ceremonial attire (top), A married Akha woman (bottom left), Lahu mother and child (bottom right)

Growing Opium

Opium is the latex of the poppy, *Papaver somniferum*. Although there are over 250 species of poppy, only one produces opium, and this one species requires very specific climatic and geographical conditions to produce as a cash crop. Opium poppies grow best between 3,000 and 7,000 feet in altitude and prefer a relatively dry climate. Rainfall during the four month growing season (September through January) averages 20 to 30 inches (500-750 mm) in the Golden Triangle area. Temperatures differ widely during growth, generally 5° C-33° C (40°F to 90° F). Opium grows best on well drained mountain slopes with a western exposure. It enjoys 'sweet' soils composed of red-brown earth with a high limestone and Ph (acidic) content. Thus, opium is an ideal crop for marginal agricultural regions such as northern Thailand and the Shan hills of Burma. Although the plant also thrives in valleys with fertile alluvial soils, such valleys are usually reserved for rice or other cash crops. It should be emphasized, however, that the opium plant is difficult to grow, being highly susceptible to adverse climatic conditions such as drought. Crop production can vary 300 percent from year to year according to the weather.

The most successful growers among the hilltribe people of Thailand are the Lahu, Yao, Meo, and especially the Haw Chinese who originated in Yunnan Province of Southwest China from where they brought generations of opium-growing experience when they migrated south into the hills of Thailand. An average of 1.4 to 1.8 kilos of raw opium per *rai* (1 rai=.4 acre) is produced by these groups as opposed to .8 to 1.2 kilos per *rai* by other groups such as the Akha and Lisu, peoples of Tibeto-Burman ancestry who took up opium cultivation after their arrival in the Golden Triangle. (Ten kilos of raw opium are required to make one kilo of refined heroin. In general the hilltribe people have a high incidence of opium addiction (5% to 25% of any village's population) and often consume much of their crop, after which they must look for additional income elsewhere. An extensive crop substitution program which has been underway for more than twenty years in northern Thailand is finally starting to show results. Opium production in Thailand has fallen from a high of about 250 tons per year during the peak years of the 1970s to only 15-30 tons a year recently, although the country is still a conduit for much of the Burmese and Lao crops which total as much as 2,000 tons per annum. A wide variety of crops have come to replace the poppy (everything from asparagus and strawberries to pyrethrum, a plant used in organic insecticides) and, although nothing can replace the profits generated by opium, the hilltribes never received a large share of those profits and consequently seem to be slowly but willingly adopting the new crops.

mountain dwellers. Trekkers, always so keen to visit an Akha village, should be aware of the discomforts offered by Akha hostelries, ranging from the expected fleas and bedbugs to breakfasts of raw dog meat and bedrooms filled with pungent opium.

History of Northern Thailand

Pre-history

While the rich cultural traditions and sophistication of the Buddhist art of Southeast Asia have been recognized since the first Westerners visited this region, until very recently orthodox scholarly opinion depicted the protohistoric period of the region as a sort of cultural backwater of India and China—if not as an absolute vacuum. Not one scholar was able to perceive that an advanced early civilization could ever have sprung up in Southeast Asia. But now, excavations at Ban Chiang in the northeast of Thailand have revolutionized the traditional view of prehistoric Southeast Asia and forever changed the recognized time of the emergence of the world's first metallurgy. At Ban Chiang the first appearance of metals has now been pushed back to the third millennium before Christ, and a period when bronze was the only metal widely used has now been clearly identified.

Similarly, research in northern Thailand by Chester Gorman, the same American archaeologist who discovered Ban Chiang, has thrown new light on the early development of agriculture in the region, including establishing a very early date for the domestication of a food plant, rice.

The study of prehistory in Thailand is still in its infancy, and an organized outline of the presence of man on its soil is still far from possible. Excavations in the Chiang Mai Valley, however, have proven that the area was a paleolithic complex, and further research at Chiang Saen has uncovered a site belonging to the Pleistocene, indicating that the Mekong Valley was inhabited by hunters and gatherers a long time ago.

A huge gap separates the first traces of a human presence in northern Thailand from the Hoabinian finds. The neolithic period of Southeast Asia is know as 'Hoabinian', a term devised by Madame Colani in the 1920s after excavations in northern Vietnam revealed simple river cobbles flaked on one side and often associated with bones of wild animals. Academics at that time conveniently convinced themselves (so as to not disrupt any dearly held prejudices) that the users of these tools, who lived approximately 10,000 years ago, were barbaric hunters without any organized society, and that any 'culture' must have come in a package from China or India at a much later date.

When Chester Gorman excavated the Spirit Cave near Mae Hong Son, the staunch French school of archaeologists was dismayed. Alongside the simple Hoabinian tools, Gorman discovered seeds of a large variety of cultivated plants, including betel nut, almond, black pepper, bottle gourd, and cucumber. These botanic fossils evidence horticultural skills that prove a cultural and technological development far beyond simple hunting-and-gathering.

The domestication of plants and animals must have developed in Southeast Asia quite independently from India and China. The fertile valleys of the Ping River, of the Mekong and the Salween, were likely inhabited by communities of inventive farmers descended from ancient settlements of the Stone Age, peoples which gradually evolved into organized societies capable of assimilating new migrations of people.

The Dawn of History

It is practically impossible, given the present state of knowledge, to outline clearly the evolution of various civilizations and peoples during the first stages of the historic period. The first known inhabitants of the region spoke Austronesian languages such as Lawa, Mon, and Khmer. (Apparently the Tai only began to filter in at the beginning of the second millennium after Christ.) The exact routes of these migrants, their origins, and their interrelationships with the long established Hoabinian farmers are not known, and such questions are still the source of endless debate among scholars. There are several indications, however, that the cultural milieu of the settlements of northern Thailand in the first millennium was not as primitive as originally envisioned, and that artistic, cultural and commercial ties existed with central Thailand, the Mon country of lower Burma, and China.

The paramount power of Southeast Asia in the first millennium was for a long time the empire of Srivijaya which, from an as yet undiscovered capital in the South (Palembang in Sumatra or perhaps Nakorn Si Thammarat in southern Thailand), controlled all of the major sea trade routes. The northern regions of Thailand had to funnel their products through the same channel, but being so far from the coast, they probably received very little of the profits derived from the trade. Culture and religion, however, travel along with merchandise, and along the sea routes of Srivijaya and then via the Mons of central Thailand, Buddhism found its way to the the North, together with the more sophisticated Hindu concepts of kingship that slowly modified the organization of the region's small principalities.

In the seventh century the Mons established an independent kingdom in the Ping Valley. According to tradition, Princess Chamadevi, daughter of the King of Louvo (modern day Lopburi), left her home to establish Haripunchai on the site of the present day city of Lamphun. The city eventually prospered and was to remain for many centuries the main cultural and religious centre of the North.

Haripunchai was a fortified town protected by moats and ramparts, and was joined with a series of settlements entrusted to relatives of Chamadevi, who had by then become a queen. According to tradition, the town of Lampang was founded by a son of Chamadevi; and a series of fortified little towns, of which Lampang Luang still survives, formed a small federation associated with Haripunchai.

When the Srivijaya empire declined, the Khmer empire of Cambodia became the paramount power in the region, gradually expanding to cover most of present day Thailand. The Khmer influence in the North was, however, quite limited, and although there are records of wars between Khmer armies and northern chieftains, Haripunchai remained independent.

The decline of Srivijaya also caused China to trade directly with the inland regions that had previously sent their products by sea, and new overland trade routes brought prosperity to inland trade centres such as Haripunchai. This economic trend is ultimately responsible for the emergence of great principalities in areas quite distant from the seas (such as Pagan and, later on, Sukhothai).

The Days of King Mengrai

The conventional history of the northern Thai kingdom begins in the mid -thirteenth century with King Mengrai, but evidence now surfacing suggests that two centuries before a unified Thai state in the North, there were already small Thai principalities flourishing as centres of Buddhist learning and art. The kingdom of Phayao may even have been in direct contact with India, if we are to credit the Pala influence evident in much of Phayao's sandstone Buddhas and stupikas. The Thai presence in the region may have grown slowly for quite some time, and it was not until the mid-thirteenth century that a political vacuum left by the death of a Khmer king, Jayavarman VII, allowed Thai chieftains to reject Khmer suzerainty and establish their own political entities. Sukhothai, the northern outpost of the Khmer empire, rebelled; and it was here that King Sri Intaratit formed the first Thai kingdom in the Central Plains.

A few years later, Mengrai, chief of a small principality on the banks of the Mekong, embarked upon the grand scheme of bringing the entire northern region under his dominion. Mengrai, of mixed Thai-Lawa blood, was 24th in a line of Lawa chieftains that had ruled in the Mekong valley for four centuries. He was often referred to as the King of Chiang Saen, but it now seems certain that the town of Chiang Saen was founded only in 1327, and so even though his original domains were in the same area, he could hardly have ruled over a place that did not exist until long after his death. Mengrai moved southward and in 1262 founded the city of Chiang Rai, naming it after himself, in a location well protected by the Kok River and by three small hills.

Mengrai subsequently moved to the Ping valley and after many attempts he finally succeeded in conquering Haripunchai. The city was captured intact and it retained its cultural supremacy for at least half a century. Controlling such an important religious centre enhanced the political stature of Mengrai, who became the paramount power in the North. He established alliances with Phya Ngam Muang, the King of Phayao; ten years after this king's death, Phayao was annexed to Mengrai's dominions. Mengrai soon controlled a vast area ranging from Laos to what is now the Shan States in Burma. He had made himself the King of Lanna, 'The Kingdom of a Million Ricefields'.

After the conquest of Haripunchai, Mengrai established a new capital at a fortified site on the banks of the Ping River, Wiang Kung Kam, which he proceeded to embellish with Buddhist temples. Some of them were inspired by the monuments of Haripunchai; Mengrai's Wat Si Liem, for example, is a

Important Dates in Lanna History

1259	Mengrai ascends the throne.
1262	Mengrai founds Chiang Rai.
1281	Mengrai conquers Haripunchai.
1287	Mengrai establishes the Kingdom of Lanna Thai.
1297	Chiang Mai is founded.
1317	Death of Mengrai
1338	Payao is annexed to Chiang Mai.
1340	Wat Phra Sing is founded in Chiang Mai.
1355-1385	Reign of Ku Na
1385-1401	Reign of Saen Muang Ma
1401-1441	Reign of Kham Ku (Kaen)
1423	Lanna monks are ordained in Sri Lanka.
1441	Chao Lok ambushes and captures his father to ascend to the throne as King Tilokaraja.
1451-1460	War with Ayutthaya
1455	Eighth World Buddhist council meets in Chiang Mai.
1478	Wat Chedi Luang is constructed in Chiang Mai.
1487	Death of Tilokaraja
1508-1515	Wars with Ayutthaya
1545	After a series of unworthy kings, a revolt in Chiang Mai attracts an Ayutthayan army.
1545	An earthquake destroys many temples in Chiang Mai.
1548	A Siamese army unsuccessfully besieges Chiang Mai.
1558	Chiang Mai is invaded by King Bayinnaung of Pegu (Burma).
1565	Luang Prabang (in Laos) falls to the Burmese.
1569	Ayutthaya falls to the Burmese.
1598	Naresuan recaptures Chiang Mai.
1600	King Naresuan of Ayutthaya defeats the King of Pegu, leaving Ava to become the paramount power in Burma.
1615	The Burmese regain control over Lanna Thai, a rule which lasts almost uninterrupted for one century.
1717	Phya Tun is nominated by the King of Ava to become Prince of Nan, a title his family will retain until the end of absolute monarchy in Siam in 1932.
1727-1770	Rebellions and wars against the Burmese
1727	A general named Thip defeats a Burmese army and is proclaimed ruler of Lampang under the name Phra Sulawa. His descendents will rule over Lampang, Lamphun and Chiang Mai until the 19th century.
1767	The Burmese attack and destroy Ayutthaya.

1771	General Phya Tak (who will later become King Taksin of Thonburi) dispatches an army to Chiang Mai to fight the Burmese.
1774	King Kawila, ruler of Lampang, fights the Burmese and hands Chiang Mai over to Phya Tak. The city, impoverished by long civil wars, is abandoned for 20 years.
1782	Phya Chakri becomes the first king of the Chakri Dynasty, under the name of Ramathibodi, and founds Bangkok.
1787-1801	The Burmese mount periodic expeditions attempting to regain Lanna Thai.
1796	Kawila repopulates Chiang Mai.
1804	Ramathibodi (later posthumously renamed Rama I) and King Kawila finally defeat the Burmese. The last Burmese stronghold, Chiang Saen, is razed to prevent reoccupation by the invaders, and the population is deported to Lampang.
1813	Kawila dies.
1874	A Siamese High Commissioner is sent to reside in Chiang Mai, and the Bangkok government begins to administer Lanna Thai directly.
1885	The British conquer upper Burma, ensuring peace on the western border, although the British will start to meddle in northern affairs.
1887	Siam cedes to France some provinces in Laos, which the Thais had controlled for a hundred years since the war in the North by Phya Tak.
c. 1890	Bands of Chinese Haw, many of them bandits, enter northern Thailand and Laos.
1893	Thailand loses to France some territories on the west bank of the Mekong River (Present day Laos and Cambodia).
1921	The railway reaches Chiang Mai.
1927	Rama VII visits Chiang Mai, entering the city with a stately procession of elephants.
c. 1932	Khruba Srivijaya, a highly revered northern monk, refuses to accept the authority of the national Sangha.
1939	The last Prince of Chiang Mai, Kaew Nawarath, dies. Siam changes its name to Thailand.

stepped pyramid modelled after Wat Ku Kut. Such emulation is elegant testimony of the admiration that Mengrai felt for the Mon culture which he had just subjugated. After a few years, he decided to move and build a much larger city on the opposite bank of the Ping. The new town was called Chiang Mai. The city, built on a grand layout, was to become the main cultural and religious centre of the North and to be the political and economic focal point of a large area reaching from the northern frontier of the Sukhothai kingdom to the southern provinces of China.

In fairytales, heroes never die an ordinary death, and the Thai chronicles report that Mengrai was struck by a bolt of lightning. It was the year 1317 A.D. and by that time Mengrai had established not just a well–organized kingdom—but a dynasty which would rule northern Thailand for the next 200 years.

Lanna from Mengrai to the Present

The historical annals of Lanna are much like the tales of King Arthur: an endless list of battles, sieges and wars, using neighbours and friends to wrestle power from allies and relatives. Just as in mediaeval Europe, wars were often waged for pride alone, sometimes being resolved by heroic single combat between rival kings, each mounted on his war elephant. Statesmanship was not the main prerequisite of kingship—more useful were physical strength and military skill, combined with a sophisticated sense of treachery. Supernatural help, of course, was always desirable, and many a would–be king, before setting out to steal his brother's throne, would seek a magical protection, often in the form of a Buddha image of proven potency. Having set his eyes on an auspicious talisman, the future king would first try to obtain it by means of deceit, and if even a war failed to accomplish the goal, he could always rely on his craftsmen to produce a copy of the item. The abbot of a friendly monastery would, quite fortuitously, experience some vision which would explain the miraculous appearance of the chosen statue.

Despite the restlessness of the leadership, it seems that a majority of the population remained unaffected by the continuous state of warfare, and the whole region continued to prosper for quite some time. Lanna enlarged its areas of influence, absorbing Phayao, Phrae and Nan, and managed successfully to withstand several attempts at invasion from Ayutthaya, the nascent Siamese kingdom which had grown powerful enough to conquer Sukhothai and swallow its dominions. The golden age of Chiang Mai blossomed in the mid-fifteenth century during the reign of Tilokaraja, a great warrior and stalwart upholder of the Buddhist faith who arranged for the 8th World Buddhist Council to be held in Chiang Mai in the year 1455.

The presence of such a large and prestigious congregation in northern Thailand, and the refined beauty of Wat Chet Yod (the temple that most probably hosted the council), testify to the fact that, despite a chequered political history, the region enjoyed good communications, safe travel, and enough surplus food to sustain a skilled community of craftsmen who did not have to labour in the ricefields. Unfortunately, the era of fairytale battles soon ended, and by the second quarter of the sixteenth century the political situation had become rather tumultuous. A series of rebellions against a succession of kings, each more unworthy than his predecessor, had considerably weakened the stability of the dynasty. The year 1545 was a particularly bad one, since in addition to a plethora of assassinations and executions, the city was also hit by a tremendous earthquake. Quarrels over the possession of a magically-endowed Buddha image aroused a Burmese army, and by the year 1558 Chiang Mai had fallen to the King of Pegu. Lanna lost its independence and was to remain under the sway of the Burmese for the next two centuries.

Burmese rule, however, brought no direct occupation of the country and certainly nothing approaching colonisation. The Burmese king appointed a chief of his liking to this or that city and was subsequently satisfied by an annual tribute. The life of the farmers in the fields would have remained exactly the same as long as their chief did not rebel, provoking a new Burmese army to invade destroying ricefields and villages until the rebel chief was subdued.

Contemporary Thai historians have recently stopped portraying the Burmese as bogeymen in the way of earlier schoolbooks, and now tend to interpret the aggressiveness of Burma as dictated by religious rather than economic forces. Although conflict over trade routes, particularly in the Gulf of Martaban, certainly played a role, the Thai–Burmese wars are now interpreted in relationship to the concept of chakravartin, the divine ruler. According to this concept of kingship, which many Southeast Asian peoples borrowed from Hindu philosophy, a chakravartin is the ideal emperor, one who rules with justice over all the people. At any one time, there can be only one chakravartin in the world. Burmese rulers always saw themselves as chakravartin, claiming that the valleys of Chiang Mai and the Chao Phraya fell within their mandate and sphere of influence. They felt that their manifest destiny was incomplete if they had not consolidated power over the whole area. The kings of Ayutthaya, on the other hand, never saw themselves as chakravartin and came to accept the Khmer concept of kingship. The Siamese rulers gradually evolved from a paternalistic 'first amongst equals' figure—as in the kings of Sukhothai—to an aloof, divine emperor upon whom commoners were forbidden to even gaze. It is understandable that such a ruler would never have tolerated an attempt to interfere with his sovereignty, nor paid any tribute, however nominal, to a foreign ruler.

Antagonism between the two superpowers peaked with the final destruction of Ayutthaya by the Burman King of Ava, Syn Byu Shin, in 1767. He sacked the Thai capital of most of its wealth and artisans, and the culture of the old court was nearly eradicated. The victorious Burmese army moved north to Lanna and once more brought the whole region under submission. Subsequently, the victorious Burmese coerced the northern people into joining them in attacking Luang Prabang (in present day Laos). The last phase of Burmese occupation was the most oppressive for the people of

Lanna. Frequent destruction of villages and towns, confiscation of crops, forced labour, and deportation of entire townships from one place to another reduced the population to a state of extreme poverty. More hardship came in the long war that followed, a war to eject the Burmese. Lanna was reduced to desolation and poverty.

Soon after the sack of Ayutthaya two figures emerged as driving forces against the invaders. One was Phya Tak, a Siamese general (though almost surely with much Chinese blood) who quickly rallied the remnants of the Siamese army against the Burmese. He eventually became King Taksin, the founder of Thonburi. The other was King Kawila, the young chief of Lampang who rebelled against the Burmese and managed to retake Chiang Mai, handing the city over to the Siamese army. King Taksin came to take formal possession of Chiang Mai on a Sunday during the fifth month of the year *Chula Sakarat* 1136 (1774 A.D.), the date which marks the end of Burmese influence over Chiang Mai.

Chiang Mai, however, was soon abandoned since its population had been reduced to starvation by almost continuous warfare. Kawila and Taksin continued to fight the Burmese, who still occupied Chiang Rai and Chiang Saen, sending new armies into the Lanna hinterlands. The war continued with vacillating fortunes for several years. This was the bloodiest period in the history of Lanna, and the scorched-earth tactics wrought upon the countryside by the Siamese army reached such a level that at one point Kawila rebelled against his allies, who were robbing and oppressing the villages around Phrae and Nan. For this insolence he received a hundred strokes from a rattan and had both his ears cut off. Kawila repented and, in order to regain favour, went off to sack the city of Chiang Saen, then a Burmese stronghold.

In 1781 King Taksin was officially declared insane and put to death. The throne was assumed by his best general, Phya Chakri, who became King Phra Buddha Yod Fa (posthumously named Rama I) and thus founded the present dynasty. The capital was moved across the Chao Phraya River from Thonburi to Bangkok, and it is there that Kawila went to pledge his allegiance to the new Siamese king. Kawila was appointed Governor of Chiang Mai, with one of his brothers being appointed deputy, and another brother designated Governor of Lampang.

Only in 1799 did Kawila finally return to Chiang Mai and occupy his throne. It is said that the city was in such a state of abandon that tigers had made their lairs within the very walls of the city. Kawila renamed the city with a Pali name, Muang Ratana Teung Sa Apinaburi, but this long and noble appellation failed to impress the resettled inhabitants, who continued to call it Chiang Mai.

The Burmese, however, did not relinquish their designs on Lanna until 1804, when Phra Buddha Yod Fa finally destroyed the city of Chiang Saen to prevent the interlopers from reoccupying the west bank of the Mekong. For much of the 19th century this sad state of desolation continued. After the death of Kawila, Chiang Mai was administered by a sequel of rather weak rulers who took little interest in improving the miserable conditions of their subjects. The people in turn had little incentive to improve their own lives since they were merely serfs to the princes. One of their only privileges, contrary to the pattern of serfdom in Siam, was their right to switch their allegiance to a different noble by moving to a new principality.

The Bangkok government evinced remarkably little interest in Lanna until the European powers began to colonize neighboring kingdoms during the second half of the nineteenth century. When the British deposed the last king of Mandalay in Burma, and the French formally annexed Tongkin (now northern Vietnam), it was clear that one or the other would eventually try to swallow Lanna as well. It was very fortunate that the throne of Siam at that time was occupied by two of the most enlightened monarchs to assume the throne in Thai history; King Mongkut (r. 1851-1868) and his son King Chulalongkorn (r. 1868-1910).

Through a complete modernization of the country and a masterful exercise of diplomatic skill, Chulalongkorn managed to preserve the independence of Siam as a whole, ceding to the French only the Laotian and Cambodian provinces which had been originally incorporated into Siam by King Taksin, and very small amounts of territory on the Malay Peninsula to the British. But, as the British were still claiming sovereignty over territory in Lanna populated by Shans, Siam found itself in a rather precarious position. The Siamese found it expedient to forcibly move large numbers of people northwards in order to repopulate with Thais certain long-abandoned areas which were subsequently encroached upon by the Shans.

To maintain a delicate balance between the acquisitive superpowers, more effective control was needed than that which could be maintained by the weak prince of Chiang Mai. In 1877 a Siamese High Commissioner was ordered to reside in Chiang Mai, and from this time Bangkok began to administer the North directly, although a Chiang Mai prince was nominally in power until 1939.

Under Chulalongkorn's reign the North gradually recovered. The abolition of slavery, the establishment of postal services, the construction of roads and better communications, and an efficient administration all contributed to the transformation of a demoralized Lanna into a serene and prosperous region. American missionaries, established in Chiang Mai since 1868, did a great deal to improve the education and the health of the local people. British firms were given logging concessions in the north, and their presence also contributed to the modernization and the education of the people. By the end of Chulalongkorn's reign, Lanna was such a peaceful and bountiful region that Reginald Le May, then adviser to the Siamese Government, when writing about his travel experiences in the North could find no better description for the area than "An Asian Arcady."

Religion and Society

With a chequered history of feudal wars and populated by diverse ethnic groups living within continually shifting boundaries, Thailand finds its unity in its steadfast fidelity to the Buddhist faith. Buddhism is accepted by the vast majority of the population—around 95%—and Thailand is today one of the few remaining Buddhist countries in the world. Buddhism, which originated in India over 2,500 years ago, was, at the peak of its expansion, the faith of all Southeast Asia and the entire Indian subcontinent as well as China, Tibet, Japan, Korea and Indonesia. While small Buddhist communi ties still thrive in all of these nations, few are the countries where it is practiced by a vast majority of the entire population. Buddhism was introduced into what is now Thailand from India in the third century, and from the first Indianized towns of the Malay Peninsula the vibrant new religion spread to the Mon kingdoms of the Central Plains, and from there all over the country.

Buddhism is at the same time a religion, since it proposes an explanation of man's destiny and it shows the path to salvation, and also a philosophy, since it is not dogmatic and abjures a blind faith in one or more deities. Buddhism does not exclude world visions proposed by other religions, and in many places incorporates substantial elements of Hindu cosmology. According to Buddhist thinking, one's life does not begin with birth and end with death, but one's being is linked in a chain of lives, each conditioned by one's behaviour in prior existences. Suffering, so clearly present in life, is seen to be caused by desire, which tempts man to act selfishly and often wrongly; the resulting misdeeds will bring not only immediate retribution but also suffering in the next life.

Only by eliminating desire can a person achieve peace of mind and escape the cycle of reincarnation. The ideal is to attain a state of perfection through entering Nirvana—an indescribable, immutable state in which a soul is at one with the universe, free from desire, suffering, and from the necessity to be reborn. Meditation helps man to restrain desire and to find his individual path to Nirvana. Renouncing worldly pleasures and studying the Buddha's teachings is the most direct way to achieve perfection.

In Thailand, nearly every young man spends at least a few months ordained in the monastery since monks are not obliged to remain in robes for life and may disrobe at any time they wish. Many choose to stay in robes for life.

There are over 27,000 temples in Thailand, about a third of them in the North. Although the first obligation of a temple (called a *wat* in Thai) is to aid aspirants in their search for Nirvana, the *wat* also serves many social purposes as well, usually being the focal point of the village community. Monasteries were the only common centres of education outside of the palace until the end of the last century, and even today monks conduct classes for children in the more remote areas. The senior monk is usually the most revered person in the village, his status being equal, if not superior, to that of the *phu yai baan*, the village headman. Counselling is one of the

A Lanna Viharn

Compared with central Thai temples, the buildings of the North have a sturdier look with multiple-tiered roofs, gracefully curved eaves, and a portico. Construction typically employs a number of prefabricated wooden parts. Early examples are often built entirely of wood, and many are open on three or four sides.

Aerial view of a typical Thai temple (Wat Trapang Tong near Sukhothai)

The Thai Temple

The complex of religious buildings that is known in Thai as a *wat* is both a monastery and a place of worship for the lay community, while at the same time serving many social functions: guesthouse, social center, school, playground, orphanage, hospital, and dog pound. A *wat* is in every respect the focal point of the village, as the *agora* was in the old Greek cities and the *piazza* still is in Italian towns.

A visitor may be surprised to find himself in a most casual environment with lovers sitting hand in hand under a tree, rambunctious children playing, and vendors selling colourful trinkets. Returning a few days later he may experience an atmosphere just as sacred as in any gothic cathedral—or, equally, he may find all of the local farmers happily receiving instruction about a new strain of rice from a government official.

Temples are built around a *chedi* (in English called a 'stupa' or a 'pagoda') the normally conical structure that houses a relic of the Buddha, the bones of a pious king, or any other object imbued with magical power. The relic contained in the *chedi* establishes the importance of the temple and is thought to ultimately be responsible for the preservation and security of the local community, as well as for the protection of its rulers from enemies and invaders. A *chedi* which contains a genuine relic of the Lord Buddha is called a *phra that*, and hence the temple will be named Wat Mahathat, or Wat Phra That.

A *phra that* continually attracts pilgrims from distant places; but most *chedis* receive attention only on special occasions. Sometimes monks can be seen meditating while walking around them.

Another important building in the temple is the *bot* or *ubosoth*, the assembly hall where novices are ordained. It is not distinguished by any particular architectural feature, and it may even be a diminutive structure tucked away in a corner of the compound. The *bot* is normally kept closed. Its grounds are indicated by the presence of eight boundary stones (*bai sema*) that demarcate the consecrated area. *Bai sema* are placed at the four corners and the four axes of the temple, where stone spheres are buried together with precious objects and gold.

A *viharn* is a building that contains Buddha images and is where the faithful assemble to pay respect to, and receive instruction from the monks, as well as to celebrate religious occasions. There may be more than one *viharn* in a *wat*. Other temple buildings include the monks quarters, one or more open pavilions (*sala*), a drum tower and a library, usually built of wood on a tall brick podium.

This complex of edifices is seldom arranged according to a plan, but rather is haphazardly scattered within a grounds that may also contain such prosaic items as lavatories, water tanks, and garages; the scenic effect that one would desire from sacred architecture is thus often spoiled. When the results are pleasant, it is often purely a matter of accident. Recent renovations sponsored by merit seekers have often left a collection of buildings of different epoches, discordant styles, and greatly varying architectural merit, giving a hybrid appearance to the complex as a whole. Gaudiness often predominates, but visitors should remember that temples were not built to please Western aesthetes but rather to serve practical and religious purposes essential to the well-being of the community.

Mythical Animals

Visitors who enter northern temples are surprised by the many statues of fantastic mythical animals, often painted in garish colours, that can transform the entire complex into a fabulous stone bestiary. These animals, often derived from the Khmer iconographic tradition, are found in both the Buddhist and Hindu cosmologies, and their inspiration is derived from ancient Buddhist texts, such as the *Trai Bhum*, a treatise which describes the order of the world as perceived in fourteenth-century Thailand.

Nagas Approaching a temple, you will often find Nagas showing the way in. Nagas are dragon-like, serpentine divinities dwelling in the subterranean and watery regions. These beings, although frightful looking, are benevolent to mankind and have a protective function; there are many artistic representations of the Buddha serenely meditating under the shelter of a cobra-like creature, Muchalinda, the Naga King. Traditionally, Nagas are responsible for producing the rain, a belief which is certainly a relic of the pre–Hindu belief in an aquatic god of fertility. In their role as protectors of the temple, Nagas symbolize the rainbow, which is a bridge linking the world of man to the world of gods. Nagas are found on the roof eaves of every Thai temple, and in the North are frequently used as balustrades. They are often represented as emerging from the mouth of a Makara, a colorful creature combining the characteristic elements of crocodiles, dolphins and elephants.

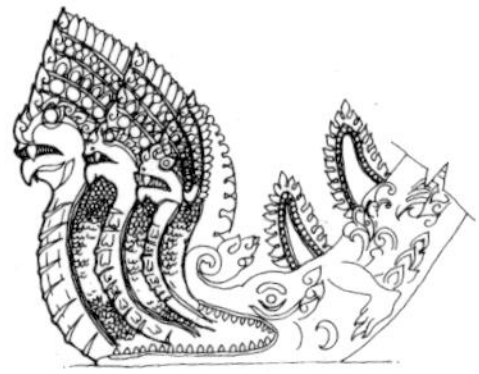

A **Makara** spewing a multi-headed Naga, frequently seen in Sukhothai art and in early Lanna temples.

Hongse (Sanskrit = Hamsa) Hongse is a mythical swan, the mount of the God Brahma. It is often found in classical Lanna art as a decoration for ceremonial gates or standing on a tall pole in front of the *viharn*. Its presence often indicates that the temple belonged to, or was founded by, a community of Mon origin.

Colorful Nagas with the reptilian scales of the body made of glazed tiles are typical of late Lanna temples and are still skillfully made in the newest *wats* of the North.

Singha Four kinds of lions (the Narashima of Sanskrit texts) inhabit the Himalayan forests. A popular symbol of strength and power, they are often employed as temple guardians. Singha are favourites of Burmese folklore and became extremely popular in Chiang Mai at the turn of the century, when Burmese style was in vogue. Burmese Singha are much more fanciful than the old Lanna–style lions and often reflect great inventiveness on the part of the artists. They are often portrayed playing, protecting a hero, or devouring a frightened victim.

Kinnari These celestial beings, half-woman and half-animal, inhabit the forests of the Himalayan region where together with the Apsaras—the celestial nymphs—they keep company to the Gods. Fanciful Burmese Kinnari are often seen in Chiang Mai temples.

Kala (Sanskrit = Kirtimuka) This mask-like creature, associated with Shiva, is often depicted devouring itself; it is therefore usually represented without a lower jaw. It symbolizes the eternal passage of time and is used as a guardian of both Hindu and Buddhist temples. In Sukhothai architecture it is often combined with Makaras or Nagas to form an arch framing the pediment. In Lanna architecture it is found above windows and doors, with the same protective function. The concept of the monster devouring its own body has stimulated many Lanna artists to create grotesque whirling shapes, often enlivened by obscene details. The examples shown here are from a classic Sukhothai stucco relief.

monks' more important functions, and they are often asked to arbitrate disputes and to give advice not only on moral issues, but on everyday problems as well. Buddhist monks are not required to work, and their simple clothing and food comes entirely from the village where they live. Offering food to the monks and taking care of the temple is done with a full heart since such support is seen as a way for the lay community to make merit and to earn a higher rebirth in a future life.

Since every individual must of necessity find their own way to end the cycle of rebirths, Buddhism is pervaded by an intrinsic tolerance and egalitarianism. Buddhism consequently does not reject alternate ways to obtain help and to alleviate suffering; a belief in spirits, both good and evil, is widely accepted.

Most Thais believe in the existence of many different kinds of spirits who are rarely seen or heard but whose influence is often felt. Animism was for long the primeval religion of Southeast Asia, and animistic beliefs are still very strong (particularly in northern Thailand) and coexist with the more sophisticated tenets of the Buddhist religion. If pleased, these spirits will help man; if displeased, they may bring harm. Three categories of spirits are regularly worshipped in rural northern Thailand: spirits of the village, spirits of the lineage, and various spirits of the house (those that reside in the land on which the house was built, those in the first post that was erected, etc.). Elaborate ceremonies to both please and appease spirits are performed at appropriate times, usually under the guidance of a medium. Mediums (shamans) are regularly possessed by spirits and know how to deal with them. The shamans use their influence and spiritual power not only to conduct ceremonies but also to disperse practical and moral advice to the community, to heal not just the physically ill but also mentally deranged people. Since men believe that the spirits are displeased by the evil acts committed by men, belief in the spirits serves a positive function in regulating or moderating social intercourse.

The negative aspects of such a belief in the supernatural—which once had strong debilitating effects—have been largely superceded today. In the past, the fear of these spirits was so strong that, according to some observers, the population lived in perpetual terror. Very often people who displayed exceptional originality or stood out from the group for any reason were believed to be possessed by evil spirits; the property of the supposed miscreants was subsequently confiscated and they themselves were expelled from the village. These outcasts, called Phi Pob, were often compelled to live together in isolated jungle settlements; Chiang Dao, for example, was once just such a colony.

Buddhism coexists with animism not only in the village, but the national religion has also unofficially incorporated in its daily practices many animist elements. Monks are regularly called in to exorcise spirits, and Buddha images are often revered more for their supernatural powers than as purely symbolic reminders of the Buddha's doctrine. Votive Buddhist tablets, small Buddha images, and relics of pious monks are worn around the neck as amulets, and their magic spells are thought to protect would–be murderers as well as reckless drivers.

The Arts of Lanna

A large part of the surviving works of art in northern Thailand are religious in nature. Although an interest in decorating objects for everyday use can be observed, at a closer inspection the intricately carved spoon, the elegant lacquered tray, or the silver bowl will often reveal itself to be destined for use in some religious ceremony. Even such mundane objects as spittoons and betel sets, for example, were considered to be symbols of status and, given the relationship between religion and divine rule, these often could even become official insignia signifying grandeur and power beyond the secular realm.

Until modern times, buildings made of brick or stone were reserved for temple architecture, and even kings used to live in quite modest wooden homes which, except for their size, were not unlike those of their subjects. Portraiture, whether in painting or sculpture, was never used to commemorate or to celebrate illustrious personages or monarchs; and to paint for a purely aesthetic purpose was quite unknown. Woodcarvings were sometimes used to decorate rich people's homes, but even here such carvings usually had a practical function as well, such as filigreed screens to allow the circulation of air.

When approaching Thai art, one should constantly be aware that it belongs to the world of religion, and not to the domain of the individual. Building a temple or painting a mural is a way to make merit, and the craftsmen who execute the commission will acquire a share of the accrued spiritual gain. No Thai artist of the past ever set out solely to create beauty, much less to express his own thoughts, feelings, or personality. Similarly, the distinction between the 'fine arts' and humble crafts is an arbitrary preconception of the Western mind that proves to be illusory anywhere in Asia, and particularly false in northern Thailand.

The history of the Thai arts is best described as a patchwork of schools and styles related to townships that flourished in various periods. The scarce documentation available coupled with the lack of a sure chronology means that a complete reconstruction of the historical evolution of Thai art can only be presented in a most sketchy and tentative way.

Styles of Buddha Images

Haripunchai (13th century). Stucco or terracotta.

Phayao (prior to the 13th century, probably 11th). Always carved from sandstone.

Sukhothai (15th century). If small, usually bronze. Large images are in brick and stucco or laterite and stucco.

Lanna (13th-15th century). Bronze.

Late Lanna (18th-19th century). Bronze. Large images in brick and stucco.

Laotian of late period (18th-19th century). Bronze, wood.

Burmese, Shan (17th-19th century). Bronze, lacquered wood.

Burmese, Shan (Buddha in Royal apparel.). Bronze, laquered wood.

Burmese, Mandalay (19th, early 20th cent.). Bronze, laquered wood, alabaster

๒๕๐๐

The Symbolism and Attire of Buddha Images

The Buddha, who renounced all worldly goods, is usually depicted in monk's robes. Monastic dress consists of three items: an undercloth for covering the lower part of the body, a large robe draped around the body, which may cover one or both shoulders (in sculpture it is usually depicted leaving the right shoulder bare), and a kind of shawl used as a cloak in cool weather. The shawl-like cloth, or *uttarasanga,* is usually represented as simply thrown across the left shoulder when presented in sculpture. Although these garments are not depicted realistically, but rather in an idealized manner, they still evidence changes in style that evolved through the centuries over the region.

For example, the shawl as depicted in the classic Lanna images of the golden period is most often quite short, hardly reaching the breast. In contemporary Sukhothai statuary the same garment reaches the waist.

The physical features of the Buddha are an idealized representation of a philosophical abstract. Sculptors relied on ancient texts which indicated the characteristics (*laksana*) by which future Buddhas could be recognized. They included 108 auspicious signs such as fingers of equal length, a protuberance on top of the head (*ushnisha*), and arms long enough to touch the knees without bending. Long ears are a reference to the Lord Buddha's royal upbringing: royalty used to wear heavy earrings that stretched the lobes. The *ketumal*, a halo-like shape above the *ushnisha*, symbolizes the energy emanating from his body—the spiritual glow of a superior being. In northern Thailand this flame is usually depicted in the form of a lotus bud, quite differently from the statuary of lower Siam.

In some works the Buddha is portrayed in royal garments, reflecting the particular beliefs and legends prevalent at the time of their creation. Representations prior to the 15th century are usually assumed to be related to the Mahayana Buddhism of the Khner and to represent the Transcendental Buddha. The Buddhas of later periods, especially in the north of Thailand and Burma, are related to the legend of Jambupati. Jambupati was a very proud king who initially refused to heed the teachings of Buddha. Buddha then manifested himself to Jambupati as Rajadhiraja, King of Kings, emerging from flames and dressed in full splendour. Jambupati converted instantly and became one of the Buddha's disciples.

Lanna Buddha

Lanna Buddha in royal apparel

Sukhothai Buddha

One of the earliest schools to flourish in the North was that of the Mon kingdom of Haripunchai (the present day town of Lamphun) during the seventh to thirteenth century. Although independent, the town obviously had contact with the Mon kingdoms of lower Siam, as well as with the Mon of Burma, who had already absorbed numerous elements of Pala Sena of north-eastern India.

A small number of exquisite stone and bronze images show that Haripunchai art is a continuation of the Dvaravati tradition of central Thailand, exhibiting delicate feminine features and smooth surfaces. The majority of the surviving sculpture is, however, terracotta and stucco that was part of temple decorations. The images of Buddha and his disciples are characterized by strong and square faces, curving eyebrows connected together, bulging eyes, and well–designed curling mustaches—elements that combine to create a rather enigmatic expression. Giants (*yaksa*) and mythical animals have decidedly fiery expressions, with spirited eyes like those of grotesque masks. Haripunchai sculpture is highly mannerist and in the later period degenerates into almost caricature–like figures. The architecture is best seen in the two *chedis* of Wat Ku Kut in Lamphun, each of rather unusual design: one is a stepped pyramid, the other is an octagonal tower. Both are enriched by a series of standing Buddhas.

After annexation to the Lanna kingdom of Mengrai, Haripunchai continued the same production for more than one hundred years. This fact should not be surprising since most of the sculpture was cast from moulds, and moulds last for a long time. The school ultimately died out in the fifteenth century, although the town continued to be a thriving artistic centre with its later sculpture being similar to that of Chiang Mai.

Another school of art that pre–dates Mengrai's unification of the North is that of Phayao, which according to recent discoveries may be the oldest truly Thai school of art in the region. No systematic excavations have been conducted so far, and no buildings survive; there is only a collection of fragments of Buddhas, basements full of statues, and *chedis*. The Phayao school was obviously heavily influenced by the Indian tradition of Pala art, which reached its apogee in that country during the ninth century. The Buddha heads, always carved from sandstone, are characterized by a pointed nose and very prominent upper lips. Fragments of Phayao sculptures are found scattered in temples in various places in the North, suggesting that during its heyday the school was a large production centre. This tradition died out after Phayao was annexed to Lanna and subsequently lost its economic importance.

The city of Chiang Saen, located on the banks of the Mekong where the modern borders of Thailand, Laos and Burma meet, was the site of a very important school of bronze casting. The name 'Chiang Saen' has often been incorrectly applied to the entirety of the sculptural production of the North, which is a misleading generalization; the name should be reserved solely for the production of Chiang Saen artisans. (The cultural centre of the North was Chiang Mai, and the artistic production of the North in general should be

Chedi of Northern Thailand

Ratana Chedi of Wat Ku Kut, Lamphun.
Haripunchai style, 12th–13th century

Chedi of Wat Phra Sak, Chiang Saen.
Haripunchai influence, 1275 a.d.

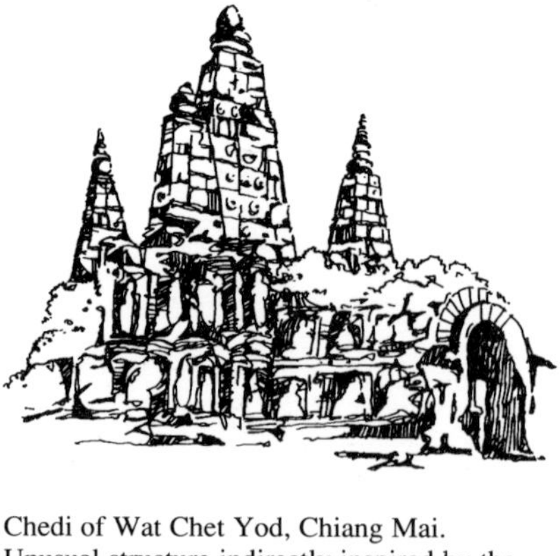

Chedi of Wat Chet Yod, Chiang Mai.
Unusual structure indirectly inspired by the temple of Bodgaya in India through Burmese replicas.

Chedi of Wat Chedi Luang, Chiang Saen.
Early Lanna style, late 14th century

Chedi of Wat Lok, Chiang Mai. A frequently encountered type of *chedi* in classic early Lanna-style, 14-15th century.

Chedi of Wat Phra That Haripunchai. Lamphun circular type, derived from Sri Lanka patterns *via* Sukhothai, late 14th century (Restored).

Chedi of Wat Kutao, Chiang Mai. A unique type showing Yunnanese influence, late 16th century.

A typical Burmese-influenced chedi. Common in the North in the late 19th century.

termed 'Lanna Art'). A group of statues of great beauty was once identified as in the classic Chiang Saen style and attributed to a very early date, but it now seems that this type was a production of the early Chiang Mai period. Such Buddha images are characterized by a plump, round face with a prominent chin, downward gazing eyes, and large curls in the hair. Such Buddhas are usually seated, legs crossed and with the soles of the feet turned upwards.

The golden age of Lanna art was in the fifteenth century, and particularly the period of King Tilokaraja, a great patron of both Buddhism and the arts. After the fall of the Mengrai dynasty, sculpture became progressively less fluid as well as less innovative. Buddha images of the later period tend to be rather stiff, with stereotyped faces which lack that inner breadth so evident in the work of the golden age. Some similarity with Laotian images—such as the so–called 'bat ears', which have a curved point at the top— can also be observed. This influence is not ascribable to any direct input of Laotian artists into Lanna art, but simply to the fact that both regions were part of the same cultural milieu.

Several buildings survive from this later phase of Lanna art. A number of ceremonial gates in Lampang, built in brick and stucco, can be related to the tradition of the golden period; they show elegant proportions with gently tapering finials and are enlivened by stucco decorations that emanate the same vitality as the great masterpieces of the early Lanna period. Their subdued exuberance makes us regret that so much of Lanna art has been lost.

While there are no surviving examples of wooden architecture from any of the early periods, there remain a number of wooden *viharns* which can be dated to the seventeenth century, the opening phase of the late Lanna period. These fragile buildings exist in precarious condition and, again, Lampang is the place where most of the best examples can be found. Such structures give us a hint of an architectural tradition which, although never grand, was undoubtedly very innovative. When compared to the architecture of lower Siam during the same period—so pretentious and so stereotyped—Lanna buildings have a refreshing intimacy and naïveté. Their honest, sturdy, squat proportions are graced by a sense of openness lent by extensive use of wood, an openness often enhanced by the absence of side panels between the columns which support the roof.

With the exception of a few fragments at Wat Umong in Chiang Mai, all surviving examples of Lanna painting are quite recent. Bright colours and a graphically naïve interpretation of the subject are the main characteristics; figures are always outlined in black and then filled in with colours. The subjects are most often the usual Jataka tales, though strong emphasis is also given to the accompanying vignettes, and consequently a mural complex usually presents a vivid portrayal of contemporary life. The two main examples of Lanna pictorial art easily accessible to the general public are the murals of Viharn Laikam at Wat Phra Sing, Chiang Mai, and the murals of Wat Phumin in Nan.

Northern artists excelled in the decorative arts. Flower motifs reminiscent of the European Baroque are very common, as are geometric elements such as lozenges and the Greek stripe. A typical medium of Lanna decorative art is a red lacquer finish applied to wooden surfaces and then overlaid with gold leaf in various motifs, such as floral patterns or a series of Bodhi trees alternating with flying deities. The showpiece of this interesting technique is in the old *viharn* at Wat Pong Yang Kok in the grounds of Wat Lampang Luang south of Lampang near Kokha village.

Burmese art in northern Thailand merits a chapter to itself. Although Burmese influence was long present, it becomes evident in art only at the end of the nineteenth century when Burmese immigrants came to work in the timber business and Burmese carpenters and craftsman were hired by British teak firms. These immigrants were responsible for the construction of many Burmese-style buildings and temples, as well as for the foundation of some Burmese monasteries. In addition to pure Burmese creations, there are many hybrid buildings incorporating a melange of Lanna, Burmese and Victorian motifs (such as the arch). Such Burmese temples of the late nineteenth century are found primarily in Chiang Mai, Lampang, and Phrae.

Even before this late Burmese influence, Shan communities had already been established in various parts of northern Thailand, and these Shans had built their own temples in their own style. (One such marvelous wooden edifice which used to be at Wat Chongkham in Ngao has now been saved from decay and moved to Muang Boran, an open air museum near Bangkok commonly known as 'The Ancient City'.) The largest Shan communities in Thailand are in Mae Hong Son and Mae Sariang, and these provinces host a number of typical Shan monasteries, as well as examples of Shan sculpture. Elaborate decoration typifies the Shan artistic idiom, and this rococo taste manifests itself even in bronze Buddha images. The Lord Buddha is often garbed in royal apparel with an extremely elaborate crown spreading horizontally to resemble a pair of giant ears. The facial features of Shan Buddhas are quite peculiar: a baby–like expression with very small lips and a small, pointed nose.

The ceramic art of the North during the later Lanna period is represented by the production of several kilns which operated from the end of the fifteenth century onwards: Wiang Kalong (Chiang Rai), San Kamphaeng (Chiang Mai), and Wang Nua (Lampang). According to the local chronicles, these kilns employed artisans abducted from Sri Satchanalai as spoils of war. The production, however, lacks the quality of the Sri Satchanalai kilns. The raw materials appear to have been of inferior quality, and the designs are repetitive and merely ornamental, lacking the vivacity and creativity for which the wares of Sukhothai and Sri Satchanalai are justly famous. Most of these northern kilns ceased operations in the seventeenth century.

Chiang Mai

An Introduction

Travellers say there are places one simply passes through because one cannot do otherwise, places where one visits because to be there is chic, and finally places where one is simply happy to be, never wanting to leave. Thailand used to fall entirely within the third category, but it seems to have now regressed into the second class, leaving unspoiled only a few isolated spots—most of them islands—where young travellers hang around for ages and go completely native. Chiang Mai, though not an island, is one such place, and its popularity is such that it is now becoming increasingly difficult to find a seat on the plane and a room to sleep. Why so? Is it because it is the proverbial "Rose of the North", set in a verdant valley amidst lush tropical forests? No, nearly all the forests have gone, and the city is now swathed in a cloud of dust. And Chiang Mai's allure is not because of its nightlife, which is rather tame compared to that of Bangkok or Pattaya (although in this respect 'The Rose' is quickly learning to emulate her brash, southern sisters). Culture? Northern culture is an ephemeral thing, hard to find and even more difficult to comprehend—the monstrosities being built nowadays make a mockery of the old culture.

And yet—despite the busloads of Taiwanese tourists, despite the dust lingering over the city, despite the ugly shophouses with the obligatory but ridiculous *galae* on the roof—all visitors are happy in Chiang Mai and nobody wants to leave. Each person has their own reason, the only common denominator being the fact that Chiang Mai is indisputably different from the rest of Thailand. For some, it is the beautiful girls that drive zig–zag sitting three on a moped; for some, it is the people hanging out in streetside cafés chattering away as if they actually have something to tell each other; for some, it is nothing more than the weird grin of the old lady in a starched blouse walking to the temple carrying a fuchsia-coloured paper flag; and for others it the hot air balloons lofted to the sky on New Years Day, each balloon carrying a piece of paper enscribed with some childlike request to the Siamese equivalent of Santa Claus.

Like the Italian towns where everybody gravitates to the piazza to talk politics over an ice cream or a glass of wine, Chiang Mai is made of its people, not of its buildings, and tourists who get the spirit are as much a part of the city as the locals. As in Florence or Rome, visitors come to see the monuments—but they stay for the cafés. Sitting at the riverside with a beer in hand, the modern vagabonds become as much a part of the landscape as the *chedis* on the mountains. They sit and plan adventures into the hills, cerebral odysseys that will never go further than Doi Suthep. They bargain for hours over a piece of lacquerware that would be half the price in a London department store. They wax poetic on mysterious dances and obscure rituals that have not been performed for fifty years. If you listen to the talk long enough, there appears, after a long march through the jungles on elephant back, the walled city of Zimmè, full of teak mansions inhabited by bejewelled and bare-breasted princesses. The riches of the North, as real as those of Xanadu, lay before your feet.

The North is a world in itself, and Chiang Mai is its centre. Northern people call themselves *khon meuang*—'People of the Principalities'—even when they live in the forest. They go to Bangkok only for school or for business and are probably more likely to go work in Saudi Arabia than to emigrate to their own capital.

Proof of the North's estrangement is the fact that Chiang Mai is infinitely more exotic to Bangkokians than it is to any Westerner. The Central Thais know nothing about it and are truly convinced that it is a very bizarre and a very cold place. *"Naaw, mai?"* ("Was it cold?") is the invariable question you are asked when you say that you have just returned from Chiang Mai. Even though "98° Fahrenheit!" might well be the answer, the citizens of the capital do not seem to grasp the reality, and when they go to Chiang Mai, Bangkok ladies inevitably wear a scarf, a visible sign of preparation to brave the utmost hardships.

As Thailand's third largest city after Bangkok and Khon Kaen, Chiang Mai is still just a small city with a population of no more than 150,000 people. However, it is considerably larger than any other of the towns in northern Thailand and thus is bound to be your base—so you might well choose to spend a few days getting acquainted with it.

The first goal is to understand how the city is laid out and what is where.The dominant feature of Chiang Mai is the square moat that encompasses the old town. The moats that one sees today are not, however, those dug at the command of King Mengrai when he first founded Chiang Mai; the present moats were excavated at a later date during the protracted wars with the Burmese. Remains of the fortifications, recently restored, are still visible at the corners, and parts of the old wall still stand near Tapae Gate. The survival of these remnants contributes to preserve the identity of Chiang Mai in the face of rapid changes.

According to tradition, Mengrai consulted the Kings of Sukhothai and Phayao about a plan on which to build the city, and the three monarchs are said to have pondered upon the fact that Haripunchai and Kelang Nakorn (the name of the earliest town sited at Lampang) were shaped like a conch shell, the symbol of Vishnu.

The centre of the modern city, just east of Tapae Gate, may be considered to be Tapae Road, especially around Charoen Prathet and Chang Klan Roads, which cut the town transversely. This is the main shopping area and also where many of the big hotels are located: the Chiang Inn, the Pornping, the Suriwong, the Diamond, and the Chiang Mai Plaza. Guesthouses are scattered everywhere but tend to concentrate along three roads: Charoen Prathet Road, Charoen Rat Road on the opposite side of the river, and the area around Tapae Gate.

Moon Muang Road, inside the moat near Tapae Gate, is the site of what the Thais call 'Farang bars' (farang means foreigner of Caucasian descent),

Chiang Mai
National Museum
Wat Chet Yod
Superhighway
To Zoo, University & Doi Suthep
Huay
Kaeo
Road
Rincome Hotel
YMCA
Chiang Mai Orchid Hotel
Chotana
Road
Wat Kutao
Stadium
Bus Station (Fang, Hot, Lamphun)
Rattanakosin Rd.
Chang Puak Gate
Mani
Noparat
Road
Si
Phum
Road
Wittha
Wat Chiang Man
Ratchaphanikai
Road
Chaiyapoom Rd.
Sithiwong
Wang
Kaeo
Road
Singharat
Road
Phra
Jhaban Rd.
Ratchawithi Rd.
Chang
Nimanhemin
Road
Suan
Kulap
Road
Road
Wat Phapong
Inthawarorot Rd.
Suthep
Road
Suan Dok Gate
Wat Phra Sing
Phra Sing Rd.
Ratchadamnoen Rd
Pokklao
Muang
Tapae Gate
To Wat Umong
Wat Suan Dok
Wat Chedi Luang
Road
Road
Ratchamanka
Road
Wat Mengrai
Road
Road
Loi
Wat Puak Hong
Samlan
Moon
Kotchasan
Park
Chiang Mai Gate
Suan Prung Gate
Bamrungburi
Road
Changlo
Road
Sri
Bunruangrit
Road
Wualai
Road
Banyen Folk Art Museum
Suriwong Rd.
National Theatre
Nantharam Rd.
Thipanet
Chiang Mai Cultural Center
Airport
Immigration Office
0 250 500 750 1000 m.
0 250 500 750 1000 yards
N

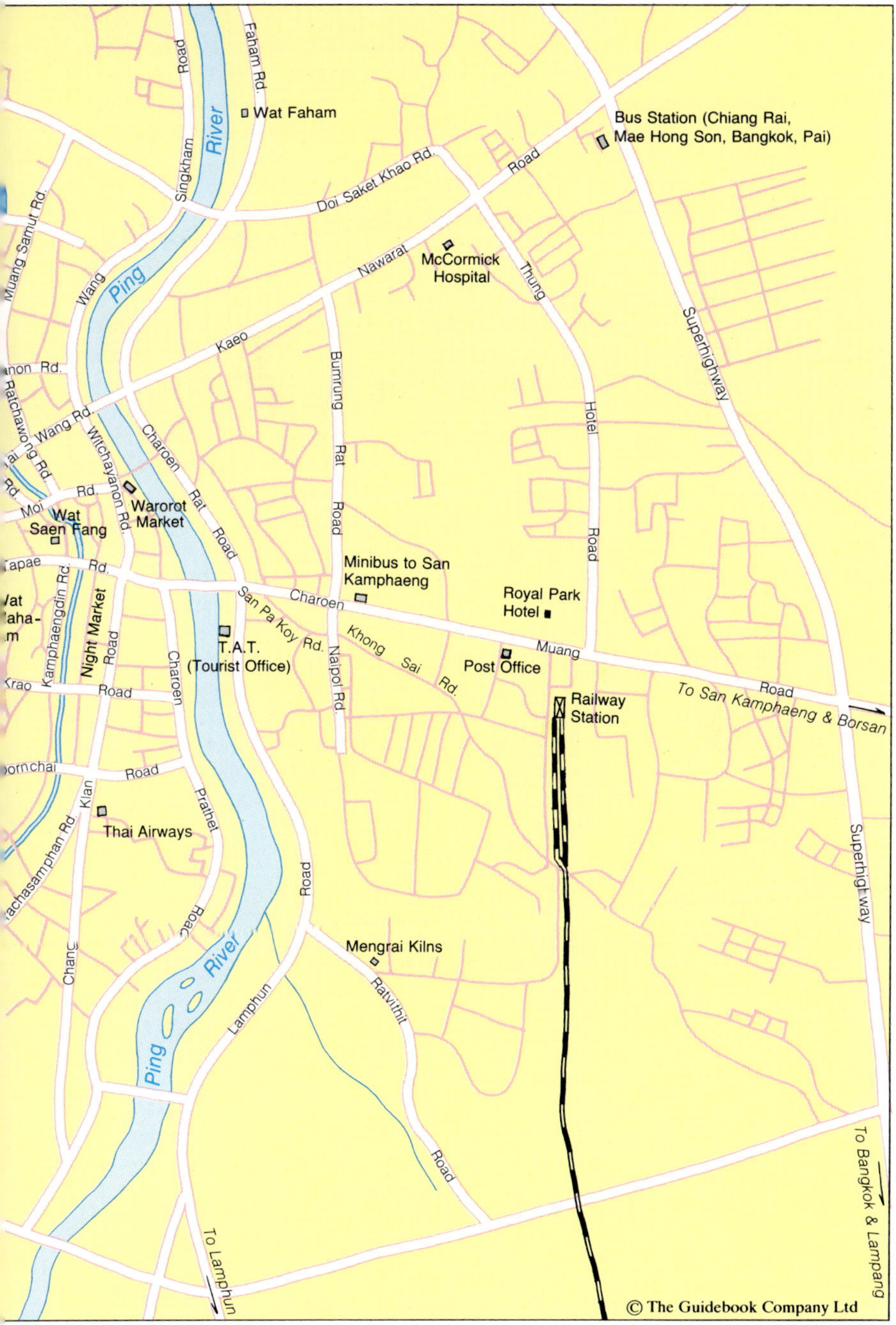

For Hotels, Restaurants and Nightspots see map on pages 228-229

establishments that cater mainly to Westerners and most especially young travellers. Nearly all of these places are on the cheap side, and they tend to be rather seedy. The atmosphere is decidedly better on the opposite bank of the river, where businesses such as the Riverside Cafe and the Teahouse attract a convivial crowd of expatriates and young Thais.

Huay Kaeo Road leads to Chiang Mai University and a number of cafés where young people meet in a rather lively environment; here are located the best and quietist hotels, the Orchid and the Rincome. Further along is a fashionable area which has recently sprung up near Wat Umong. (When looking for a place to stay, keep in mind the noise and the pollution, both of which are becoming increasingly difficult to avoid.) Most residents prefer the peaceful surroundings of the eastern bank of the river, the old Farang quarter, where there are still many old houses, big gardens, and a relative lack of noise.

Transportation around town is easy. In the cool weather you can walk nearly everywhere, as the town is still rather small. There are no proper taxis; mini–buses ply certain routes and will drop you off more or less where you want—though sometimes only after having detoured around your destination a few times to drop off other passengers. Tuk–tuks, the noisy and unstable three-wheelers so ubiquitous in Bangkok, have now arrived in Chiang Mai—along with their imported drivers, many of whom still have to learn the names of Chiang Mai's streets. Short hops can be done by tricycle (samlor), if you are not Socialist-minded and feel no guilt at having an albeit healthy, man pedal you around in the sweltering heat. Jeeps, cars, motorcycles and bicycles can be rented everywhere at reasonable rates and with a selection to suit all budgets. Having your own transportation makes life much easier. Motorcycles especially give you freedom to roam about, and the traffic in Chiang Mai is not nearly so murderous as it is in Bangkok. Expect to pay 100-150 baht per day for a 100-150cc motorbike.

The History of Chiang Mai

The city which King Mengrai built was at a considerable distance from the Ping River —exactly how far we do not know, since the river has shifted its course during the centuries. When Mengrai established his capital here, the valley was already inhabited. As late as the end of the last century it was still possible to see the moats and ramparts of Muang La Maing, an earlier Lawa stronghold built at the base of the slope of Doi Suthep at the western end of present day Chiang Mai.

Mengrai's walled town contained the royal palace, the houses of the nobility, and several important temples. What was for long considered to be Mengrai's palace has now been entirely razed to make place for the Yupharat School. Holt Hallett, who saw the building at the turn of the century, describes it as a "substantial one–storeyed building, slightly Chinese in aspect, with brick walls, plastered over with excellent cement, and a tiled roof." What Hallet saw was certainly a late reconstruction, as the Lanna kings always resided in wooden buildings.

At the end of the eighteenth century, sacked by the Burmese and impoverished by continuous wars, the city saw its population shrink and was even abandoned for a time. When peace returned, the city expanded and an L-shaped wall and moat were added to the south and east sides, embracing the old city. Remains of these fortifications can still be seen at Wat Saen Fang and in Kamphaengdin Road (where until recently a redlight district nestled under the earthen ramparts).

The outer town, where the markets were located, was the busiest area. "After passing through the gates," wrote Hallett in 1890, "we entered the market, which extends for more than half a mile to the gates of the inner city, and beyond them for some distance towards the palace. On either side of the main road, little covered booths or stalls are set up; but most of the women spread a mat on the ground to sit upon, and placing their baskets by their side, expose their provisions upon wicker work trays or freshly cut plantain-leaves. It is a very pretty sight in the early morning to watch the women and girls from the neighbouring villages streaming over the bridge, their produce dangling from each end of a pole of bamboo over their shoulders, or accurately poised on their heads ..."

"As in the island of Bali," noted Carl Bock, "the women do all selling. The pork stalls alone are kept by men, but they always seem to have more dogs around than customers."

Old Chiang Mai Moats

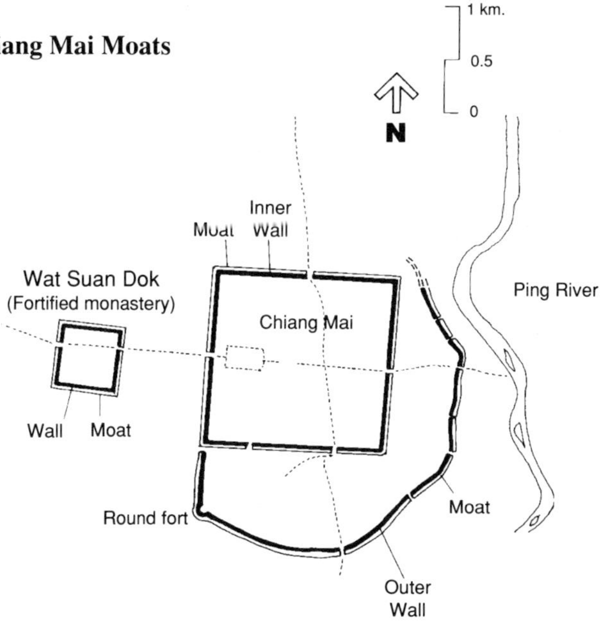

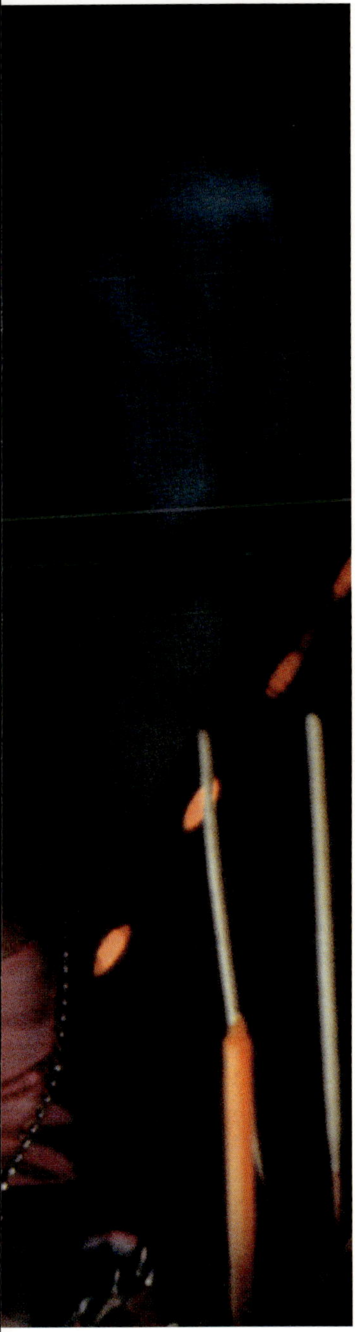

During the Loy Kratong festival small floats are elaborately constructed of banana leaf and adorned with flower petals to bear offerings of coins and incense. The floats are set adrift upon rivers and lakes to thank the spirit of the waters for providing a successful rice harvest. (left)

In Chiang Mai, aside from the purely religious activities associated with Loy Kratong, there is a grand parade of colorful floats graced with local beauties. The parade is followed by the inevitable beauty pagent to select a Miss Loy Kratong. (above)

"It is no unusual thing to see an elephant stalking down the market amidst a crowd of Karens, Shans, and Kamuks from across the Mekong, and even Tai from the distant Sipsong Panna, and Haw traders from Yunnan..." wrote a British surveyor who visited the city in the same period. Trade with the neighbouring kingdoms was brisk. Every year Chiang Mai was visited by caravans regularly employing 1,000 mules from Yunnan and 7,000 from the Shan states; 5,000 porters were engaged in the trade with lower Burma and another 4,000 travelled into the Shan states and northern Burma. Over 3,000 laden oxen plied the trade with Lampang, and more than 8,000 elephants were employed as beasts of burden in the region.

Communications with lower Siam were quite difficult, and it was very time consuming to journey to and from Bangkok. Until the establishment of the railroad in the late 1920s, trade was scanty and few officials from the South visited the town. During the rainy season, the journey took 17 days from Chiang Mai to Bangkok, and 50 days from Bangkok to Chiang Mai. In the dry season it took 35 days from Chiang Mai to reach Bangkok and 66 to return. To avoid the rapids in the upper part of the Ping, the section from Hot to Chiang Mai during the rainy season was always done on elephant back.

Very few foreigners visited Chiang Mai before the second half of the nineteenth century. In 1867 an American Presbyterian Mission was established in Chiang Mai, and their work was instrumental in improving the education, health, and material prosperity of the region, which had been misruled for centuries—the populace having been kept as private slaves by the local chiefs. Although the missionaries never seriously attempted to convert the Northerners to Christianity, they did do much to extirpate superstitious beliefs in witchcraft which had rendered the life of the villagers miserable, afflicting them with perpetual fear. The Presbyterians opened schools and hospitals, introduced modern agricultural methods, and taught carpentry and shipbuilding.

Realizing the importance of their work, the central government in Bangkok supported their activities and in a few decades there were mission stations all over the North, from Chiang Mai to Nan. The MacCormick Hospital, the McKean Leprosary Center, and the Payap College are just a few of their achievements which are still noticeable today. The histories of the missionaries can be read on the tombstones of the Christian cemetery, where one can pause and ponder upon the hard life and, all too frequently, the early demise of these selflessly dedicated people.

The missionaries' quarter was located on the east side of the river, and when the British, after conquering upper Burma, gained logging concessions in Siam, the area turned into a small foreign community of many nationalities. Of the 'Teak Wallah' era, quite a few vestiges remain, and visitors who want to savour the atmosphere of the old times should cast a glance at the old British Consulate, the Borneo compound (where the managers of the Leonowens Company used to reside), the Queripel house (now a cultural centre near the Superhighway), and many other colonial-style buildings awaiting demolition in the back alleyways of Chiang Mai. Such buildings are silent reminders of a saga that spanned only a few decades but dramatically changed the life and the economy of the North.

The British were actually trying to establish themselves in northern Siam, having planned a railroad from Burma to China that would pass through Chiang Mai, but they finally abandoned the idea, deciding that Siam should remain a buffer state between British dominions and those of the French in Indochina.

The activities of the British spurred the government in Bangkok to realize that Chiang Mai was worthy of attention. This decision was visibly manifested by the royal visit of King Prachadipok in 1927, who entered the city with a cortege of 87 elephants, heralding a new era. He was the first Chakri king to ever visit Chiang Mai.

Since then, the North has been rapidly integrated into the mainstream of the Thai nation. Today, Chiang Mai is one of the most prosperous provinces of Thailand, and modernization is evident everywhere: in the new residential complexes, the huge hotels and, lately, the industrial estates sprawling along the Superhighway.

Temples of Chiang Mai

Chiang Mai was the principal religious centre around which coalesced the life and culture of a vast region stretching as far as China. Quite naturally, then, Chiang Mai is a city of temples. Today there are 36 *wats* within the moats alone and more than 85 in the metropolitan area, not to speak of those in the surrounding countryside. Very few, however, survive intact in the original Lanna style in which they were built. At the end of the last century Burmese influence was very strong, due not only to the presence of wealthy merchants but also to a community of craftsmen and builders employed by the British to work in the logging industry. Their presence resulted in a number of atypical additions, transformations and restorations to the local temples, and the results of their efforts are numerous hybrid buildings which over time have become so typical of Chiang Mai as to be considered almost a local creation.

More changes came in the 1930s when the venerated monk Khruba Srivijaya initiated the restoration of several major monasteries, emulating grandiose design concepts inspired by the taste of administrators newly arrived from Bangkok. The new architecture was completely alien to both local style and local sentiments. When the Bangkok ('Rattanakosin') style was forcibly introduced in the North, it was already at the very end of its period of vitality; new buildings were often designed by Western architects and many have a tangible Art Deco flavour, which in Chiang Mai is particularly evident in the figures of Devas (female celestial beings) on many of the temples' door panels.

The introduction of ferroconcrete and other modern construction techniques have forever vanquished the charm of the traditional architecture, with contemporary creations most closely resembling the pavilions of a Tiger

Balm Garden. Gracious, ancient structures are continually being demolished to be replaced by concrete monstrosities painted in garish colours. Murals are whitewashed and then repainted without any spirit, while delicate carvings end up in antique shops—if they are not burned as fuel in the monastery's kitchen.

The most pathetic note is the degeneration that took place in traditional mural painting. As usually happens when a new vogue is introduced, the capital gets the first choice and the countryside gets the leftovers and cheap imitations. At the turn of the century, Bangkok employed a number of Italian painters to 'revitalise' the tired Rattanakosin art. What reached the countryside was only a vulgar imitation of their already vulgar style, a popularized art much like that of the cigarette cards and meat extract advertisements of Europe at that time. The murals of Doi Suthep, for example, look like huge enlargements of those cards given away in Italy in the early 1920s to the faithful consumers of Liebig Stock Cubes.

Despite all of these sad changes, temple sightseeing remains a major tourist sport in Chiang Mai, and seeking 'your' pristine temple in the back alleys of the old town is still an exciting treasure hunt. The following is a list of temples, including all the major ones and the most obviously notable (because they are located on roads where they are unlikely to be missed), plus some less obvious recommendations. At the present rate of destruction, this list is destined to be out of date shortly, so don't be be surprised if you find a concrete 'renovation' instead of the old masterpiece you were expecting.

Wat Phra Sing Located at the junction of Singharat and Phra Sing Roads (an extension of Ratchadamnoen Road), this temple has been one of Chiang Mai's most important sanctuaries. Founded in 1345 to house the ashes of King Kham Fu, the main *viharn* is a lofty building erected in 1925 and recently restored; although nicely decorated, it feels much like the atrium of a railway station. Behind the new *viharn* there is a *bot* (an old Lanna wooden structure with a stuccoed gate) and the famed Viharn Laikam, possibly the finest building still surviving in Chiang Mai. Built in late Lanna style in 1806 or 1811 by a brother of King Kawila, it houses the Buddha Phra Sing. This famous image, the origin of which is shrouded in incredible legends, was one of the palladia of the Lanna dynasty. Brought from Chiang Rai to Chiang Mai by King Saen Muang Ma, it is an early Lanna bronze image. (Unfortunately, the original head was cut away and the present one is a replica.) On the walls of the *viharn* there is an interesting complex of late 19th century mural paintings, depicting the story of the Jataka San Tong and also the story of Suwannahonse, the golden Hamsa (a mythical bird-like creature). These paintings, probably the work of a local artist named Jek Seng, are the best preserved in the city and constitute the best available documentation of everyday life in the North a century ago. Observers of human nature will discover humourous vignettes of children playing, lovers hiding in the bushes, and ladies gossiping behind a screen; social scientists will find a complete visual catalogue of textiles, costumes, tattoos, baskets, and kitchen utensils. Most of the buildings depicted in the murals quite faithfully reflect the style of northern houses and palaces, with realistically painted curtains, lamps and chandeliers. The royal personages portrayed are usually wearing Burmese clothes, following an artistic convention of the period.

The Nagas and the Singha in front of the *viharn*, as well as those of the nearby *bot*, are in pure Lanna style, showing none of the Burmese influence so pervasive in Chiang Mai. The library is a delicate wooden building of dainty proportions, raised on top of a tall whitewashed podium decorated with stucco Devas; it was rebuilt in 1920 on an older base.

Next to Wat Phra Sing, (on Singharat Road) is a tiny temple with beautifully carved windows, **Wat Phapong**. Right behind it is **Wat Prasat**, an interesting building in the old Lanna style, especially worthy of attention because the *viharn* is connected to the *chedi* by a tunnel, a very ancient architectural form.

Wat Chedi Luang, located on Phra Pokklao Road, is famous for its gigantic, ruined *chedi*. Built in 1401 and subsequently enlarged to the height of 90 m by King Tilokaraja, the *chedi* was destroyed by an earthquake in 1545 and never restored. Remnants of beautiful stucco figures flank the steps. The other buildings are modern and hardly worthy of attention. Of great beauty is a tall gum tree which stands the best chance of survival among all its fellows in the valley: according to legend, the city of Chiang Mai will last only as long as this tree stands, and so thus far it has been spared by rapacious developers. The City Pillar is housed in a small building under this gum tree, supposedly on the spot where King Mengrai was struck by lightning. (The **Monument to King Mengrai** lies on the opposite corner of the Ratchadamnoen intersection.)

Wat Pan Tao, located on Phra Pokklao Road just a few metres from Wat Chedi Luang, is a small temple preserving an old *viharn* in pristine condition. The walls are made entirely of wooden panels, none of which support the roof which rests entirely on wooden columns. Above the door and windows of the facade there are stuccoed-and-gilded decorations of exquisite workmanship in the classic Lanna tradition.

Wat Mengrai, on Ratchamanka Road, Lane 6, is a modern temple done entirely in cement. Still, there is an interesting stuccoed ceremonial gate and also a standing Buddha image which was cast during Mengrai's reign and is reputed to be in his likeness.

Wat Puak Hong, located not far from Suan Prung Gate on a lane off Samlan Road, has an interesting old *chedi*. Similar to that of Wat Rampoeng (a temple outside the city) and displaying an unusual Chinese influence, the *chedi* dates from the sixteenth to seventeenth century and is a round, stepped pyramid with decorated niches sheltering meditating Buddhas.

Wat Munyongkorn, also on Samlan Road is—despite its disorganized, scruffy appearance—well worth visiting. The main *viharn* is an old wooden Lanna edifice in need of skilful restoration. A diminutive *bot* of much more recent construction features elegant woodcarvings decorated with glasswork.

Chiang Mai temples: the skyline of Wat Suan Dok (top)
Viharn Laikham at Wat Phra Sing (bottom)

The *chedi* is a Lanna structure topped by a Burmese bell–shaped finial. Thus, the full architectural history of Chiang Mai is represented on this one site.

Wat Chiang Man is on Ratchaphanikai Road and is probably the first temple built by Mengrai. It is purported to be the site of his camp; but the buildings are obviously not nearly so old, apart from the *chedi*, which is probably a fifteenth century reconstruction of the original. It features strong Mon (early Pagan) characteristics, the base being decorated with rows of buttresses shaped like elephants. To the left of the *chedi* is a small library, recently rebuilt and painted in garish colours, and an old *bot*, a nineteenth century Lanna wooden structure containing a fine collection of bronzes, some Lanna, some Uthong. The two *viharns* are more recent and architecturally insignificant, though they do contain a number of revered Buddha images; the Phra Setang Khamani is a tiny crystal figurine supposed to be very ancient and endowed with rainmaking powers, and the stone Phra Sila is an Indian image in the Pala style.

Wat Saen Fang, on Tapae Road facing the intersection with Kamphaengdin Road, is approached by a Naga-flanked lane and incorporates part of a second ring of city walls, lending the temple a fortress-like appearance. There is a tall Burmese-style *chedi* decorated with several Singha created in a spirited manner as well as golden parasols and a collection of old guns. The monks' quarters are in a large Burmese building, with arches and Victorian fretwork, while the *viharn* is a brightly painted Lanna-Burmese amalgamation.

More or less opposite,**Wat Bupparam** presents an even more heterogeneous collection of buildings: the main *viharn* has a facade with arches of Burmese flavour set under a Lanna roof. Alongside it is a fragile example of Lanna art; a tiny old wooden *viharn* with stucco decorations applied on the wood. The dark and somehow magical interior enshrines three large Buddhas which are crowded under a curving roof. In the same compound is a tall, ferroconcrete preaching hall, a garish reminder that the days of good taste are gone.

Further along the road, **Wat Maharam** is distinguished by the witty, Burmese-style figures that adorn the wall. The *chedi* and the large *viharn* are both Burmese, while the *bot* is Lanna. Opposite to it, **Wat Chedowan**, now in a state of disrepair, has three small Burmese *chedis*. A tall Burmese mansion still towers in the middle of Tapae Road, replete with Victorian fretwork and gracefully ornamented balconies. More Burmese temples can be seen along the northern wall of the city, notably **Wat Papao**, a Shan monastery with a rather romantic atmosphere due to its abandoned state.

Wat Chiang Kong, on Kamphaengdin Road, is a unique, well–preserved Chinese building. With paintings on the upper-floor balcony and beautifully carved door panels in Lanna style, it is a most unusual combination. The stucco decorations on the walls recall those of temples built in Bangkok during the third Chakri reign.

Wat Bua Krok Luang is located on the other side of the river, on a side lane off the road to San Kamphaeng. (Follow the arrow for the Ban Suan

Restaurant and you will not miss it.) Wat Bua Krok Luang houses the second important mural complex of Chiang Mai. There is an old Lanna *viharn* which appears to have been modified in the first decades of this century by cutting windows and doors into the murals, which were done some few years earlier than the renovations. The murals are enchanting—fresh and naïve, with strong outlines and bright colours—although in a very poor state of preservation. Painted at the turn of the century, they are in late Lanna style but the treatment suggests Shan (Tai Yai) craftsmanship. The subjects are, as usual, the life of the Buddha and scenes from the Jataka tales. The presiding Buddha image is huge and wholly unartistic, showing strong Laotian influence and a very rustic look.

Wat Suan Dok lies 1 km after the city gate off Suthep Road and it is a favourite spot for sunset watchers, although recent additions to the skyline may disturb more sophisticated visitors. Despite recent changes, the temple is spaciously laid out and very picturesque. It was once a fortified monastery, a *wiang*, built on the site of a royal garden. (*Suan Dok* means "Flower Garden" in Thai.) Tall ceremonial gates still mark the limits of the large compound. The main feature is a huge bell–shaped *chedi* (similar to those of Sukhothai) built at the end of the fourteenth century by King Ku Na, who had sponsored the famous monk Maha Tera Sumana to come from Ceylon and teach in Chiang Mai. The monk's presence explains the Singhalese shape of the building, which was extravagantly restored in the 1930s. Next to the *chedi* is a vast complex of the tombs and cenotaphs of the royal family of Chiang Mai, memorials which contribute to the intriguing skyline of the temple. The main *viharn*, unfortunately, is not unlike a railway station; it is a ferrocement creation of the illustrious restorer of Chiang Mai, Khruba Srivijaya.

Wat Umong lies at the end of a long winding lane, also off of Suthep Road, and is recommended if you have your own transportation. It is one of Chiang Mai's oldest monasteries, with underground cells for meditation. Of the oldest buildings very little is left to see above ground, although a few fragments of Nagas and *yaksas* (guardian giants) hint of lavish stucco decoration in a style similar to that of Haripunchai. The *chedi* is a recent hybrid built above the old meditation cells. The cells contain traces of the oldest surviving painting (fifteenth century) of early Lanna style. Floral decorative motifs and Buddhas of the past are the most common images. Sadly, today they have nearly entirely vanished.

A new monastery has sprung up in the compound, and it is very active in proselytizing to judge from the many moralizing signs scattered around the garden. Wat Umong is one of the few Thai temples which actively encourages artistic endeavours on the part of the monks. The monastery is also popular with Western Buddhist practitioners; some of the monks give sermons in English and anyone is welcome to come for retreat and meditation.

Wat Chet Yod (Wat Potharam Maha Viharn) is located along the Superhighway, not far from the National Museum. The *chedi* here is unique,

Examples of traditional Lanna wooden houses: the Kamtieng House, moved to Bangkok (bottom), the house of Kunying Wualai Leelanuch in Lampang (top), and the Banyen Museum in Chiang Mai (right).

quite unlike anything else in the North. It is actually composed of seven *chedis* erected on a rectangular laterite base which contains a barrel-vaulted room. This shape was inspired, most likely indirectly, by the Indian temple of Bodgaya, probably through Mon replicas seen in Burma. According to the Chronicles, however, it was copied direct from India and built by King Tilokaraja in 1455 to house the Eighth Buddhist World Council. These traditional beliefs have often been questioned by art historians both as to date and to provenance. The stucco decorations, which are the most enjoyable part of the structure, certainly date from Tilokaraja's reign. They represent 70 celestial deities, sumptuously adorned and serenely flying in the sky; the faces are of a delicate beauty indicative of the high refinement reached by the Lanna school of art at its peak. In the same compound another *chedi*, in classic Lanna style, houses the ashes of King Tilokaraja.

Wat Kutao, not far from the National Stadium, is renowned for another unusual *chedi*, this one evidencing Chinese influence. Probably built around the sixteenth-seventeenth century to contain the ashes of a Burmese ruler of Chiang Mai, or perhaps a Chinese warlord, it is shaped like hemispheres arranged in descending order of size.

Doi Suthep

The sentinel which watches over the city and, indeed, the very symbol of the city, the mountain of Doi Suthep is the most popular excursion from Chiang Mai, combining a glimpse of local colour and culture with a bit of fresh air. Only a few hundred metres above the valley floor, but being partly covered in forests, the mountain is considerably cooler than the city and provides a much needed recreation spot for the local people.

The trip takes some twenty minutes by car, and can be done with the local minibuses that leave from Chang Puak Gate (White Elephant Gate). Just past the entrance to Chiang Mai Zoo, Huay Kaeo Road begins to curve and climb and here, on the left, is a statue commemorating Phra Khruba Srivijaya, the famous monk who, in 1934, initiated the construction of the first proper road up to Doi Suthep in order to make the temple more accessible to pilgrims. The steep and winding road provides spectacular views back down over the city. At KM 6.8 a turning on the right leads 3 km to Doi Suthep National Park and the small waterfall of Konthathan.

The road reaches the foot of the peak and the temple, **Wat Phra That**. (The parking area has become a little village inhabited solely by professional tourist hasslers, hilltribe vendors, and beggars; they collectively produce enough garbage to have attained notice several times in the local press.) The temple is reached by a steep flight of steps leading from the parking area; the balustrade of the stairway is in the form of Nagas with brown and green tiles laid to resemble a snake's scales.

According to legend, the site of Wat Phra That was chosen in the late fourteenth century when King Ku Na (*r*. 1355-1385) was seeking a repository for holy relics that had been discovered at the same time as those enshrined at

Wat Suan Dok in town. The precious relics were placed in a howdah on the back of an elephant which was then set free to wander at will. The noble beast proceeded to climb Doi Suthep and near the summit it stopped, trumpeted, and turned around three times before kneeling, indicating that this was the proper site. The holy objects were accordingly enshrined in a *chedi*.

The present temple, comprising two sanctuaries and cloisters, was constructed in the sixteenth century, although the original buildings have been either expanded or restored several times by later Chiang Mai rulers. The gables of the sanctuaries are superbly decorated, and the *chedi*, constructed in typical Lanna style and flanked by four ornamental umbrellas, is covered with engraved gold plates. On a clear winter day, the terrace around the temple offers magnificent views of the surrounding countryside. The temple is also renown for the massive celebration of certain Buddhist holidays, such as Maka Bucha and Visaka Bucha, when hundreds of monks congregate to pray here.

From the parking area at Wat Phra That, the road continues to rise through the mountain forest for another 4 km before reaching **Phuping Palace**, the summer residence of the Thai royal family. The palace buildings are closed to the public, but the extensive grounds, with flower beds (blooms seen best in January) laid out as in English gardens, can be viewed Friday to Sunday and on public holidays from 8:30 a.m. to 4:30 p.m. whenever no members of the royal family are in residence. The main gates are at KM 18 but the visitor's entrance is 1.2 km beyond, where there is a parking lot and a path leading 200 m to the palace grounds.

Some 3 km beyond Phuping Palace is the **Meo village** of Ban Don Pui, reached by a rough track that is often muddy and generally only passable by truck or jeep. (Vehicles are easily hired in the parking area at Wat Phra That, but the drivers are almost invariably reckless, making the trip quite unpleasant.) The village, although at an unusually low altitude for the Blue Hmong tribe, is authentic, but its proximity to Chiang Mai has attracted a large number of visitors and turned the place into a tourist trap. Hundreds of souvenir stalls line the entrance, most of them selling strange and misplaced curios (such as fake Nepalese antiques and imitations of Tibetan Tankas) which have nothing to do with tribal crafts. A pathetic note is introduced by a miniscule garden of opium poppies with an educational sign explaining how opium culture has been forsaken in favour of more honest pursuits. Although unpleasant, a visit to this village is of some sociological interest since it is a textbook example of how a primitive community can totally lose its traditional sense of identity without being successfully integrated into the mainstream of society.

Other Places of Interest

The Chiang Mai Zoological Park Although rather modest by world standards, this zoo is the largest in Thailand and contains over 500 animals in pleasantly wooded grounds at the foot of Doi Suthep. It began as the private collection of Harold Young, an American working as an instructor with the Border Patrol Police; Young used to shelter wild animals brought in by hilltribesmen and hunters. Upon his death in 1965 the zoo was taken over by the Zoological Organization of Thailand.

Chiang Mai University Founded in 1965, it occupies spacious grounds and often stages exhibitions and performances. Of particular interest is the Tribal Research Centre, open from Monday to Friday, which houses a small museum of tribal crafts and an excellent library on the people of the hills.

Chiang Mai National Museum Located on the Superhighway, near Wat Ched Yod, it contains an interesting collection of northern art, as well as representative items of other schools of Thai art. The showpiece of the collection is a large Buddha face which once belonged to a complete statue which must have been one of the biggest bronzes ever cast in Thailand. This image is still believed by many to possess magic powers. Other noteworthy exhibits are multi-tiered shelves for votive tablets (dating from Tilokaraja's reign) and the famous Lord Buddha's footprint of Chiang Mai, decorated with glass and gold leaf on black lacquer. Several interesting terracottas of the Haripunchai school are also on display. Folk and hilltribe arts and crafts are exhibited on the upper floor.

Banyen Folk Art Museum Banyen, the noted handicraft centre, has now established a little museum of woodcarvings and objects of everyday use. Housed in a traditional northern building which is open to the public, the collection coalesces a life of painstaking search by Mrs. Banyen Aksonsri, who began her career selling curios to tourists, pedalling around town on a bicycle which is now displayed in the museum. She was to become a prominent antique dealer. When she realized that it was no longer possible to find goods of the quality she had once sold so freely, she turned to marketing handicrafts and retained the antiques as a private collection.

Kantoke dinners A *kantoke* dinner is the traditional northern way of entertaining friends: sitting on the floor around a small round table, eating spicy food, and enjoying dance or musical performances. The food served at the *kantoke* dinners of tourist-oriented establishments is rather bland, and the company of large tour groups makes the experience similar to that of dining in an army mess hall, although the dances may be graceful and amusing. The two most famous venues are the **Old Chiang Mai Cultural Centre**, a cluster of reconstructed northern houses on Wualai Road, and the Diamond, a magnificent old Burmese mansion near the river behind the Diamond Hotel.

Shopping Areas

Shopping in Chiang Mai is great fun—and watching other people shop is even more amusing. Since walking is so easy—there are even sidewalks, unlike almost any other city in Thailand—examining exotic and useless merchandise will be the major pastime after you have seen enough temples.

Tapae Road is the main centre for serious shopping. Here you find supermarkets for trekking supplies, tailor shops for clothing, grocery stores, stationery stores, and antique shops. (Fortuitously, most banks are also located around this area.) If you want to see where local people shop for strange vegetables, unusual fruits, dry spices, primitive kitchenware, baskets, mats, poultry, fish, frogs, insects and even more bizarre items, go early in the morning to the **Warorot Market**. There is not much to take home, but lots of fun in the looking.

Many travellers nowadays seem to be more interested in seeing how people live rather than visiting temples and museums. If you are a people watcher, you should miss neither the Saturday Market at San Patong (on the road to Hot) nor the cattle market at the town of Sansai, which provides an interesting window onto the life of the farmers. (See page 114.)

A big attraction in Chiang Mai is the **Night Bazaar**, which in recent years has expanded enormously to become a kind of permanent fair, seemingly spreading over half of the city from 6 o'clock to midnight. The market is so engrossing that in the morning the town often seems quiet and deserted —all of the vendors are gathering their strength for the big battle of the night. The market gravitates around two large shopping centres, The Chiang Mai Plaza, a three storey building in distinctive 'Neo–Northern' style, and the Ying Ping Bazaar, a covered area for stalls run mostly by hilltribe vendors. Stalls are also set up along the streets and the small lanes between Chang Klan and Charoen Prathet Roads. Literally everything is sold at the night bazaar, but the focus is on hilltribe handicrafts, local crafts, fancy northern food, music cassettes, and cheap T–shirts and clothing. Antiques and silver items are found along **Wualai Road**, where the community of silversmiths was once located. Many smiths are still there, while others have moved to San Kamphaeng Road which has become a main centre of handicraft production and should be the object of an excursion.

Handicraft production used to be a widespread cottage industry and, up until a decade or so ago, one could see craftsmen at work nearly everywhere in Chiang Mai Valley. Today craftsmen tend to work in cooperatives or be employed by modern factories that mass produce handicrafts for export as well as for the local souvenir market. Everything, however, is still done largely by hand, although inventiveness and originality are now rare. Along **San Kamphaeng Road** and on to the village of **Borsan** all of the traditional crafts of the North are represented, everything from lacquerware to handspun textiles to paper umbrellas. Modern showrooms line both sides of the road, each welcoming visitors to observe production. The meeting point of tourist buses is the Borsan Umbrella Centre, where thousands of tourists meet, each one returning home with an indispensable red–fringed parasol, a treasured memento of Kitsch Avenue.

Trekking

For the past fifteen years one of the main attractions of Chiang Mai and Northern Thailand has been trekking to the various hilltribe settlements in the mountains along the border between Thailand and Burma. At one time an authentic adventure, trekking has now become a regular feature on tourist itineraries with brochures beckoning, "See hilltribes now cheap!" Unfortunately, the effects of all this on the hilltribes is mixed. While tourists help to supplement the hill peoples' meagre income, the massive invasion of travellers also introduces consumerism and erodes traditional values.

As for where to arrange a tour, a plethora of new trekking agencies in Chiang Mai has led to territorial disputes between competitors, encouraging some shady characters to enter the business. At one time, trekking company owners went so far as to hire gunmen to hold up the clients of a rival agency as they marched through the forest. Apparently these disputes have largely been settled with the agreement that specific trekking agencies now specialize on only one or two villages for which they maintain exclusive visiting rights. This means travellers cannot go to an agency and request a visit to a specific village or area of their choice but must stick to that agency's normal agenda. If you should request a particular destination, the booking agent will probably say "No problem" in order to make the sale; you will not, however, get a refund even if you have been lied to, much less if you have had an unsatisfactory experience. Also be wary of guides claiming to be hilltribe people themselves; there are no hilltribe people working as trekking guides in Chiang Mai.

Most organized treks these days are far from satisfactory. After hiking for hours through denuded hills and valleys, you finally arrive in some poverty stricken village where you are greeted by an expensive, warm Coca–Cola. Distance from civilization does not necessarily correlate with the degree of authenticity, interest, or 'innocence' of a village. Conversely, if you go to a truly remote village on your own, you may not be welcome unless you've brought all your own food and some gifts as well.

It is wise, in any case, never to trek without a guide in northern Thailand. Not because you might get lost, although that is a distinct possibility, but because sometimes unescorted foreigners are considered 'fair game' by robbers or, less often, by some hilltribe people who can't resist the temptation to fatten their wallet with impunity. Also, many of the villages have an arrangement with some trekking agency to receive their clients exclusively. Many villages are not prepared or able to deal with visitors who do not speak the local language or, at very least, Thai. Therefore, the success of a trek in the hills boils down to choosing the right guide and agency. In the worst case scenario—which occurs all too often— your guide turns out to be an insensitive lout who can speak neither the local language nor English, and generally

Labour Negotiations

Next morning, feeling very king-like, I repaired to the office to see a veritable crowd of courtiers in the shape of headmen, fierce-elephant mahouts and coolies awaiting audience of me. Seating myself at Orwell's desk, I commanded our Siamese clerk to let him in one by one.

"Lord," said the first, a headman, "I desire a rise in my pay."

It struck me as rather curious that he should want one the first day Orwell was absent, and I took up the notes that Orwell had left for my guidance. One or two employees were marked for rises, but certainly not this gentleman.

"That," I answered, "thou canst not have."

"Then do I desire to leave the service of the Great Company," said the headman, respectfully but firmly.

I hesitated for a second. I had yet to feel my way, to learn the ropes, and were I to begin by losing one whom I knew was the firm's best headman, it would be a bad start. Was the man bluffing, or wasn't he?

I took my decision. To give in would be arrant weakness. And what about that kingship of mine? I said. "Thou canst go tomorrow."

He salaamed and withdrew. The next was the head compound coolie.

"Lord," said he, "I wish for an increase in my wages."

"Impossible," I answered.

"Then I wish to go."

"Certainly," I replied without hesitation.

He departed. After him appeared a fierce-elephant mahout.

"Lord," said he, "it is time my wages grew."

"It is not yet time."

"In that case it is my wish to return to the home of my parents over the hills."

"May thy journey be safe and thy parents pleased to see thee," was my answer.

And so it went on the whole morning. By the time the tiffin hour had arrived, every single employee of any consequence had signified his decision to leave on the morrow as I would not grant him a rise. Since there was nothing else to be done, I walked over to Orwell's bungalow and sat down to lunch.

Though I had taken over Orwell's cook, an excellent Lao we had nicknamed the Prince, and the meal was therefore as good as one could get out in the wilds, I didn't enjoy it in the least, for inwardly I was confoundedly worried. You couldn't train a head coolie, much less an elephant headman, in a week or even a month, and with the whole of the work of the forest coming to a standstill I should be very properly in for the sack. On the other hand, to give in would prove equally fatal; the men would feel, I reflected, that they could do anything they liked with me, and directly Swan or the F.M. saw the rise in the pay-sheet, which would be enormous, again I would get into trouble.

After tiffin, instead of returning to the office, I remained in the bungalow, pretending to read a book but in reality just sweating, both mentally and physically. The men, I guessed would be holding a palaver in the coolie lines, and I was wondering what the outcome would be.

After tea I strolled leisurely back. As I entered the office from the bungalow side, I saw with satisfaction that the whole pack of them were crouching in the porch at the other side, evidently in mind for an interview. I kept them waiting purposely for another half-hour, busying myself on some rice and chili accounts, then told the Siamese clerk that I would see the first.

The headman appeared and salaamed deeply:

"Lord," said he, "I think that my pay is sufficient as it is. Wherefore do I not desire to leave the services of the Great Company."

"Very well," I answered, looking as though the matter was of very little interest to me one way or the other.

"Lord," said the head compound coolie, "my wages are all that I could wish for."

"Lord," said the fierce-elephant mahout, "my wages have grown enough. Wherefore shall the home of my parents across the hills not yet see me."

And so on down through the whole pack. By nightfall I had the satisfaction of having proved myself King.

Reginald Campbell, Teak-Wallah *(1935)*

behaves like a bored circus barker.

On the other hand, a successful trek can be a fantastic experience you will treasure for the rest of your life. A memorable trek requires a memorable guide, somebody who is familiar with the most interesting and beautiful villages, is genuinely liked by the tribal people, who can speak their language and your language, and—very important!—can cook.

The only way to find out which agencies are reliable is simply to ask other travellers who have already been out in the hills. Specifically ask them the name of their guide if they were particularly impressed. This book cannot make any recommendations since today's greatest agency can quickly become tomorrow's biggest rip–off.

Many travelers go trekking in the hope they will find opium fields, but opium is not nearly as prevalent as it was a few years ago, thanks to the vigorous eradication and crop substitution efforts of the Thai government. Still, in some villages you may be offered (for a price) some pipes of opium to smoke. Smoke at your own risk! Remember it is against Thai law even up in the hills and, although you are unlikely to suffer arrest, you are likely to suffer nausea and to have a crushing hangover in the morning—a most unpleasant feeling as you endeavor to climb the mountains in the searing heat.

Travel as lightly as possible. You don't need much since the village will provide you with a place to sleep, and your guide should be carrying all the food necessary beyond what the village can supply. Your main needs are toilet paper, mosquito repellent, sunglasses, a hat, a canteen (filled with purified water before you leave the city), a raincoat or poncho in the June-October rainy season, a complete change of clothes (including a sweater or jacket between December and February, when it can even frost in the high mountains), band–aids, sneakers for walking, and a swim suit and towel. Malaria pills are a must, especially if you are trekking in the area that borders on the Karen State of Burma, where you will surely contract malaria if no precautions are taken. (Meflaquine is considered by many to be the best prophylaxis.) It is wise to bring a disinfectant as well. If you bring gifts for your hosts in the hills, try to bring something useful rather than candy and cigarettes. Bring no jewelry or expensive watches and carry very little money; 500 baht should suffice for a normal three or four day outing. Leave your passport behind, but <u>do</u> bring your credit cards along since a common scam in Chiang Mai seems to be 'borrowing' credit cards from the hotel safe while their owners are up in the hills.

As far as etiquette is concerned, let common sense be your guide. Do ask permission before sticking your camera in someone's face. Don't, for instance, feel obliged to eat the proffered raw dog meat topped with a sauce of bile. The hilltribe people have a good sense of humor and enjoy seeing polite foreigners think that they must not reject hospitality; the villagers can then get a good laugh over the expression on your face as you try to chew the noxious stuff.

The best time of the year to trek in Thailand is November through

February, after the rains but before the heat and haze of March through May. Generally speaking, the mountains to the west and southwest of Chiang Mai are more beautiful and less visited than the hills to the north and northeast of the city.

One should also try to visit a hilltribe at the time of a festival, as at such times the people dress up in all their finery and many different groups may be found at the same place at one time. A good time is around Chinese New Year, which is celebrated across most of Southeast Asia; most hilltribe villages also celebrate this annual event which varies slightly with the lunar calendar. The Karen, many being Christians, celebrate Christmas and other Christian holidays, though in their own unique way. A Yao wedding is a most festive occasion and not to be missed should the opportunity present itself.

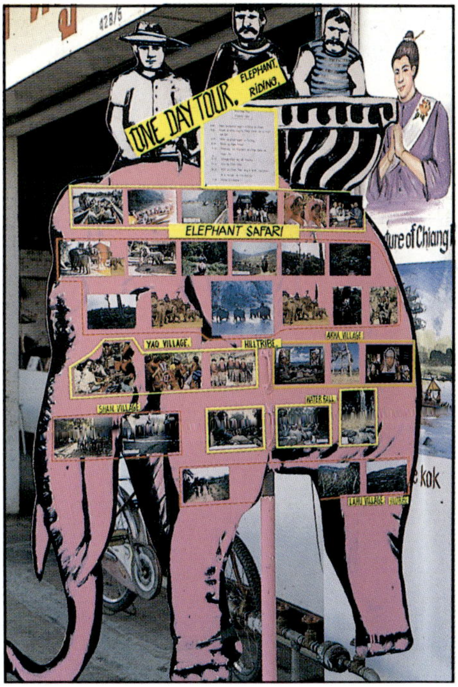

Chiang Mai Environs

Lamphun

The historic town of Lamphun, 26 km south of Chiang Mai, lies on H106. Before the Superhighway was opened, this road was the only link between the northern capital and the nation's main north-south highway. Public buses plying the route leave Chiang Mai from the terminus on the east bank of the Ping River just across from Nawarat Bridge.

By car, turn right after crossing Nawarat Bridge onto H106, which parallels the river. Past the Gymkhana Club and the foreign cemetery, begins the old road to Lamphun, flanked most of the way by tall and beautiful trees. This is one of the few tree-lined avenues left in the North and has the charm of another world. The trees are 30 metres (100 feet) tall and meticulously—and cleverly—pruned. Each trunk has been fitted with pegs that allow the pruners to climb up, just like scaling a ladder, to vertiginous heights. The road passes through the village of Saraphi, renown for the baskets it produces. Lamyai plantations are common on both sides of the road all the way to Lamphun.

Lamphun, a small and quiet town on the right bank of the Kwang River, has been a very important site in the history of the arts in Thailand. Founded in 660 as the capital of the Mon kingdom of Haripunchai, whose first queen was the legendary Chamadevi, Lamphun was an independent principality until it was conquered by King Mengrai in 1281 and incorporated into the Lanna kingdom. The town on the present sight was begun in the early nineteenth century, when it was fortified by walls and a moat.

Wat Phra That Haripunchai is one of the major temples of the North. The compound backs onto H106 as you enter the town and a left turn should be made to reach the main entrance, which faces the river. The temple was founded in 1044 by King Athitayaraj of Haripunchai on the site of the former royal palace. Two ornamental lions guard the gateway, next to which is a *bot*; unfortunately it is usually locked although it contains two fine bronze Buddha statues seated beneath a spire-shaped canopy.

First encountered inside a compound is the modern v*iharn* built in 1925 (the original having been destroyed by fire in 1915). With deep porticos and a low, sloping three-tiered roof, it enshrines a large Chiang Saen-style bronze Buddha, **Phra Chao Thongtip**, plus a number of smaller images. Contemporary mural paintings above the doorway and in the interior depict scenes from the lives of the Buddha, but they are of scarcely any artistic value.

Outside the *viharn*, to the left is a Lanna–style manuscript repository dating from the early nineteenth century and containing religious texts and accounts of local history. To the right of the *viharn* is a giant bronze gong cast in 1860; it is claimed to be the world's largest gong. In the centre of the

compound is an imposing 50 metre high Lanna–style *chedi* covered in copper plates and topped by a gold umbrella. The most sacred part of the temple, it was built in 1467, though subsequently enlarged to the present height. To the right and slightly behind the main *chedi* is a stepped-pyramid *chedi* called the Suwanna Chedi, built in 1418 as a replica of that of Wat Ku Kut. (Another ancient *chedi*, Chedi Chiang Yan, located outside the main compound close to the school, shows unusual Srivijayan features, probably transmitted through the influence of Sukhothai.) In the rear of the compound is a *viharn* enshrining the standing Buddha known as Phra Chao Tan Jai, and nearby is a *sala* housing four Buddha footprints (*Phrabat Si Roi*) one inside the other.

Given the religious importance of this sanctuary, it is not surprising that a large number of Buddha images and precious objects have been donated to the temple. A small museum within the temple compound houses a spectacular collection of Buddhas in the Lanna style, all in pristine condition and with a splendid patina. Other fine statues have been placed at the four sides of the main *chedi* and are objects of worship, but these have been 'restored' and regilded, and somehow seem to have lost their former beauty.

The **museum,** located outside the temple compound on the opposite side of the main road, is the perfect adjunct to a visit to Wat Phra That Haripunchai. It is small but extremely well laid out and contains a valuable collection of bronzes from Wat Phra That Haripunchai as well as a number of archaeological finds, mostly stuccoes and terracottas of the early Haripunchai period, including masks of monstrous figures which all display fierce eyes and the enigmatic grin that is the hallmark of the Haripunchai school, as can be seen in the images remaining *in situ* at Wat Chamadevi.

Wat Chamadevi (also known as **Wat Ku Kut**) is Lamphun's most important temple. Lying on the western side of town, 1 km down the road towards Sanphathong village, this is the site of the oldest monuments in Lamphun; these are two brick *chedis* decorated with stucco figures of Buddha, built (according to J. Boisselier) in 1218 and considered to be the last surviving examples of Dvaravati architecture. The larger of the two is a stepped pyramid, 21 m high and 15.4 m wide, built on a square plan; the design is possibly related to a similar reliquary found in Polonnaruwa, Sri Lanka; this monument, the Sat Mahal Pasada, was once famed as a model for the design of similar structures throughout the region. (See, for example, Chedi Si Liem in Chiang Mai, the Suwanna Chedi in Wat Phra That Haripunchai in Lamphun, Wat Phya Wat in Nan, and another stepped *chedi* in the compound of Wat Mahathat in Sukhothai.) Another *chedi* dating from approximately the same period, of smaller proportions but equal beauty, is built on an octagonal plan.

The new *viharn* has been carelessly sited very close to the two ancient *chedis*, obstructing a full appreciation of the monuments. Further attempts to disfigure these national treasures were made by some pious but misguided believer who donated large neon lights to embellish each step of the *chedi*.

Most of these have fortunately been removed by the Fine Arts Department, but the episode illustrates the dangers which threaten Thailand's heritage when preservation is left to the taste of individual abbots.

Also worth visiting is **Wat Phra Yeun** which is located about 1 kilometre from the centre of Lamphun across the Kwang River on the road to Lampang. It is noted for a Burmese-style *chedi* shaped like a *mondop*. This *chedi* was built in 1900 on the site of a *mondop* constructed in 1369 by the Lanna King, Ku Na, to shelter four standing Buddha statues.

Pa Sang, 12 km from Lamphun along H106, is a one–street town noted for cotton weaving, batik, lamyai (a favourite fruit), and girls who some Thais say are even more attractive than those of Lamphun. The town was founded by King Kawila after the liberation of Chiang Mai from Burmese

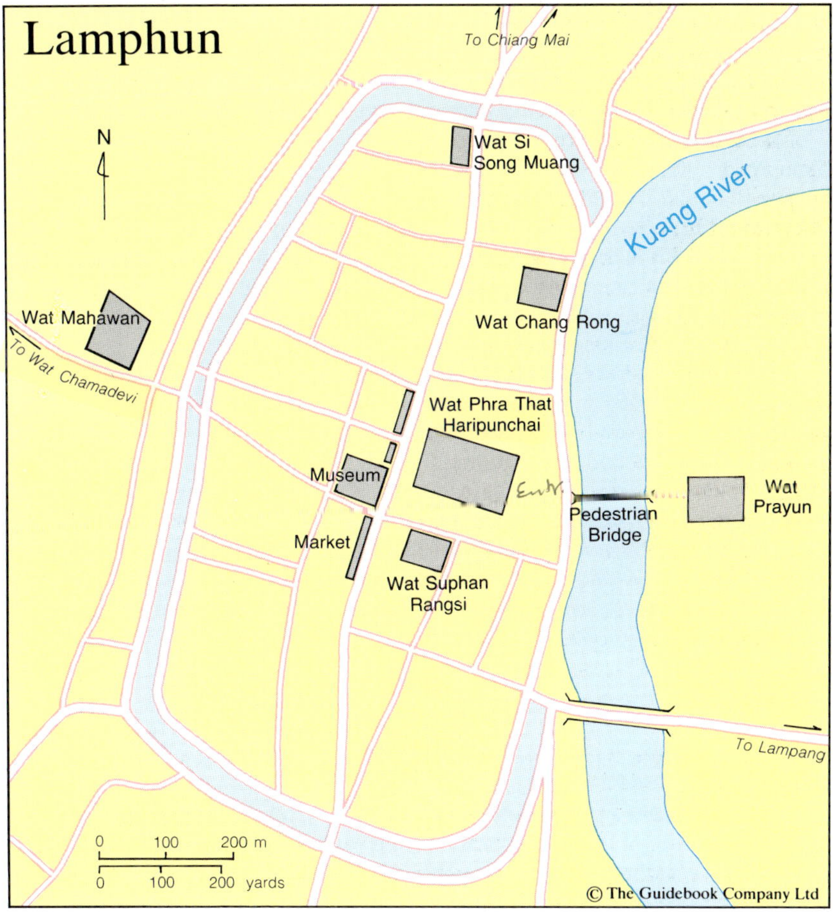

control in the late eighteenth century. At **Wat Pa Sang Ngam**, on the main street, there is an interesting manuscript repository dating from the beginning of the nineteenth century, but the town's unaltered way of life is still its main attraction. A few kilometres to the east, set amidst lush rice fields between Lamphun and Pa Sang, lies a sizeable settlement of Karen hilltribe people, **Ban Mae Kanard Luang**.

To detour to **Wat Chedi Liem** and **Wiang Kum Kam**, the ruins of a recently unearthed ancient city, visit the village of **Ta Wang Tan** (Saraphi district), not far from the Old Chiang Mai Road. These monuments can be visited during the excursion to Lamphun and are historically related to the monuments found there. The ruins are hidden in a thick lamyai grove, but the site is obvious from a distance because of the tall *chedi* of Wat Chedi Liem.

The city of **Wiang Kungam** was built by King Mengrai a few years before he built Chiang Mai. He resided there for six years and then, finding the site inconvenient, moved across the river to build the new city. Several temples are found today within the area that was once the city of Wiang Kungam most of them recently excavated ruins, though two *wats* are still in use. Wat Chedi Liem is noted for a tall *chedi* (a stepped pyramid built on the model of Wat Ku Kut) which was restored early in this century by a wealthy patron who added several Burmese-style decorations. The second old temple is **Wat Chang Kham**, where there is a spirit house supposed to contain the soul of nobody less than King Mengrai himself. Wat Chang Kham has a beautiful *chedi* in Lanna style, restored, and a *viharn* which although very new, shows some excellent craftsmanship. Next to Wat Chan Kham are excavations of the Fine Arts Department.

Also in this area is the **McKean Institute**. The Institute occupies a small island in the Ping River and covers 160 acres of landscaped grounds. In addition to a clinic and wards for the treatment of leprosy sufferers, there are also physiotherapy and occupational therapy units as well as a church and pleasant cottages for the more than 200 in-patients. The Institute was founded in 1908 by a Presbyterian missionary, Dr. James W. McKean, who nurtured it to become an internationally recognized model of its type. Today, the visitor need have no fear of leprosy since the disease is not so fearfully contagious as once thought. The Institute remains a living testament to the pioneering achievements of Dr. McKean.

Chom Thong

Highway 108 leads to the southern part of the valley of Chiang Mai, following the Ping River, which is sometimes visible from the road. The excursion to Chom Thong, the main attraction, is most fun on a Saturday morning, the day of the cattle market. A morning visit to Chom Thong can be combined with an afternoon trip to Doi Inthanon, Thailand's highest peak, though it will not leave enough time for a long walk in the woods there.

Chiang Mai and Environs
Meo Nong Hoy
To Hang Dong
orchid farms
To Chiang Dao, Fang
Mae Rim
Mae Jo
To Chiang Rai
Doi Saket
Mae Sa Valley Resort
San Sai
Don Kaeo
Doi Pui 1690
Royal Palace
Doi Suthep 1668
Wat Jed Yod
Museum
Chiang Mai
Wat Umong
Airport
Handicrafts
Borsan
Wiang Kungam
Superhighway
Muang Kung (pottery)
Ko Klang
San Kamphaeng
To Mae Rim & Samoeng
Saraphi
Hang Dong
Bantawai Handicrafts
Mae Ping
N
San Pa Tong
Wat Pha Lam
0 2 4 6 km
0 2 4 miles
Lamphun
To Doi Inthanon, Chom Thong, Hot & Mae Sarieng/Mae Hong Son
To Lampang & Bangkok
Pa Sang
To Bangkok
© The Guidebook Company Ltd

Sights en route Just after KM 10 on the Chiang Mai-Chom Thong highway, a dirt track on the right leads directly into the tiny village of **Muang Kung**. Virtually the entire population here is engaged in pottery making—but making pots for household use, not souvenirs—and the practice of this traditional craft can be seen while strolling around the 50–odd wooden houses. Each house is built up on posts and the craftsmen huddle in the area below, shaping the clay on primitive wheels. The naturally light brown clay is sometimes given a characteristic reddish hue by mixing it with iron minerals, and sometimes blackened by mixing it with charcoal from the kilns.

Shortly before Hang Dong lies the turnoff for Samoeng. A new road has been opened to join the Mae Rim Road and give access to various resorts in the hills. It is 38 km from Hang Dong to Samoeng, and from there 30 km to Mae Rim. This road is a possible alternative route back to Chiang Mai after an excursion to Chom Thong.

The village of **Hang Dong** is noted for its bamboo weaving, and a number of shops sell baskets and other items along both sides of the road. If you are interested in woodcarvings, turn left along a small country road to reach **Bantawai**. This once sleepy village has over the past few years developed into a large mass production centre for handicrafts. What used to be a cottage industry has now become a major industrial enterprise; while virtually every household is churning out some sort of woodcarving, several larger establishments produce wooden horses and opium-smoking headrests by the thousand. Burmese, Nepalese, Indian and Tibetan 'antiques' wait by the side of the road to age a bit before reaching the border market of Mae Sai, where they will be 'discovered' by eager tourists.

Huge shipping containers of carved items are sent everyday to all parts of the world, though as yet there is no proper road to support this industry. The village, with its thousands of wooden horses and Mandalay Buddhas, is perpetually shrouded by a cloud of dust.

The highway continues to traverse the flat and fertile plain, now and then passing small hamlets. Just 2 km beyond San Pa Tong, wooden pens on the right mark the side of the *kadwua* or **cattle market**. The market which is held only on Saturday mornings, is possibly the largest market of its kind in the North. Besides cattle and buffalos, virtually everything is sold in a rather picturesque setting of leaf–thatched huts. Exotic foods and spices, herbal medicines, betelnut, and homegrown tobacco lie alongside motorcycles, T–shirts and the latest Japanese tape recorders.

One kilometre beyond the Doi Inthanon turnoff, H108 enters the small town of **Chom Thong**, renown for **Wat Phra That Si Chom Thong**, a beautiful temple in Lanna style. The main *chedi*, also in Lanna style and dating from the fifteenth century (though rebuilt several times), is a very impressive structure sheathed in brass plaques. The guardian figures have a rather primitive appearance vaguely reminiscent of the school of Lampang. A more recent Burmese-style *chedi* lies just behind the main entrance.

The *viharn*, originally built by King Muang Keo in 1516 and rebuilt in 1817, is a graceful old building distinguished by a two–tiered roof with gables and facades decorated with intricate woodcarving. Inside, ten sturdy pillars support the roof. The interior is dominated by a tall, highly ornate reliquary which enshrines a Buddha relic surrounded by some exquisite Buddha images and carved elephant tusks.

The small town of **Hot**, 88 km from Chiang Mai, was formerly sited 15 km farther downstream on the Ping river but had to be relocated some years ago when the land was submerged by the reservoir following the construction of Bhumipol Dam.

The ruins of the ancient city of Hot—little more than the remains of a few *chedis*—can be seen a few kilometres further along on H1012. A Karen village, Ban Huai Fan, is easily accessible along a laterite road a few kilometres after Wang Lung, but it is hardly worth the visit.

Doi Inthanon

Doi Inthanon, Thailand's highest mountain at 2,565 metres (8,514 feet), makes a pleasant one–day excursion from Chiang Mai. It is best to have your own transportation—and it should be reasonably good transportation—in order to ensure that it will take you safely to the top and back, as there are no repair shops or petrol stations on the way to the summit.

The turnoff to Doi Inthanon National Park and to the Mae Klang Waterfalls is just before KM 57 on the Chiang Mai-Chom Thong highway just before entering the town of Chom Thong; from there it is 8 km to the waterfalls and 48 km to the summit of Doi Inthanon.

Mae Klang, a picturesque spot, is a popular picnic area with the people of Chiang Mai, and there is a small village of restaurants, foodstalls, and souvenir shops around the parking area. The 30 metre (100 foot) waterfalls are a few metres away. Footpaths lead to various viewpoints, and it is possible to climb above the waterfalls to a fine panorama of the valley. There is also a cave, Tham Borchinda, but it is more than one hour's trek away and, in any case, of interest only to the speleologist. To get there safely it is is necessary to hire a guide from the Royal Forestry Department office near the entrance to Mae Klang.

Driving up the mountain there is a large area between kilometres 28 and 35 which has been completely cleared of forests by slash-and-burn agriculture. More than 3,000 Meo and Karen tribespeople live here, and a royally-sponsored project is helping them to improve their traditional systems of cultivation, introducing new crops that promise better standards of living.

At the top of Doi Inthanon there is a Royal Thai Air Force radar station and a small plateau which on a clear day affords a spectacular vista of the

'Clash'

On my way into the busy, well-lit bus station I saw a monk I knew standing by himself and asked him where he was going. I wasn't out to make money off a monk. I thought that if he was going to a place nearby or if he lived along the road to my house, I could do him a good turn and gain a little merit in the process, but when he named a distant town, however, I forgot the merit business. I got into the car and was about to take off when three men hurried out of the bus station and asked how much it would be to hire the car. I answered offhand, a hundred and fifty baht; it was twice the regular fare. Without hesitation, they opened the door and all three got in. This seemed odd but as the monk wanted to go a little beyond their destination, I asked permission to take him along since he was going the same way. They said it would be all right so I backed up, opened the door and invited the monk into the car. At first he was bewildered but then murmured a blessing and climbed in. . .

We had not driven very far before two water buffaloes, one chasing the other, lunged out of the bushes onto the road. As I swerved to the opposite side, my headlights picked out the rear end of a dead lorry in the dark. It was too close to brake. I spun the wheel and smashed with a terrific noise into a bridge railing. The door must have come off because I felt I was being whirled into the air. Then I was aware of being on a raised path by a paddy field. I could make out cries of pain, moans, calls for help, but they soon became faint.

So there I was in a very bad accident. It could not have been avoided. An angel (if there is such a thing) could have been in the driver's seat and still it would have happened. I was completely stunned. I couldn't help myself, much less the others. Suddenly I was aware of people running and I could see them shining their flashlights about. Four or five men snatched up the things that lay scattered around the car. On the other side of the wreck, the moans began again. The men moved toward the sounds.

'This one's not dead yet,' someone said. Then there was the klunk

of something hard, like a lump of earth or rock, striking something. I could almost see what was happening. The death throes of the Samurai swordsman in the movie I had seen at noon told me in a flash what to do. I turned my face up and held my breath. My mouth hung open, eyes rolled up and frozen fingers seemed to clutch at the air. Just in time. Two shadows approached and loomed above my head. They yanked the watch from my wrist and a sharp pain creased my neck when they tore off my gold chain. . .

The braking sound of an approaching car broke off the conversation. A villager replied to an inquiry from the driver. The engine stopped.

'Police, police,' they passed the word along softly.

I tried to raise myself but could not.

My whole body was in pain and I thought something must be broken. A police officer swept his light among the bodies.

'Hey, sergeant, take a look at this one! It looks like him.'

The sergeant and the others examined one of my passengers. After some hesitation, another voice confirmed the first opinion.

'Yes, that's him, that's the Tiger. Not much to be afraid of now.'

'Now that we've got him do we get the reward?'

'Sure, if we show we cornered him.'

'Hell, that's easy, I'll put a hole through his head, all their heads.'

It was quiet again. This time I did not think of the Samurai but concentrated on the image of Buddha and began my prayers.

'Don't be a fool!' the first voice that had called over the sergeant broke the silence crossly. The policemen then lackadaisically inspected the scene. I could make out only that they were talking about a group of bandits.

'How many were there, exactly?'

'The guy they held up said six.'

'Then one is missing. And when did the monk join the gang?'

I felt like crying for shame.

Khamsing Srinawk, from The Politician and Other Stories

forests and the valley below. Many rare birds, mostly from north Asia, have been observed by ornithologists in this confined spot. Near the parking lot, in a grove of moss–covered trees, lies the tomb of one of the last rulers of Chiang Mai, King Inthanon, who chose to be buried here and thus gave his name to the mountain. The slopes of the mountain above 1,800 metres (6,000 feet) are covered by extensive evergreen forests which, because of the persistent mist, are rich with ferns, orchids, moss, and a staggering variety of epiphytic plants. Although nearly all of the large mammals have been extirpated, the aviafauna is still rich and the trip will be particularly rewarding for the birdwatcher. A partial list includes tree partridges, woodcocks, sunbirds, laughing thrushes, babblers, and flowerpeckers.

Many trails, some of them old hilltribe trails, crisscross the park. The most interesting trails start at KM 31 near the bungalows and the park outstation, where it is possible to hire a guide. A trek may take the entire day, and, in order to avoid retracing one's steps, hikers can arrange for a car to pick them up at a point selected by the park guides.

About ten kilometres before the summit, shortly after the road passes the military checkpoint, there is a turnoff to **Mae Chaem**. This road eventually joins H108 between Hot and Mae Sariang. Very steep and narrow, it winds through thick rainforest before descending across increasingly open deciduous woods into the fertile valley. The sleepy little town of Mae Chaem is spread out in a number of smaller sub–villages overlooking the valley. Mae Chaem was once renown for its weaving and still has some charming old temples. Of particular interest is **Wat Pa Daet**, where there are two untouched buildings in old Lanna style. The scripture repository contains lively murals awaiting restoration.

Mae Sa Valley

Mae Sa Valley has been 'developed' only recently but is fast becoming popular with Thai tourists seeking fresh air and a quiet place to relax with the family. A number of little country cottages and many resorts have sprung up amidst the rather modest scenic attractions. Mountain slopes have been landscaped, flowers have been planted, and the villages have been spruced up. Every house has its little English garden, and even the hilltribe residents wash their faces. The valley does not look very tropical, but it is certainly very civilized, and one senses a degree of prosperity that would be nice to see extended to the whole region, even at the cost of losing all of its exotic charms. Mae Sa Valley is not the kind of scene that attracts foreign tourists, but, while a prolonged stay must be deadly boring, a short drive around the circuit is an easy and pleasant diversion from Chiang Mai city life.

The excursion starts at **Mae Rim**, some 12 km out of Chiang Mai on the road to Fang, where one turns left. The volume of traffic along this section of H107 is so great that it had to be enlarged to become what is, by Thai standards, a real superhighway. The town of Mae Rim, fattened by the money brought in on tourist buses, has recently been entirely rebuilt.

The first 'tourist attractions' to be encountered are orchid nurseries, all of which are open to the public with a few charging a modest entrance fee. For the foreigner, the nursuries will probably be the most genuinely interesting part of the day. The variety of native orchids and the myriads of hybrids grown here—combined with the sheer size of the nurseries—cannot fail to impress even the most jaded of travellers. Visitors can see how orchids are propagated and how hybrids are created in the laboratory. The shop of one nursery, Mountain Orchids, makes gold–plated flowers and also features a small 'butterfly farm' to breed specimens for collectors.

Further on, **Mae Sa Waterfall** is the most scenic spot of the valley and boasts the most tourist buses. After driving through a bunch of resorts in dubious rustic style, one reaches the 'Elephant Camp' where shows are given every morning. Interestingly, all of the mahouts here are Karen.

Mae Sa Valley Resort is a complex of typical English cottages replete with flower gardens, and although it feels like it has been dropped from another continent, it is quite pretty. It will be renovated soon and have a new look.

Erawan Resort is the biggest attraction in the valley, embodying the very essence of beauty according to Siamese taste: imitation English gardens with flower beds of garishly-colored blooms filling every possible space, each species being duly labelled in Latin. It is the perfect background for Thai people to photograph each other under a scorching sun and, for a fee, have a portrait taken with local villagers masquerading as hilltribe people. A cultural show is staged twice a day (or any time enough people show up) in a large thatched pavilion. Pretty bungalows swathed in creepers can be rented for the night at reasonable rates.

Fang and the Ping River Valley

The valley of Fang was for centuries one of the major trade routes of the North, linking Chiang Mai with Chiang Tung (in what is today the Shan States of Burma) and with the Kingdom of Lane Xang (Luang Prabang in present day Laos) by boats trafficking the Ping River. The short excursion to Fang (152 km north of Chiang Mai) and beyond to Tha Thon holds many of the attractions for which the North is famous: mountains, caves, waterfalls, hilltribes, and perhaps the most exciting river trip possible in Thailand.

Public buses plying the route depart Chiang Mai every 30 minutes and take approximately 3 1/2 hours to cover the distance. Some 38 km from Chiang Mai the highway temporarily leaves the valley of the Ping River and briefly enters that of its tributary, the Mae Nam Taeng. This whole area has been extensively developed by the Irrigation Department and owes its fertility to a complex system of dams and irrigation channels. Two sites in

particular, **Mae Taeng Dam** and **Mae Faek**, have been landscaped and are picturesque areas ideal for picnics.

Chiang Dao Elephant Show After KM 49, H107 makes a sharp downhill curve and the road leaves the fields and the alluvial plains, entering a gorge carved out by the Ping River. A little before KM 56 there is a turn to the right which leads to the Chiang Dao Elephant Show, situated on the banks of the Ping River. The performance (daily at 9:30 a.m.) features elephants displaying basic work skills. The display begins with the elephants' daily morning bath in the river, following which the animals are led to a primitive amphitheatre where they demonstrate the various methods of pulling, dragging and lifting logs.

Hilltribes Development and Welfare Centre At KM 61.5 a signposted track on the left leads to the Hilltribes Development and Welfare Centre, a project run by the Department of Public Welfare which provides the hilltribes living on or near Doi Chiang Dao with agricultural assistance, medical care, and other services to help raise living standards. The station, including a nursery for the propagation of a variety of cash crops is located on the hillside at an altitude of over 1,000 m (3,300 feet). The 7 km track is rough and steep; while passing through superb tropical forests and affording magnificent views, it is passable only by motorbike or truck.

Beyond the agricultural station are several hilltribe villages. The closest, a Lahu (Muser) settlement, lies only 1 km away and is easily visited, but the others necessitate lengthy treks.

Continuing northwards, **Doi Chiang Dao** comes into view on the left, although its peak at 2,285 m (7,540 feet) is often shrouded in cloud. This is Thailand's third highest mountain after Doi Inthanon and Doi Phahompok. Doi Chiang Dao is a distinctly impressive sight and dominates the landscape for the next stretch of the journey. A number of hilltribes live on the slopes of Doi Chiang Dao and it is possible to trek to Lisu, Muser and Karen villages, although it is essential to have a guide.

From the Ping River gorge the road levels out as it enters the valley of Chiang Dao. The little town was once a settlement of people believed to be possessed by spirits of a type called Phi Pob, particularly grisly ghosts who ate the entrails of their victims. Such persons were driven from their homes and sent to live together in far away locations set apart for them. Only a long stay in the village would reveal if the old superstition still holds true, and most travellers are contented with a quick stop.

The **Chiang Dao Caves**, nestled at the foot of the mountain, lie 5 km further along a partly paved track that passes through teak plantations, fields, and tiny hamlets. Adjacent to the parking area is an old Burmese-style *chedi* and a small stream which flows into a pool containing tame fish. An ornamental royal barge, made of stone, 'floats' in the pool, and small *chedis* in the looming rock face complete the fairyland ambience. At the top of a covered stairway is the narrow mouth of the cave, from where a few steps lead down into the first chamber. The cave was venerated by Shan people, as is evident from the style of the myriad statues, offerings, and decorations—in various states of disrepair—left in the cave by worshippers. The first chamber, which receives some light from an opening in the ceiling, is the most impressive, with a number of large Shan Buddhas. A long Naga flanks the steps leading down into the dark cave, where there is a curious pair of gong holders, a large Siamese Buddha, and a statue representing the Nirvana of one of Buddha's disciples.

King Naresuan's Monument, off to the left of H107 at KM 78.3, has a *chedi* and a reconstructed wooden fort commemorating King Naresuan of Ayutthaya. This monarch, in 1593, repelled a Burmese invasion and slew the Burmese Crown Prince in an elephant–back duel at Nong Sa Rai, near Suphan Buri. He later travelled north to lead an offensive against Burma, winning a sizeable amount of territory between Chiang Mai and Fang. During this campaign King Naresuan rested his army and prepared for battle near the present–day village of Mengrai which is located 4.4 km away down a partially surfaced track.

The landscape through the watershed area is punctuated by some spectacular rock outcrops, especially between KM 89 and KM 94. Just beyond, at KM 95, a small hamlet on the right of H107 hosts an agricultural site of the Royal Northern Project; here farmers are experimenting with the cultivation of temperate climate vegetables as potential cash crops. At the far end of the village a track (muddy and impassable in the rainy season) forks left 900 m to **Huay Luk Waterfall** which, in truth, is hardly more than a stream passing down the hillside.

From Huay Luk the road rises steeply and the sheer rock formations are reminiscent of the fantastic limestone mountains of Guilin in China. The climb continues beyond the Muser village of **Ban Hua Toa,** where the highway begins a long descent into the broad plain of the Fang valley.

The **Tubtao Caves** lie 3 km (not two, as the signpost does indicates) down a laterite track off to the left at KM 117.8. (Along the way are fine views of Doi Chiang Dao.) Here, in a tranquil leafy glade, is a small wooden hut inhabited by a solitary monk and behind, at the foot of the cliff, are two staircases leading to 'Light Cave' (Tham Pha Khaw) on the right and 'Dark Cave' (Tham Pan Jeak) on the left. 'Light Cave' is so named because it is illuminated by a hole in the roof of a largish vault. A giant seated Buddha reaching almost to the roof faces an open–sided shrine containing a 10–metre high brick-and-cement image of a reclining Buddha surrounded by statues of kneeling devotees. 'Dark Cave' has a main chamber where there are four seated Buddhas placed adjacent to a curious limestone formation. From here one needs a torch to go farther; there is an ancient *chedi* in a large grotto inhabited by bats at the end of a 1.4 km-long passage, but this is rarely visited. This cave was— and still is—an important centre for pilgrimages.

The Asian Elephant

The Asian elephant (*Elephas maximus*) is along with its cousin, the African elephant, one of the last two survivors of a zoological Order, the Proboscidea, which has included some 350 species throughout its evolution. In Thailand, Asian elephants once probably numbered in the hundreds of thousands, and Lanna Thai, 'The Land of a Million Ricefields', might just as well have the name of neighbouring Laos: 'The Land of a Million Elephants'. Today there are only 2,000 to 3,000 wild elephants remaining in Thailand. (In all of Southeast Asia and the Indian subcontinent there are probably about 35-40,000 wild elephants surviving in 13 countries.) The Asian elephant has been officially declared an Endangered Species and the animal receives full legal protection in Thailand, but numbers are plummeting nonetheless, though more from destruction of the elephant's forest habitat than from the direct pressure of poaching. Shy and secretive in spite of their immense size and strength, it is very difficult to see Asian elephants in the wild, even in places where they are found in good numbers.

Northern Thailand has always been a bountiful home for domesticated elephants. Surprisingly, the superficially clumsy-looking beasts are wonderfully agile—slower, but far more sure-footed than either horses or mules even on the most precipitous mountain trails. Posing other advantages—such as having superb night vision and being able to perfectly remember trails—they

King Rama VII visiting Chiang Mai, c 1920

were the favoured pack animal in the North. In fact, a hundred years ago far more elephants were employed to carry goods than to drag logs, the more glamorous job for which they are best known. Elephants employed as draught animals are able to carry about 300 kilograms (660 pounds), a large amount but only a small proportion of their body weight.

As late as the turn of the century there were over 100,000 domesticated elephants in Thailand. A great many of them were in the North; in the 1880s there were 20,000 elephants employed in regular caravan routes around Chiang Mai alone. Today there only about 2,500 domesticated elephants living in northern Thailand, the highest number being 488 animals in Chiang Mai Province, with Tak close behind at 484.

Today (or at least until a recent logging ban) most Thai elephants work at dragging logs in the forest, a task for which they are ideally suited since they can drag carefully selected logs, particularly teak and other valuable hardwoods, through thick forest without the necessity of building roads which unnecessarily destroy the environment. Elephants are able to drag about half their body weight (much more than they can carry), a big bull capable of dragging a log of two tons; while worked in tandem, pairs can drag even heavier logs. The best place to observe elephants at work and undergoing training is at the Young Elephant Training Centre outside of Lampang. (See Page 161)

White elephants are thought to bring good fortune. This representation is in a rare manuscript at the National Museum.

Carl Bock, the Scandinavian traveller who visited here in the late nineteenth century, describes the amazing number of offerings piled up in the cave.

Fang, comprised mostly of two–storeyed wooden shophouses, is a small and undistinguished district centre close to the Burmese border. Originally founded by King Mengrai in 1268, Fang's position along an important trading route made it a prosperous and independent city. It was destroyed by a Burmese incursion at the beginning of the last century and lay deserted until 1880. A British surveyor who visited it in the last decades of the nineteenth century left this descripiton, "The town is an old one, irregular in shape, with a moat and wall of half burnt bricks with a backing of earth 12 feet thick. The walls were originally crenellated, and trees not less than sixty years old are growing on them. A great deal of the inside is jungle, with a street or two roughly laid out. The ricefields surrounding the town are extensive, but very little is under cultivation. The few pagodas are more than half in ruins."

Fang, being close to Burma and deep within the infamous Golden Triangle, is inevitably part of the opium-smuggling pipeline. The surrounding border district is occupied by diverse, and often clashing, rebel factions: remnants of Chiang Kai-Shek's Kuominatang troops, Karen Liberation Armies, communist insurgents, and, most notably, the Shan United Army commanded by the notorious 'opium warlord', Khun Sa. Fighting occasionally erupts between rebel factions and thus travellers should be wary about trekking in remote areas around here. Treks are organized by some of the small hotels in the town and there are some good hilltribe villages to be visited, but check on the security situation before setting out—tourists have been robbed and even killed. Advise the Tourist Police of your itinerary and, if necessary, ask for an armed escort.

The town of Fang is primarily useful simply as a base, though it does afford the simple pleasure of people-watching. Being a bustling border post, visitors include Burmese as well as colourful hilltribe people down from the mountains to market their goods. The Ku Charoen Chai restaurant, just across from the market, is a good vantage point for taking in the scene—as well as the best eating place in town.

Horticultural Station and Hot Springs By KM151 at the entrance to Fang a signposted turnoff on the left leads (after about 7 km on a laterite track) to Fang Horticultural Experimental Station. Crops such as coffee, apples, peaches, and various vegetables are grown to provide seedlings for the neighbouring villages.

Another 2.6 km beyond the horticultural station are the **Ban Nam Rawn** sulphur springs. Water near boiling point bubbles out of the ground in many places scattered over a rocky field, and the air is permeated with the stench of sulphur. At present it is a pleasant location with forested hills providing a scenic backdrop, but this may change since the government is planning to build a geothermal power station to tap the energy of the hot springs.

The small settlement of **Tha Thon**, on the banks of the Kok River, lies

24 km north of Fang on H1089 (in reality an extension of H107). It is a pretty drive and the beautiful scenery gets even better with the river excursions available from Tha Thon. Basic accommodation is available at the Chankasem Bungalow and Restaurant along the riverside. Thip's Travellers House and various guesthouses can also organize longtail boats or rafts for a rivertrip.

Entering the hamlet, just before the bridge spanning the river, **Wat Tha Thon** stands on the hillside to the left while on the right a short track leads down the river bank to a boathouse. From this landing, longtail boats leave daily at 12:30 p.m. for the 3 hour trip downstream to Chiang Rai. The one-way fare is 160 baht per person or, alternatively, travellers can hire their own boat, taking up to eight passengers, for 1,600 baht. (A word of warning: boats have occasionally been held up and robbed.)

For the adventurous, the trip downriver to Chiang Rai can be made by bamboo raft in three days with two nights spent aboard. With a crude cabin housing up to six passengers, passage on these custom-built rafts costs 2,200 baht per person; this price includes the construction costs, the services of a boatman, plus a supply of blankets, mats and a stove. (Food is extra.) Rafts should be commissioned at the boathouse ten days ahead of their planned use. The trip is best between October and January.

Whether by longtail boat or by raft, the journey down the Kok River to Chiang Rai is one of the finest river excursions possible in Thailand. The natural scenery is exceptionally beautiful, passing over a number of rapids (not 'white water', but fun nevertheless) and coasting by several hilltribe villages, mostly Muser and Yao. **Tham Phra Cave** lies just 15 minutes upstream from Chiang Rai. The regular daily boat stops only once at the passport check of Mae Salak, one hour from Tha Thon, and travellers are therefore better off taking their own boat or raft in order to be able to stop at any places of interest, such as the cave.

For travellers with neither the time nor the inclination to make the full trip to Chiang Rai, there are shorter boat excursions, the most popular being to the village of **Ban Mai Mork Charm**, one and a half hours from Tha Thon by longtail boat. Akha, Lahu and Lisu hilltribes can be seen, and it is possible to stay overnight in this village at little expense.

Thai Orchids

There are over 1,000 species of wild orchids in Thailand, and most of them are found in the North. Botanically speaking, northern Thailand belongs to the Trans-Himalayan region or, more specifically, to the transition zone between the southeastern tentacles of the Himalayan range and the monsoon tropics. An interlacing of the flora of these two distinct climatic regions has therefore given the orchid world of northern Thailand a distinct flavour not to be found elsewhere.

To define such a flavour is not an easy task, as it hinges upon subtle variations of minor features of the plants. Sikkimese orchids, for instance, in a very general sense possess a finely carved elegance of certain floral parts that distinguishes them from orchids native to other regions. Thinking of northern Thai orchids, the pre-eminent characteristic that comes to mind is the captivating fragrance of many species. While orchids of other climes can rival those from northern Thailand in many ways, few—if any—can match their lovely scent. This attribute applies especially to the species in the genus *Dendrobium*, the grouping which dominates the orchid scene in the northern hills. The *Dendrobium* are also among the most flamboyant species known.

To the uninformed cold-climate visitor, these orchids possess a rather peculiar annual lifestye. For the drier part of the year, particularly during the flowering season, many of them may not have any leaves at all. This leaflessness makes their vibrant colours stand out even more vividly, since during the dry season the general colour hue of the forest is of drab ochres, pale yellows, and greys set against hazy skies. The reason the orchids have shed their leaves is to preserve moisture in the characteristic bulbs that can be seen attached to many rough-barked trees. Most, but not all, of the species found in the North are fine-tuned to the area's unique climate: extreme aridity alternating seasonally with heavy dew, regular early morning mist, clouds wafting through in the afternoons, and chilly nights. It is easier, in fact, to duplicate this cool and humid environment in a greenhouse in Europe or America than in a torrid spot like Bangkok. However, the export of native wild orchids is severely restricted by law, and some species have become extremely rare, such as the only blue Vanda in the world, the famous 'Famui' or *Vanda cerulea.*

The orchid admirer lucky enough to see an old and gigantic tree staggering under the weight of hundreds of epiphytic plants may take heart; the presence of orchids is a sure indication of the ecological health of a forest: orchids will not reproduce in polluted air!

Key to orchid varieties pictured

(with Thai names next to Latin) :

1. Dendrobium scabrilingue, (*Neung Nam Pueng*)
2. Dendrobium densiflorum, (*Ueang Kam*)
3. Dendrobium secundum, (*Ueang Beng Siifar*)
4. Vanda cerulea, (*Famuee*)
5. Rhynchostylis retusa, (*Ayaraet*)
6. Dendrobium heterocarpum

④
⑤
⑥
①
②
③

Mae Hong Son and Region

Until comparatively recently Mae Hong Son was virtually cut off from the rest of Thailand. Tucked away in a forgotten corner and hemmed in by mountains, it was accessible only by a long and difficult trek normally done on elephant back. Not until 1965 was a paved road opened to link the town with Chiang Mai. Now there are daily flights connecting Chiang Mai and Mae Hong Son which is ideal for those in a hurry, but for people with time to spare the road trip is recommended. A number of interesting places lie en route and the mountain scenery is some of the finest in all of Thailand. (If you opt to drive leave Chiang Mai by the Chiang Mai Gate and head southwest on Wualai Road which leads to H108 after crossing the airport highway. H108 eventually takes you to Mae Hong Son.)

Only 17 km from Hot along H108 is **Ob Luang Gorge**, often mis–described as Thailand's answer to the Grand Canyon; in truth it is only a narrow gorge with steep walls almost meeting at the top. Nevertheless it is an intriguing sight spanned by a rickety wooden bridge over the waters of the Chaem River hurtling through the narrows 50 m below. Steps lead down from the roadside to the bridge, or a few metres farther on, there is a right turn which leads into Ob Luang Nature Park where you can park and walk 200 m to the bottom of the gorge. The picturesque scenery is enhanced by many colourful birds and butterflies.

After here, the road rises steadily to a plateau and the views of the mountains on either side are magnificent. Suddenly pine trees appear in profusion, transforming the scenery into something reminiscent of Scandinavia. In this area the government is experimenting with the cultivation of pine trees (all introduced species) in an effort to stem the deforestation caused by the destructive slash-and-burn farming of the hilltribes. This denuding of the hillsides of their natural vegetation can be seen all along the journey to Mae Sariang; whole hillsides are bald, as if shaved by a gigantic razor, and only a few charred, stubbly tree stumps are reminders of the vanished forest.

Pine trees have been chosen for reforestation because they grow faster than the many indigenous timber trees. Pine wood has a number of uses, notably in paper-making, but, unfortunately, it has little value for wildlife and is thus, in effect, a green desert. At Baw Keow Nursery, young pine trees can be seen on the left planted in neat rows just like a rubber plantation. Another 15 km along the road, on the right is the entrance to the Pine Improvement Centre, a Thai-Danish co–project for the propagation of pine forests.

Mae Sariang After switchbacks and stunning scenery, H108 gradually descends into the valley of the Yuam River and reaches Mae Sariang, 104 km from Hot.

Mae Sariang is a small town that offers only two inexpensive and rather dirty hotels for overnight accommodation. However, the food sold by a row of simple restaurants along the main road is not as bad as one might expect. Old wooden shophouses abound in the older part of town. A rickety wooden bridge crosses the Yuam River and leads to the mountains bordering Burma. Although Mae Sariang has often been in the newspaper headlines because of frequent border fighting, opium smuggling, and refugee problems, there is little evidence of these troubles in town.

A quick stroll around shows that a couple of Burmese temples is all that Mae Sariang has to offer. **Wat Utthayarom** (Jong Sung), built in 1896, and the more impressive **Wat Sri Boonruang**, dating from 1939, are fascinating for their Burmese-style architecture that typifies many of the religious buildings in the region. To the right, inside the main gate of the compound, is Wat Utthayarom, containing three *chedis,* the last of which has nine spires. Beyond is Wat Sri Boonruang—the more decorative of the two temples—while nearby is the monks' quarters in the typical form of a long wooden building raised on stilts, painted yellow, and covered with the inevitable corrugated tin roof.

From Mae Sariang a dirt track leads south, running along the Burmese border all the way to Tak. This area is not entirely safe and is seldom travelled by foreigners.

From Mae Sariang H108 turns northward towards Mae Hong Son. Three kilometres beyond the town, the road passes the Huaychompu Teak Arboretum on the right. There is generally very little traffic, which is fortunate since some 54 km from Mae Sariang H108 narrows to barely a two –car width and rises and falls steeply through a difficult series of S–bends. The mountainous forest breaks only now and then to allow glimpses of small, tucked–away farming valleys, although entering the district of Khun Yuam the landscape does open up briefly to reveal the lush and fertile upper valley of the Yuam River.

Beyond the valley, H108 passes through the hills until 18 km before reaching Mae Hong Son (55 km after Khun Yuam) where it begins to descend. There is a superb view down into the steep, V–shaped valley of the Cha River, a tributary of the Pai. From here the road enters the valley of the Pai and the town of Mae Hong Son.

Mae Hong Son

Cradled by forested and often mist–shrouded mountains, Mae Hong Son is a sleepy little settlement made up mostly of two–storeyed wooden shophouses. Two reasonable modern hotels—the Myitniyom, on the left just before the town centre, and the Mae Tee, on the right in the heart of the town —offer decent accommodations.

Mae Hong Son did not exist as a permanent settlement until the mid – nineteenth century, but long before that the area was visited by Shans from

who migrated seasonally to work the forests, and by various hilltribes—notably Lisu, Lawa, Hmong, Musur, and Karen. This ethnic mix survives today and the province of Mae Hong Son, of which the town is the capital, has a population of only 2% ethnic Thais, the rest being Shan or Tai Yai (50%) and hilltribes (48%). The mountain folk remain mostly in their own close–knit villages although they regularly visit town, especially the morning market.

The settlement of the area began in 1831 when the king of Chiang Mai, finding himself short of domesticated elephants, ordered an expedition led by Chao Kaew Muang to capture and train the beasts for work—and for war. A base was established at Ban Pon Mu (now called Ban Pang Mu) on the banks of the Pai River, but later a large number of elephants were caught a few

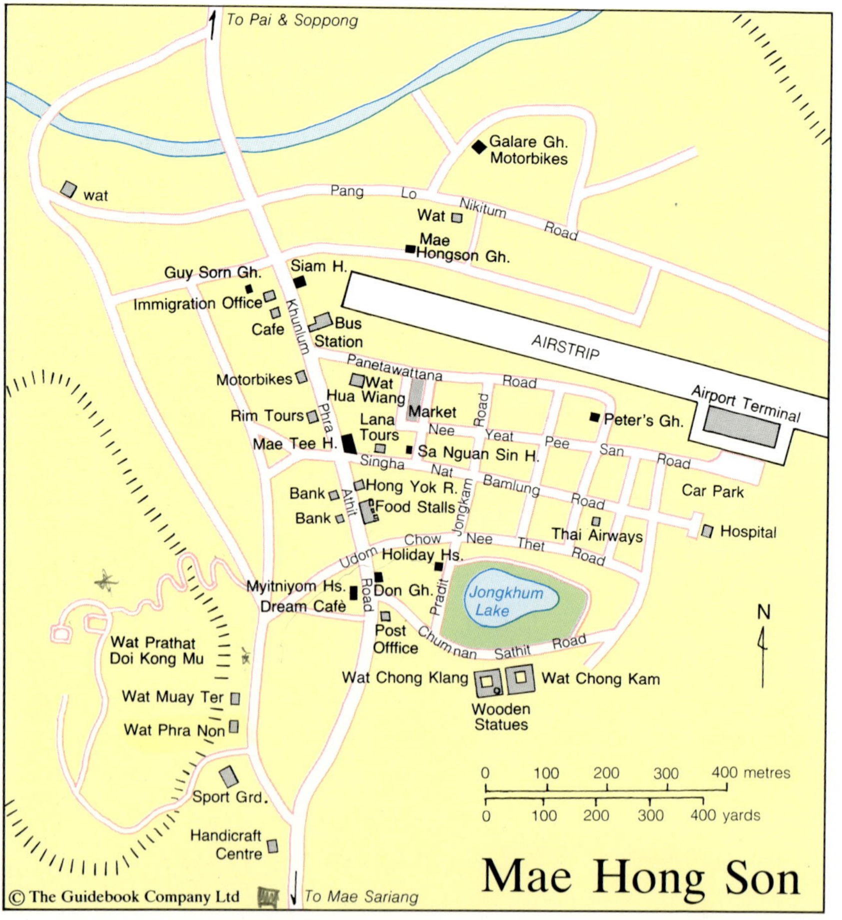

kilometres farther south and so Chao Kaew Muang had the Shans build a trapping corral on the site of what was to become Mae Hong Son. The elephant camp grew into a village, and gradually more and more Shans made a permanent home where they had once visited only seasonally.

So rapid was the development of Mae Hong Son—and so great the influx of Shans—that in 1874 the ruler of Chiang Mai deemed it wise to constitute it as a city, appointing Phraya Singhanatdraja as resident ruler. In 1893 the area was made a province by Siam's Ministry of the Interior, and Mae Hong Son was designated provincial capital.

The principal attraction of Mae Hong Son is a feeling of tranquility in a Shangri–la setting. Nothing much happens here, and that is precisely its charm: you feel pleasantly cut off from the rest of the world. The town is close to the Burmese border and, while there is no official crossing, some smuggling does take place, adding a certain spice to the air.

To see the town at its liveliest—in fact, the only time it is lively—make a visit to the morning market behind the Mae Tee Hotel. Between 6 and 8 a.m. there is a flurry of activity around stalls laden with fruit, vegetables, spices, meats, clothes, and household goods. Sellers with no stalls lay their produce on leaves along the roadside. Hilltribe people mix with townfolk, presenting a kaleidoscope of faces ranging from pretty young girls to wizened grannies contentedly puffing away on fat, hand–rolled cheroots.

Close to the morning market in the centre of town is **Wat Hua Wiang**, a temple even more dilapidated than most, built in the 'wood and corrugated tin' architectural style. Appearances can be deceptive, however, and the *wat* enshrines a fine brass seated Buddha, a copy of a statue in Mandalay. The copy was cast in sections in Burma and then transported by land and river before being assembled in Mae Hong Son.

The most picturesque spot in Mae Hong Son is a small lake surrounded by a palm grove, which has been a park for twenty years. On the shores of the lake are two intriguing temples, **Wat Chong Kam** and **Wat Chong Klang**. Of particular interest here is the collection of wooden dolls housed in a small barred room to the right just inside the entrance to the *viharn* of Wat Chong Klang. These 33 statues, the tallest being about 1 m high, represent figures from the story of Vessantara Jataka (the Jataka are stories of the previous lives of the Buddha). They were brought to Mae Hong Son from Burma in 1857. Beside Wat Chong Kam is a building enshrining the revered statue of Luang Pho To, a 5 m high sitting Buddha made of brick and plaster

Mae Hong Son is dominated by a small hill, **Doi Kong Mu**. In the morning it is usually covered in mist, but late in the afternoon its summit affords a spectacular vista of the town and the entire valley. To reach Doi Kong Mu turn right onto H1095 and then, after 200 m, take a turn to the left onto a good paved road for the 2.4 km to the summit. About halfway the road forks; keeping straight leads to a radio relay station, while turning right leads to two *chedis* on the crest of the hill. These two *chedis* of Wat Phra That Doi Kong Mu, built in 1860 and 1874 respectively, and the several surrounding images are fascinating but the real reward of Doi Kong Mu is the magnificent view of the town, the valley and the surrounding mountains. The enchantment is heightened by the tinkling of the bells atop the *chedis,* which at night are lit up like Christmas trees. (Loy Krathong festival—usually in November, according to the lunar calendar—is celebrated in the Burmese way here; the krathongs, instead of being floated on rivers and ponds, are attached to hot gas balloons made of paper and sent floating skyward from the hilltop.)

At the foot of Doi Kong Mu, on the right of the turning off of H1095, is **Wat Phra Non**. The temple, which has been rebuilt, houses two large plaster-over-brick Buddha statues, one a 12 m long reclining image and the other a seated Buddha. With their painted, realistic faces, these are typical of the Burmese style. Behind Wat Phra Non are two stone Burmese lions of great size which guard the entrance to the old footpath up Doi Kong Mu. A few metres farther along is a row of six *chedis* built on a raised platform—all that remains of **Wat Muay Toh**.

Directly across the road from Wat Phra Non is the more interesting **Wat Kham Kho**, built in 1890. Both the covered walkway from the main gate and

Mist enshrouds Wat Chong Klang in Mae Hong Son (top) and the famous wooden statues inside the temple (bottom)

the *viharn* are roofed in the inevitable corrugated tin but are unusually enlivened with tottering tiers of intricate filigree work on the eaves. Inside the *viharn* are five main Buddha images, the central one being in the Burmese style, and the one on the right being typically Thai with its pointed headdress. Behind these are many old religious objects including a number of small carved 'Buddha Palaces' containing images. In front of the altar is a beautifully carved 80 year–old Peacock throne decorated with inlaid coloured glass. The rest of the interior is festooned with paintings, photographs, and the usual clutter of objects that make northern temples seem so lovingly inhabited—the raised corner where the abbot sits is equipped with a telephone and refrigerator.

Excursions From Mae Hong Son it is possible to make excursions to Tham Pla (Fish Cave), Pha Sua Waterfall and, further afield, the large cave of Tham Lod. However, all but the first are difficult to reach by ordinary car and the traveller is best advised to hire a minibus truck in town.

Tham Pla Leave Mae Hong Son from the north via H1095 and at KM 17.6 turn left down an unsurfaced track that leads 200 m to a parking area. From here a small, narrow suspension bridge crosses a stream to a path which, after a 5–minute walk through an attractive grove, leads to Tham Pla or 'Fish Cave'. The cave is actually a rocky pool where a subterranean stream surfaces at the base of a cliff. The pool contains tame fish (*pla muang* or *pla pluang hin*), the biggest up to a metre in length, which rise to the surface to be fed. (Fish food can be bought at the park keeper's hut on the right, halfway along the path.) An alcove in the rockface houses a small shrine, and so the fish are considered holy and thus protected. The whole area is pretty and peaceful, and a few wooden picnic tables are scattered about the grove.

Pha Sua Waterfall Travel north on H1095 and just before KM 17, at the bottom of a steep incline, turn sharp left onto a dirt track. After 2 km the track crosses a wooden bridge and 300 metres later enters the Shan village of Mok Cham Pae. Having passed the village, the rough track now rises and falls sharply, giving good views of the surrounding mountains. The parking area for the waterfall is on the right, 8.7 km beyond. (The road continues to climb for another 10 km to reach the King's residence at Pang Tong). Rough steps cut out of the earth lead down to an impressive waterfall. The water tumbles over a broad ledge in half a dozen separate flows during the dry season, although in the rainy season (when, unfortunately, the track is virtually impassable) water falls in a continuous curtain.

Tham Lod The rarely visited cave of Tham Lod lies off H1095 some 80 km from Mae Hong Son. It is difficult to reach since the highway is unsurfaced after the first 28 km, rapidly deteriorating into a steep, winding, rocky track. The views of the mountains, however excellent, are even more impressive than those seen on the drive from Mae Sariang to Mae Hong Son—and they get better in direct proportion to the deterioration of the road. Especially spectacular panoramas can be seen off to the left (looking toward

Burma) between KM 49 and KM 51. After KM 52, thick jungle encroaches on both sides of the track, obscuring the view, and 8 km farther along the road passes through a cultivated valley. Just beyond lies the Lisu village of **Soppong,** where the tribespeople are a colorful sight in their bright green or blue pantaloons.

Roughly 72 km from Mae Hong Son (the kilometre markers ran out a long time ago!) there is to the right a small Lisu village, opposite which a trail leads to Tham Lod. One kilometre down the trail there is a stream which has to be forded; only a truck or jeep can manage it. Hemmed in by jungle, the track continues 5 km beyond the stream and then forks; the right–hand fork leads to a Shan village where guides to the cave can be hired (the going rate is about 30 baht for men and 10 baht for boys). Guides are essential as there are no lights in the cave, and the guides provide torches made of bundled pinewood kindling.

The entrance to the cave is one kilometre beyond the village, and nearby is the house of the Forest Department keeper, who will also act as a guide if necessary. From the parking area it is a 300 m walk—half uphill and half down—to the mouth of the 300-400 m long cave. Not far from the cave entrance there is a cosy guest house named, appropriately enough, **Cave Lodge**; it has inexpensive rooms and bungalows, as well as a highly recommended restaurant.

The cave itself is high and broad with a shallow stream running through it. There is no good path, and it is necessary to wade back and forth across the stream. Inside the cave are some interesting limestone formations believed to be 9,000 years old, and high up in niches near the rear entrance there are the remains of recently discovered prehistoric wooden coffins. (You have to be part mountain goat to make the climb, although there are some bamboo ladders to help.) Emerging from the rear entrance of the cave it is a 20–minute walk along a jungle trail back to the parking area. A visit to Tham Lod, though not easy, is rewarding for people with a taste for adventure.

H1095 goes from Mae Hong Son to Pai and then continues southeast to join H107 near Ban Mae Malai (from where it is 35 km back to Chiang Mai). Buses cover the route but the road is in poor condition and, while improving somewhat beyond Pai, a car can make the journey providing there has been no rain, but the driver should be prepared for a nerve-racking ordeal. The area is populated mostly by the Lisu tribe, who are often seen along the road.

Pai

Pai is one of the newest destinations on the traveller's itinerary, made more accessible by the paving of the northern loop of the Mae Hong Son-Chiang Mai highway. The village rests in a quiet and pleasant valley surrounded by mountains and hilltribe villages, making Pai probably the best starting place for treks in the North. The main attraction of Pai is undoubtedly its proximity to the hilltribes, but there are a few other sights worth mentioning. **Wat Mae Yen**, also known as 'the temple on the hill', is a 30-minute walk east of town past a Shan village and up a 350–step staircase. The buildings are all of recent construction but the venue provides a fantastic view of the surrounding mountains, especially at sunset. **Morepang Waterfall** is a two hour (7 km) hike east of Pai along a trail which passes several hilltribe and KMT settlements. The well–known **Hot Springs** of Pai are about 15 km east of town and are best visited by motorcycle or bicycle (which can be rented in town). A very pleasant ride through the forests is made all the more fun by knowing a refreshing mineral bath and hot tub await you at the journey's end. Pai is such a small village that it is not worth recommending any one hotel or restaurant; just walk around and choose what looks like the most popular places—and join the crowd.

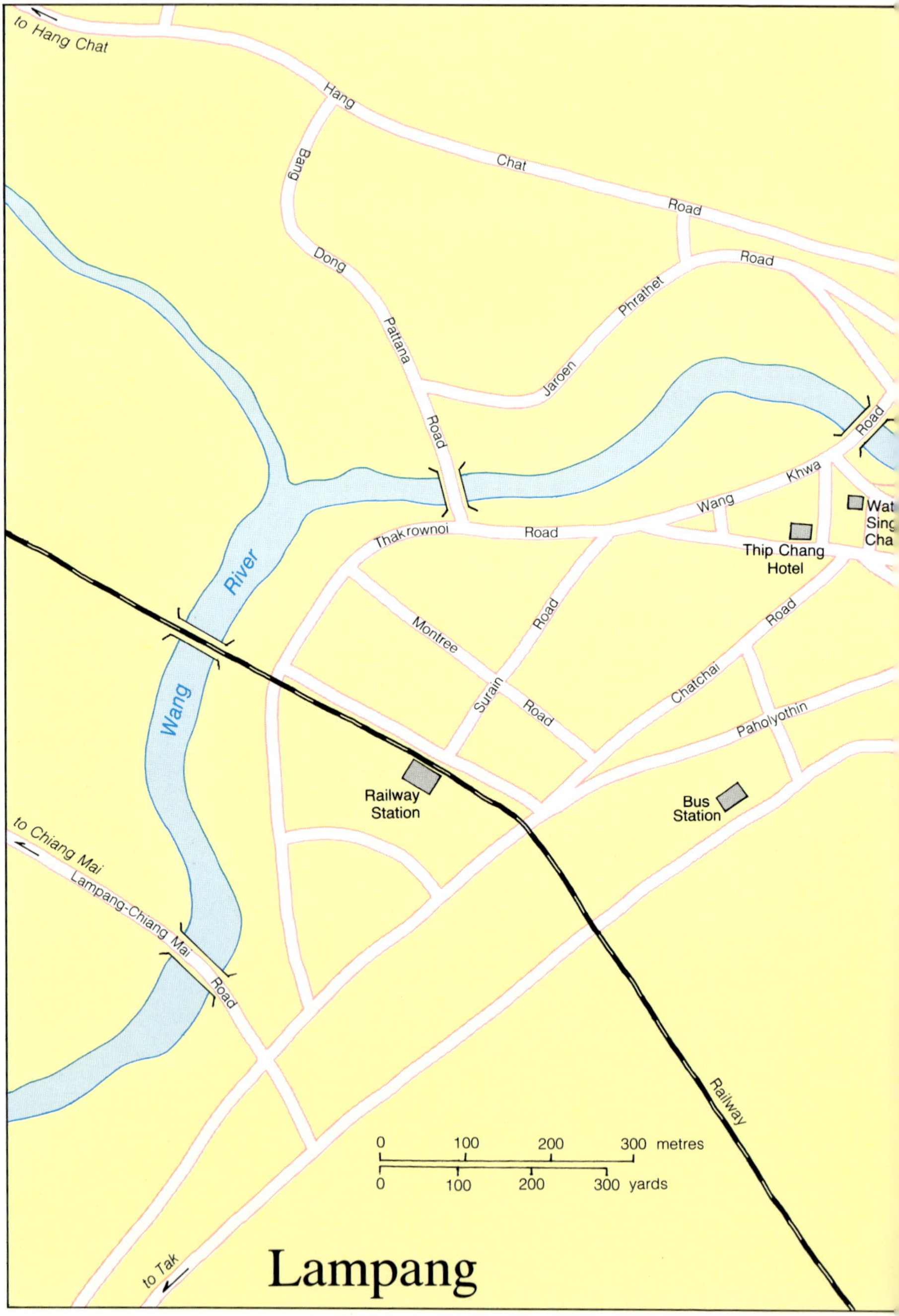
to Hang Chat
Hang
Chat
Road
Bang
Dong
Pattana
Road
Road
Phrathet
Jaroen
Road
Wang
River
Wang
Khwa
Wat
Sing
Cha
Thakrownoi
Road
Thip Chang
Hotel
Montree
Road
Surain
Road
Road
Chatchai
Road
Paholyothin
Railway
Station
Bus
Station
to Chiang Mai
Lampang-Chiang Mai
Road
Railway
0
100
200
300 metres
0
100
200
300 yards
to Tak

Lampang

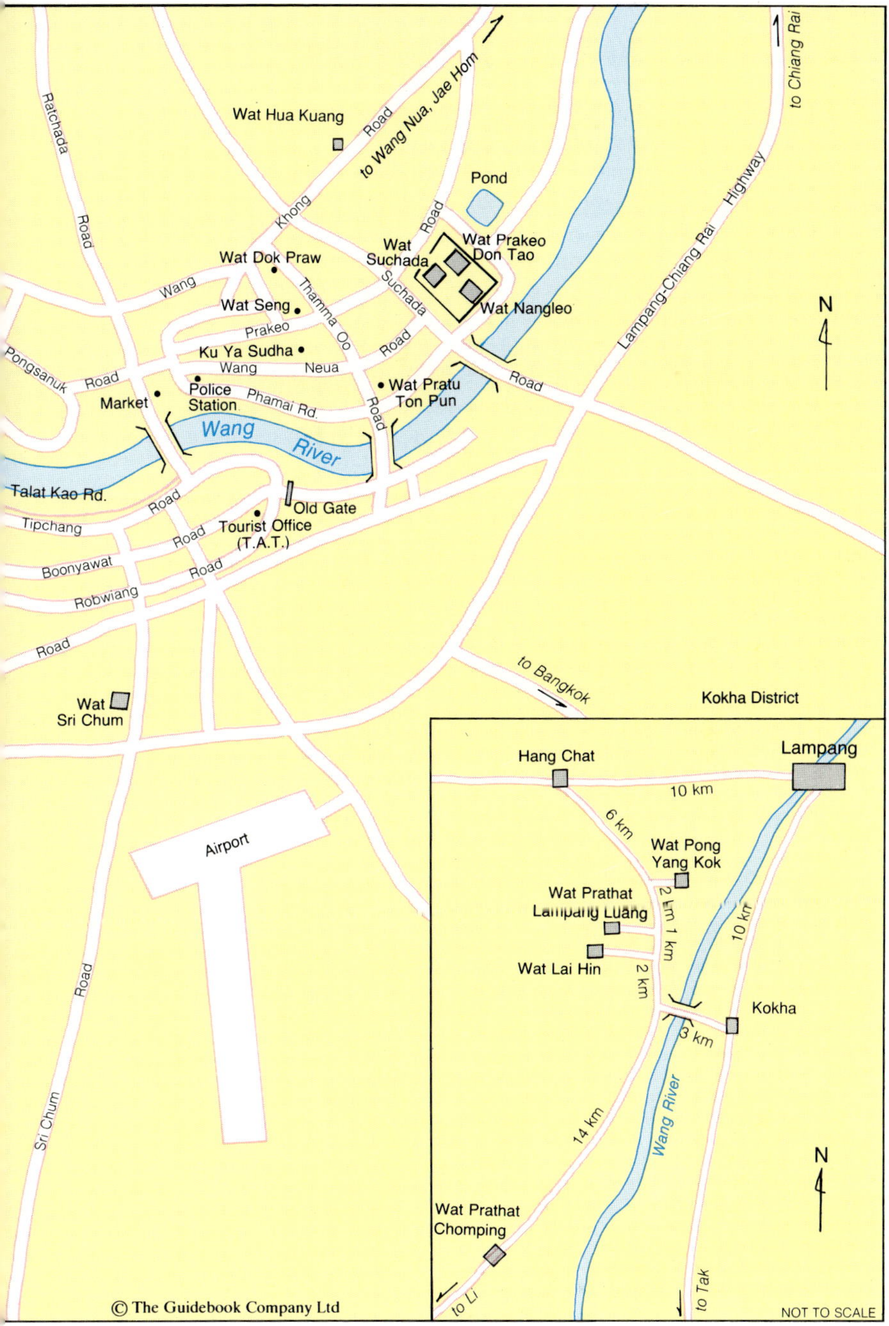

Ratchada Road
Wat Hua Kuang
Khong Road
to Wang Nua, Jae Hom
Pond
Wat Suchada
Wat Prakeo Don Tao
Wat Nangleo
Wat Dok Praw
Wang
Thamma Oo Road
Suchada Road
Wat Seng
Prakeo
Ku Ya Sudha
Pongsanuk Road
Wang Neua Road
Police Station
Market
Phamai Rd.
Wat Pratu Ton Pun
Road
Wang River
Talat Kao Rd.
Old Gate
Tourist Office (T.A.T.)
Tipchang Road
Boonyawat Road
Robwiang Road
Lampang-Chiang Rai Highway
to Chiang Rai
N
to Bangkok
Kokha District
Wat Sri Chum
Airport
Sri Chum Road
Hang Chat
Lampang
10 km
6 km
Wat Pong Yang Kok
Wat Prathat Lampang Luang
2 km
1 km
10 km
Wat Lai Hin
2 km
Kokha
3 km
Wang River
14 km
N
Wat Prathat Chomping
to Li
to Tak
NOT TO SCALE

Lampang and the Wang River Basin

Lampang, the second largest town in northern Thailand, lies in the middle of the valley of the Wang River, a tributary of the Ping. This fertile area produces cotton, tobacco, rice, and fruit. The Wang basin is separated from that of the Ping by Doi Khun Tan, a large mountain range still largely uninhabited. The eastern side of the valley is bordered by Doi Bussaracum, which separates the Wang from the Ing and Yom valleys. Thus isolated, Lampang has over the centuries developed its own cultural idiosyncracies and its own characteristic style.

The scenic journey from Chiang Mai, a trip that used to take several days through thick forest on elephant back, now takes only one and a half hours by car on one of the best roads in Thailand. Lampang is also connected to both Chiang Mai and Bangkok by railway, and to Pitsanulok and Phrae by air.

Halfway between Chiang Mai and Lampang at KM 48 lies the turnoff for **Doi Khun Tan National Park**. The condition of the 18 km road is rather poor, so the park is more easily reached by train; the small station of Khun Tan is right in the middle of the park. Bungalows can be reserved through either the Chiang Mai or Bangkok (Hualampong) Railway Stations. Although several species of large mammals inhabit the park, they are elusive creatures and rarely seen. The main attraction of Doi Khun Tan is the beautiful scenery in an atmosphere of tranquility. The main trail climbs from the railway station to Park Headquarters, and then continues to the bungalow site and yet further on to the peak (1,375m/4,540 feet). The arduous walk to the summit and back takes at least one full day but is more enjoyable if done in two days.

The town of **Lampang** has a long history dating back to the Haripunchai kingdom and was probably founded in the seventh century by a son of Queen Chamadevi, who established a Mon principality in the northern region. There is archaeological evidence of a series of settlements that flourished along the valley of the Wang River long before the establishment of Chiang Mai and the Lanna kingdom. The town was then called Kelang Nakorn and was linked with four outlying fortified settlements (*wiang*), of which Phra That Lampang Luang still stands.

When the kingdom of Haripunchai was annexed by Mengrai, Lampang ostensibly became part of Lanna, though in fact it was often governed by local rulers who acted autonomously. The region shared more or less the same historical vicissitudes as Chiang Mai, including three hundred years of Burmese occupation.

The specific site of the town of Lampang has shifted over the centuries; while the location of Kelang Nakorn is not known, the prosperous town of the Lanna era was located on the opposite side of the river from the centre of the modern town. The Lanna town covered approximately the area that today comprises the neighbourhood of Wiang Neua. It is here that the oldest temples are found, and one can still see remains of the ancient fortifications. Testimony to a long and rich history are a number of well–preserved temples that constitute better examples of Lanna architecture than any buildings still surviving in Chiang Mai. Although the town has an unassuming appearance, an attentive visit will uncover a wealth of interesting old houses, some of them very well maintained and adapted for modern living while others are decaying in hidden orchards and overgrown gardens. The traditional house design of Lampang is quite different from that of Chiang Mai and is recognized by the absence of the *galae* and a more austere appearance, as well as the presence of a fan–like motif on the fronton. This classic type was already disappearing by the turn of the century, and most of the old mansions reflect the Western influence introduced by Burmese carpenters during the reign of Rama V.

The busy market area of Lampang is today located along Boonyawat and Robwiang Roads. In the old days the market was located by the river, and this shift has somehow preserved nearly intact a quiet residential area known as *talat kao* or 'Old Market'. The street is lined with many lovely shophouses displaying a fascinating melange of Chinese, Burmese and Western styles. Victorian gingerbread abounds, imported by Burmese carpenters. Indeed, buildings that today appear quaint and traditional—at least compared to modern ferrocement constructions—were the avant–garde at the turn of the century, displaying the same eclecticism that one sees today in the bizarre hybrids of Bangkok housing estates, true testament to the passion for novelty that is so typical of Thai taste. At the turn of the century, Lampang, or Nakorn Lampang, as it was then called, was a prosperous town of more than 20,000 souls and over 4,000 working elephants employed in the logging business and transportation. The Old Market was annually visited by ten caravans from the Shan States, each comprised of more than 100 mules carrying lacquer, furs, steel, copper, tea, and opium. 10,000 bullock carts came to the market every year, and 20,000 porters were engaged in the trade with Burma and China.

A period photograph portrays the characteristic silhouette of the Ratchada Bridge, still a prominent landmark of Lampang, arched over massive rafts of logs floating on a then majestic Wang River. Those were the heydays of the 'Teak Wallah' era, and Lampang was right in the middle of it. Today the Wang River is little more than a stream, and it is difficult to imagine that it was once a major thoroughfare: a dike has been built upriver and deforestation has further reduced the volume of water.

In addition to a handful of old Lanna temples (and, of course, modern Thai temples), Lampang also hosts a number of Chinese and Burmese temples, reminders of the cosmopolitan ethnic mix of any booming trading post. Some of the Burmese monasteries still house small communities of Burmese monks, and these little 'islands' of Burma should interest visitors with no opportunity to visit Thailand's more exotic neighbour.

For most Thais the symbol of Lampang, and the image most often associated with it, is the horse drawn cart. Colourful carts still ply the streets, and one can rent them most pleasantly early in the morning or in the evenings for a cool and leisurely ride around the old town. Lampang is also a fine place to witness northern festivals, as the people are quite conservative and take pride in wearing traditional handwoven textiles and old fashioned jewelry on festive occasions. The Songkran and Loy Krathong festivities are celebrated in true Lanna style; and an historical parade, called the Wiang Luang Lakon, is now held every year, usually in February, to recreate the splendours of Queen Chamadevi's court.

For the shopper, Lampang is a noted centre for the production of blue and white pottery, and there are a number of factories located around town. Normally it is possible to observe the craftsmen at work and to buy at very reasonable prices.

With so many attractions to offer, Lampang easily justifies a pleasant sojourn of two or three days. Convenient accommodation is guaranteed by the Thip Chang Hotel and the Asia Lampang Hotel, both moderately priced but very decent. Nightlife is limited to a number of open air 'garden restaurants' (*suan ahaan*) located along Thakrownoi Road. Many foreigners prefer the quaint atmosphere of the Riverside, which is under Italian management. Two special restaurants worth trying are the Sri Wang (on Thakrownoi Road) and the Wiang Lakon (on Paholyothin Road), both in interesting buildings.

Temples of Lampang

Built on high ground, **Wat Prakeo Don Tao**, is the main temple of Lampang and is reputed to have been founded by the first ruler of the town. There is evidence that this temple was an important religious centre in the fifteenth century, when, according to the local chronicles, it for some years housed the Emerald Buddha, now enshrined in the Royal Chapel of Wat Prakeo in Bangkok. Another related image, also made from jasper (and not from emerald), the Prakeo Don Tao—of which the more famous Emerald Buddha is supposed to be a copy—was also housed here and gave its name to the temple. (Today this statue is nearby in Wat Prathat Lampang Luang.) There is a local legend about the Prakeo Don Tao and the founding of this monastery. The Buddha image is said to have materialized miraculously out of a large emerald found in a watermelon by a lady named Suchada, who had brought the fruit to a venerated monk. When the two discovered the gem, they tried to carve a Buddha image out of it—without success. Finally, the God Indra came to their aid and produced the marvelous statue. The townspeople, however, disbelieved the story and, suspecting an illicit relationship between Suchada and the monk, put the woman to death, thus bringing down upon the town a series of disasters.

Legends such as this were created to enhance the charisma of images that local rulers chose as their palladia; the images were then jealously preserved as sources of magical power and strength. Similar legends were created to exalt the power of chedis, thereby ensuring their maintenance by the rulers and the support of the monastery by the local population. The *chedi* of Wat Prakeo Don Tao, for example, is reputed to enshrine a hair of the Lord Buddha.

The *chedi*, 50 metres high, is the only original structure left in the monastery. The present main *viharn*, the Viharn Phra Chao Thong Tip (which houses a splendid Buddha image), and the Hall of the Reclining Buddha were both built in ferrocement in the 1930s during the spree of renovations led by the venerated monk of the North, Khruba Srivijaya, of whom there are many realistic images in the temple. The single most interesting building is a Burmese-style *mondop* which stands directly in front of the *chedi*, presenting a striking contrast of shapes and styles. Built in 1909 as a donation by a Thai prince, this building employed Burmese artisans then living in Lampang; it is built on a square plan, and the roof is a pyramidal succession of tiers. The main image, in bronze, is in classic Mandalay style although it was cast at the turn of the century. The decoration of the *mondop* is extremely elaborate, employing mirror mosaics on every inch of the surface and deep woodcarvings over the doorways. Although most of the motifs are Burmese, there is also some Western influence evident in the incongruous use of figures of Cupid as the centerpieces of the ceiling panels. The temple charges an entrance fee to foreign visitors. A small museum annexed to the monastery contains a modest collection of Lanna furniture.

Wat Suchada Located next to Wat Prakeo Don Tao, this temple is now considered part of the same monastery, which is properly called Wat Prakeo Don Tao Suchadaram. It was built by people forcibly resettled from Chiang Saen after the destruction of that town by Rama I at the beginning of the nineteenth century. The *wat* contains a *chedi* and two *viharns* in late Lanna style. The main *viharn*, recently restored, houses a large Buddha, made of brick and stucco, and has interesting paintings on the wooden side panels, as well as beautiful lacquer decorations. Unfortunately, the *viharn* is usually closed and permission to enter is difficult to obtain.

Wat Hua Kuang Located on Wang Khong Road not far from Wat Prakeo Don Tao, this is another temple built by the resettled Chiang Saen community. An old *viharn* in late Lanna style still survives, together with interesting Chiang Saen images as well as manuscripts on the subject of casting bronze brought to Lampang by the displaced people.

Wat Seng Muang Ma Located on Thamma Oo Road, it belongs to the same group of Chiang Saen temples. It contains a diminutive *chedi* of very elegant proportions and a tall *viharn* with a large Buddha image and a series of paintings on wooden panels dating from the turn of the century.

Wat Pongsanuk Tai Located on Pongsanuk Road in Wiang Neua district (turn left after crossing the Ratchada Bridge), Wat Pong Sanuk is the most charming temple in Lampang, built in pure old Lanna style. A new monastery, shaded by tall trees, contains almost intact the old one, which is perched on a high platform accessible by four flights of steps, one on each side. The main entrance is an arched gatehouse in brick and stucco. On the platform there are a Lanna *chedi*, entirely encased in copper sheets and enclosed by a brick rail; a more recent *viharn* housing a reclining Buddha; and a marvelous open–sided *mondop* in old Lanna style. This building has a tiered roof with false upper stories, and contains a cage with four Buddha images flanking a Bodhi tree. The grace of its proportions and the ingenuity and wit of the decoration make us regret that so many Lanna temples have been demolished to make space for modern hybrids influenced by Bangkok taste.

Ku Ya Sudha Turning right after crossing Ratchada Bridge, one reaches Wang Neua Road and the remains of the gate house of a monastery, now destroyed, to which the locals have given the nickname of Ku Ya Sudha or 'The Grotto of Granny Sudha'. This gate house, decorated with stucco deities, dates from the late fifteenth century and is one of the oldest surviving examples of Lanna art.

Ho Amok (The Octagonal Tower) Of the ancient fortifications of Lampang, there still survives an octagonal tower which was part of a wall on the west bank of the river, opposite the old town. Today it lies in the modern part of the new town near Wat Si Ked on Robwiang Road.

Wat Ka Tuk Located on Tipchang Road opposite Ratchada Bridge, this is a modern temple, though it still preserves a late Lanna *viharn*. This wooden building is of the open type and is decorated entirely in gold and red lacquer with typical Lanna motifs, such as Bodhi trees and flying deities.

Wat Chedi Sao Although not very old, this is a charming temple located in the countryside, a few kilometres to the left off the road to Jae Hom. It is distinguished by twenty (*sao* means 'twenty' in northern Thai) whitewashed *chedis* in composite Burmese–Thai style. This temple must have had very imaginative abbots in recent years, as a potpourri of fanciful statues have been added piecemeal here and there, creating the appearance of a playground rather than a religious site. The collection includes the twelve animals which are cyclically associated with particular years (in the Chinese manner) and also many figures from Buddhist legends. The presiding image in the *viharn* is an old brick-and-stucco Lanna Buddha, not entirely devoid of artistic merit, while all the buildings are entirely new. A small museum houses a collection of bric–a–brac ranging from stuffed otters to crocodile skulls. There is also a golden Buddha accidentally split in two by the plough which uncovered it when it was discovered in a field by local farmers a few years ago.

Burmese Temples of Lampang

A large number of Burmese people came to northern Thailand to work in the timber trade during the latter half of the nineteenth century. People involved in this business often sponsored the construction of temples because they feared that the spirits of the fallen trees had been made homeless and would thus seek revenge. A practice became popular whereby patrons would build or restore temples in the hope that they could transfer the accrued merit to the displaced spirits in exchange for their forgiveness. Such beliefs help to account for the strong Burmese presence in northern architecture.

Wat Sri Rong Muang This is a fairly recent Burmese temple, painted in garish colours—visually dazzling but of scarcely any architectural merit.

Wat Pha Fang Located on Airport Road, opposite the Thai International Airways office, this temple has a typical Burmese *chedi* surrounded by chapels, each containing a Buddha image in Mandalay style. The recently renovated temple has spacious and clean grounds. The main *viharn* is rather plain, both inside and outside, while the *bot*, located near the *chedi*, is more elaborately decorated.

Wat Sri Chum On Sri Chum Road, opposite a mosque, this is probably the most interesting Burmese temple in Lampang, and it is still home to a community of Burmese monks. The main *viharn* contains the sleeping quarters of the monks—as is usual in Burmese monasteries—and was built in 1900-1901 in the woods outside the city at a site sacred since ancient times. A well–preserved lacquered panel inside depicts the temple in its original setting of luxuriant palm groves and wooden houses; foreigners travelling by automobile through the woods to visit the temple are pictured at a local food stall seeking refreshments. This charming turn–of–the-century vignette of Lampang is in itself enough to justify a visit to Wat Sri Chum.

The temple was built by Burmese carpenters summoned from Mandalay. Worthy of attention are the deep carvings above the doors and the lacquered door panels, which show a certain local influence overlaid upon the Burmese style. The bot, to the left of the entrance, is of the same period as the main *viharn*, while the elaborate *chedi* was built in 1949 at the behest of yet another Burmese benefactor.

Temples of Kokha District

The best temples of Lampang are located in Kokha District, some 20 km outside of town. To visit them, it is necessary to arrange your own transportation. The tour can be done in half a day, possibly en route to or from Chiang Mai or Tak.

Wat Lai Hin Coming from Lampang *via* Kokha, this is the first *wat* to be encountered. It is located in the village of Lai Hin, just a few minutes off the main road on the left. (The sign is in Thai only.) The old temple, although surrounded by modern buildings, is still intact. Contained within a porticoed enclosure (usually closed, but ask the monks and they will open it for you) on high ground by a stream, the temple overlooks ricefields. Walking around the enclosure, one can understand the strategic significance of its location in times gone by, when it was normally approached by water and commanded a defensible position dominating the countryside. The main *viharn* is old Lanna style of the open type and has good stucco decorations on the gable and good lacquerwork in the interior. The wooden parts are possibly two hundred years old; the brick basement under the Buddha images may be contemporaneous with the gatehouse, which is probably a fifteenth to sixteenth century structure. Miscellaneous artifacts—such as spirit houses, coffins and bookcases—can be seen in the portico.

Wat Prathat Lampang Luang In every respect this is the most interesting monastery in northern Thailand. Lampang Luang was once a *wiang,* or 'fortified site', protected by three parallel earthen ramparts separated by moats. Established in early Haripunchai times, it was part of a group of satellite fortresses connected with Kelang Nakorn. The ancient *wiang* is still occupied by a farming community, and the monastery lies on high ground at its southern edge, further protected on the back side by an additional circle of walls. To fully appreciate the original layout, one should stroll around the village, where remains of the old fortifications are evident everywhere, and enter the temple from the back rather than from today's main entrance.

The tall *chedi* (a *phra that*) is widely believed to contain genuine relics

Wat Prathat Lampang Luang: Main ceremonial gate (top), Buddha in the Viharn Nam Tam, one of the oldest buildings in Thailand (bottom), and the Ku housing the principle Buddha image of the complex (right)

of the Buddha. Indeed, Wat Prathat Lampang Luang has a long and uninterrupted history as an important Buddhist centre, but it is also the venue of many non–Buddhist ceremonies. Several large Bodhi trees thought to be inhabited by spirits are worshipped in an animistic manner, regularly receiving offerings in a special shrine. Ill or mentally disturbed people are often brought to these trees in search of protection and relief.

On important holidays, most especially Songkran and Loy Krathong, Wat Prathat Lampang Luang is the site of large ceremonies, attracting people from far away provinces. Its religious importance is enhanced by the presence of the Prakeo Don Tao, a jasper image believed to be imbued with magical powers; it was certainly much coveted by northern rulers of the fifteenth century, as was its companion image, the famous Emerald Buddha. The *wiang* of Lampang Luang was also the scene of a famous episode in the struggle against the Burmese occupiers. In 1736 it was the site of a duel between a Burmese general and Tip Chang, the local hero who won the battle which liberated Lampang. (The drainage supposedly used by Tip Chang to surreptiously enter the occupied *wiang* is signposted and proudly shown to visitors, although one has difficulty in imagining a warrior slim enough to wriggle through it.)

Artistically, Wat Prathat Lampang Luang is the most beautiful and well-preserved monument in Lanna style. The wealth of its decorative arts crystallizes a brilliant chapter of Asian art which is difficult to see elsewhere, due to the demolition or alteration of most of the monuments in the North.

The phra *that* and the most important buildings are all contained within a porticoed enclosure. The main entrance, along a flight of steps flanked by Nagas, is a monumental gatehouse decorated with delicate stucco work. The *phra that*, 45 metres high, owes its present shape to enlargements ordered by Chao Haan Sri Thatta, a local ruler, in 1496. The main *viharn*, squeezed between the gatehouse and the *chedi*, was also originally built in 1496, but its present large dimensions are probably more recent. It is open on four sides and contains a *ku*, a gilded brick housing for the presiding image, named Lan Tong, which was cast in 1563.

Early nineteenth century paintings of the Lampang school, recently cleaned, decorate the panels below the roof eaves. Like other northern paintings, they portray nobles and high personages in Burmese costumes. This is an artistic convention parallel to that of the Bangkok school wherein deities are shown in royal apparel—the Burmese clothing does not indicate Burmese craftsmanship.

Another little *viharn* to the left of the *phra that* houses a 5–metre high Buddha image in brick and stucco. This building, dated 1802, deserves particular attention for its exquisite decoration: inlaid mosaics on the gable, red-and-gold lacquer on the interior surfaces, a stuccoed gate, and wooden ceremonial flags. Two small open–sided *viharns* are set to the right of the main one. While the first was entirely rebuilt in 1967, the second, Viharn

Nam Tam, dates from the early sixteenth century and is possibly the oldest wooden building in Thailand. Recent restoration has revealed painting on the wood panels below the roof, also dating from the sixteen century, with strong, dark outlines of lively feminine figures illustrating the story of Indra. Within the enclosure there are also the *bot* (redone in 1924) and a brick *mondop* housing a Buddha footprint. The building containing the Prakeo Don Tao is outside the enclosure. Next to it is a small museum containing a large Lanna Buddha image in bronze, some stone heads of the Phayao school, and several other artifacts. Even more interesting is the collection of coffins displayed in the gallery of the enclosure, where a large variety of lacquer techniques and traditional Lanna decorative motifs can be observed.

Wat Pong Yang Kok Continuing along the same road towards Hang Chat there is on the right a turnoff to Wat Pong Yang Kok. This temple contains an exquisite open *viharn,* built of wood in old Lanna style, which houses a small *ku*. The interior is renown for its lacquer decorations, which feature the Bodhi tree motif repeated over all the surfaces.

Wat Prathat Chomping This temple, which lies 14 km to the left after Kokha heading towards Li, has been entirely rebuilt in recent years and is of interest only for one curiosity. The small *bot* has a hole in the window panels which acts as a camera obscura. The image of the gilded *chedi* outside is thus projected onto a piece of white cloth proudly held by the monks, who genuinely believe themselves to be in the presence of a miracle.

Phayao, Doi Bussaracum, and the Upper Wang River

Lampang is connected to Ngao, Phayao and Chiang Rai by H1. This was previously the only route from Chiang Mai to Chiang Rai, prior to the opening of the direct road via Wiang Papao.

An interesting circuit can be made in one or two days using Lampang as a base and taking advantage of two new roads which afford fine views of unspoiled country. Start early in the morning by car, taking H1 in time to see the show at the Young Elephant Training Centre, visit some interesting monuments, and then have lunch by the lake at Phayao. From Phayao you can then take the new road that climbs over Doi Bussaracum and descends into the peaceful valley of the Wang River and then return leisurely to Lampang in the late afternoon. Should you wish to spend more time, you can stay overnight in Phayao, where there is simple but adequate accommodation.

The **Young Elephant Training Centre** is definitely the most authentic place in Thailand to see elephants working in their natural environment; although frequently visited by tourists (though more Thais than foreigners), the school is a bona fide establishment and not a commercial circus. It is essential to have your own transportation, as the school is a bit off the road in the middle of the forest and reaching it might be difficult if you have just been dropped by a morning bus.

The Centre lies just beyond KM 656 of H1on a dirt road to the left which leads 1.5 km to a natural amphitheatre, a saucer-shaped plain surrounded by high, rocky hills. All of the buildings are constructed of wood and bamboo. A little stream, Huay Mae La, provides water for the elephants' daily bath—and a chance to romp before they begin the rigours of the day.

The Centre, the first of its kind in Thailand, was established in 1969 and is operated by the veterinary section of the Northern Timber Works Department of the Forest Industry Organization (FIO). Its main purpose is to train young elephants in the skills necessary for working in the government-owned teak forests—at least it was until all logging was recently banned. There is always a vet in attendance since elephants, in spite of their size and strength, are quite prone to illness. The tricky task of separating a calf and its mother are also accomplished at the training centre. Young elephants are enrolled at about five years of age, and their training will take between five and six years. Each animal is first introduced to its mahout (who will likely be its companion for life) and then taught the basic words of command; only then does it begin more advanced training in dragging, carrying, pushing and stacking logs, either on its own or in tandem with a partner.

The FIO owns 92 work elephants, though only 40 to 50 are stationed at the Centre, and only 20 or so of these will normally be at the performance grounds; old elephants and mothers with very young calves are generally left to wander free in the forest. There are usually about seven to ten calves undergoing training. The Centre is open daily except on public holidays, although there are no classes during the hot season, March through May. (Entrance is free.) Demonstrations of elephants learning their skills take place in the early morning from 6 a.m. to 9 a.m. and the show is undoubtedly the best of its kind in the North.

Tham Pha Thai At KM 666.8 there is a 1 km track off to the right which passes through a pleasant grove to the base of a cliff and the cave of Tham Pha Thai. A steep climb up 283 steps leads to the huge, arched entrance to the cave, next to which is a *chedi*. Just inside is a Buddha image set beside a gigantic stalagmite soaring almost to the roof, from where a hole allows sunlight to dramatically illuminate the fantastic formation. The cave is lit by electric light for its entire 400 m length and terminates in a cavern dominated by a large, curiously-shaped chunk of limestone.

Ngao, set in a small fertile valley surrounded by hills, is an old and pleasant town, but there is little to detain the visitor.

Near KM 673, 12 km south of Ngao, a small and crumbling Burmese-style *chedi* on the right is all that remains of the old Shan monastery complex of **Wat Chong Kham.** An unusual wooden structure combining *viharn* and monks' quarters was in danger of falling into total decay when it was fortuitously acquired by Muang Boran ('Ancient City'), an open air 'architecture museum' near Bangkok. It has been moved and reconstructed there, an excellent example of one type of northern architecture.

The town of **Phayao** is of considerable interest to the historian since it is generally accepted that a settlement existed on the site at least as early as the Bronze Age. It was later abandoned for some unknown reason and not reinhabited until 1096 when Pho Khun Chom Dham established it as the capital of a small kingdom, the arts of which have been linked to that of Chiang Saen. Phayao later allied itself with King Mengrai's Lanna kingdom, into which it was eventually absorbed. At the end of the eighteenth century, after long wars with the Burmese, the city was abandoned and remained so until 1840, when it was resettled by emigrants from Lampang. The new city was entirely enclosed by walls and remained so until the second decade of this century, when it was visited by Reginald Le May, who wrote in his *Asian Arcady*, "The northern entrance to the town was not more than ten feet wide; and the southern entrance was precisely the same, just a narrow opening in the wall which, built partly of brick and mud, surrounds the city. As we went through the gap, it seemed like entering some mediaeval castle, and one half expected to hear the massive wooden gate banged shut behind the last man."

Formerly a district of Chiang Rai, Phayao was made a province in 1977 and the town of Phayao was raised to the status of a provincial capital. The town is pleasingly placed on the banks of a large, natural lake opposite which looms a 1,856m (6,125 feet) high mountain, Doi Bussaracum. The lake has what speculators ominously call 'potential' and there have been proposals to turn it into a tourist attraction by dredging the shallows and using that earth to create an artificial island replete with recreational facilities. In the meantime, the lake has a nice promenade and is a picturesque setting for many restaurants. The main drawback of Phayao is its extremely hot climate, suffering droughts which impoverish the countryside.

Over the last ten years, the abbot of **Wat Li**, a temple in the middle of town, has collected a large number of chance finds from the surrounding countryside. These prizes have been housed in a specially constructed building and include fragments of Buddha images, stupikas, bases of statues, votive tablets, and miscellaneous metal objects.

Located just behind the market, **Wat Luang Ratcha Santhan** used to be the other point of interest in Phayao. Unfortunately, the ancient wooden *viharn*, which contained several interesting pieces of Lanna art, collapsed a few years ago.

Wat Sikom Kham is the main temple of Phayao and a must for every visitor, containing many varied and unusual things to see. The temple is located outside of town on the shores of the lake. The site, according to one of the many legends that abound in this ancient town, was chosen by the Lord Buddha himself when he saw a bird planting a seed from which a tree immediately sprang up, providing the Lord with shelter from the sun. Other legends narrate that the site was once a marsh which miraculously turned to solid land.

The present *viharn* was built in 1961 to replace one constructed in 1922. Reginald Le May saw the original old Lanna *viharn*, which was of the open type: "As you enter through the ancient gate you can see the roof of the temple, which is low in front, sloping upwards to the back; as you look closer, you see that in reality there are six partitions of roof, all with an upward slope, but each partition raised a little above the preceding one and quite distinct in itself at the end of the fourth is the curved upward tip which is a particular feature of Siamese and Lao architecture; while on each side, sloping downwards from the top, is a series of three other partitions... As is very often found in northern Siam, there are no walls, but a series of supporting pillars on either side, rising from the floor to the roof... Inside the temple I could see the great Buddha looming in the dim light..."

The Buddha image seen today is the same one seen by Le May and is possibly the largest in the North. Built of brick and stucco which is covered in gold leaf, it is about 16 m high and probably dates from the fifteenth century. Named Phra Chao Ton Luang, it is an object of great veneration in the North. The courtyard outside the *viharn* holds a large collection of Buddha heads in sandstone, all examples of the early Phayao school and all in various stages of disintegration. There are also two Buddha footprints engraved on stone slabs kept in a pavilion beside the *viharn*; these date from the end of the fourteenth century.

In a garden outside the *viharn* there is one of those bizarre educational complexes of a kind which have recently become quite popular in Thailand. Inspired by Buddhist scriptures, there are grotesque but realistic figures of the torments of Hell, modelled in cement and painted in garish colours; the figures include everything from a Chinese goddess to a dinosaur. It is rather droll and a bit ugly, but if you have never seen anything of the sort before, a visit is fun and illustrates a fad that is taking hold—quite a jump from the old Lanna art. For some reason the movie character, E.T., is also featured in this ghoulish playground.

The temple authorities, however, must not be entirely insensitive to art, as they have now commissioned a top Thai contemporary artist to paint the murals of a new and distinctively modern *viharn* built right over the lake, perched on a raised platform. The artist is Angkarn Kalyanapongsa, an award-winning poet and a painter of great sensitivity. For the first time a genuine artist has been asked to paint temple murals and, although not a Northerner himself, Angkarn has wisely chosen to utilize traditional Lanna motifs reinterpreted in his own distinctive style. The new *viharn* promises to be a masterpiece.

After visiting the temple, a turn on the right (after 1 km) leads to the lakeside promenade where there are a few restaurants offering a pleasant view over the water to the mountains beyond.

Doi Bussaracum and the Wang River Valley

A new road has been opened connecting Phayao with the Chiang Mai-Chiang Rai road, passing over the mountain Doi Bussaracum. The road reaches an altitude of 1,700 metres (5,600 feet) at a panoramic viewpoint, after passing through large areas of largely unspoilt deciduous forest. It is likely that this new accessibility will stimulate encroachment and deforestation, as is usually the case, but for the time being this is still a wonderful drive in the woods. The road ultimately descends gently into the valley of the Wang River and at Wang Nua one turns left if heading for Lampang. As the road has been improved only recently, it is little traveled and is still deprived of the Chinese shophouses and tacky garages that usually punctuate Thailand's major thoroughfares. In the Wang valley one still sees villages looking as all Thai villages used to be—without Pepsi Cola signs. The farmers tend their crops by the roadside and life goes on as it did for centuries, affording an insight into what Thailand has lost while 'developing': verdant forests, peaceful rural life, and a rustic but rich artistic heritage.

Quite a few ancient temples, most of them related to the style found in Lampang, still dot the valley and not all of them have been redone in cement. Of particular interest is the side trip to Muang Pan, in Jae Sorn District. In the small village of **Soplee** there is an old Lanna structure that has recently been restored to pristine condition, either utilizing the original parts or, where necessary, making new elements exactly identical to the deteriorated originals. The project was completed in 1986—not by the Fine Arts Department, which is rarely so scrupulous about faithful restoration—but by volunteers from the Lampang Heritage Preservation Group. This endeavour by private citizens has established an interesting precedent and created a model to be emulated by the authorities. A few kilometres away is **Wat Jae Sorn**, another remarkable example of old Lanna art, though still awaiting its turn for careful restoration.

Chiang Rai, Chiang Saen, Mae Sai and the Mekong

The journey northeast to Chiang Rai and then beyond to the Golden Triangle is probably the most popular excursion from Chiang Mai. This region is the most northerly part of Thailand and for many travellers it epitomizes the ultimate travel adventure. It has all the classic ingredients—mountain scenery, hilltribes, temples, work elephants, exotically beautiful women, etc.—but most especially it has the romance of the 'Golden Triangle'.

The drive from Chiang Mai is quite pleasant, passing through a series of hills and valleys. The road crosses the valley of Chiang Mai, passing by the small hill of **Doi Saket** (where a venerated temple is built on top of the hill) and then starts ascending a larger hill, **Doi Nang Kaew**. Along the road there are often caravans of mules which carry supplies to the tea-growing villages inaccessible by road. At the peak of the hill many drivers honk their horns to salute the spirit of Nang Kaeo, a much revered female spirit who is supposed to haunt this area. Her statue is housed in a shrine on the left side of the road, and villagers used to bring offerings in the form of wooden phalluses and place them in the many 'spirit houses' around the shrine. Recently, fervent

Buddhists have tried to discourage this practice and have cleaned up the site. A Buddha statue has been installed and there is a sign that reads, "Nang Kaeo has gone to paradise and doesn't need penises anymore." Villagers, however, continue to bring phalluses to the ephemeral lady, hiding them behind the Buddha statue.

Descending into the valley the road reaches the small town of Wiang Pa Pao, the halfway point between Chiang Mai and Chiang Rai, before crossing another set of hills and descending into the large, irrigated valley of Chiang Rai.

Chiang Rai

Chiang Rai has in recent years awaken from being a quaint and sleepy town to become a large, modern and cosmopolitan tourist center where even the *samlor* drivers speak French. The allure of the Golden Triangle clings to this drab, cement town where thousands of French visitors desperately search for opium poppies and Chinese warlords in the dining rooms of five star hotels. A huge crane now stands brazenly in the middle of the Mae Kok River to help construct an enormous resort complex on the island in front of the town, irretrievably scarring one of the most romantic places in northern Thailand. One can imagine the dismay of intrepid backpackers who, after two days of trekking through the hills and rafting down the Mae Kok River, reach their hard–fought destination to be welcomed by a box of cement.

Efforts have been made to recreate or restore ancient monuments and to stimulate a sense of history by reconstructing parts of the old walls. A monument erected to King Mengrai, and a *lak meuang* (city pillar) has also been raised. But all these cosmetic changes regularly fail to impress visitors. The town is drab and dusty and evidences very little of its ancient history. Founded by King Mengrai in 1262, Chiang Rai was, until the nineteenth century, an important trading centre and thus a bone of contention between Siam and Burma. At the end of the Burmese Wars the city was reduced to a state of complete abandon with only a few hundred families remaining within the walls. The establishment of a mission and a hospital at the end of the century injected a little bit of hope into the community, but it is only since the late 1970s that Chiang Rai has developed into a modern town. It is a convenient base for excursions but has very little to offter visitors who are not interested in exploring the surrounding countryside. Besides the early morning market, the only attractions are a handful of temples, none of which are architecturally interesting.

Wat Prasing, on Singhakai Road near the Town Hall, formerly housed the important image of Phra Buddha Si Hing. Though the original is now enshrined in the temple of the same name in Chiang Mai, a copy of that statue resides here at present day.

Wat Phra Kae, near Wat Prasing on Trirat Road, has a bot in late Lanna style built in 1890. Though gaudily restored, this temple does boast some half a dozen fine bronze images. The presiding image is Phra Chao Lang Tong, an early Chiang Saen statue which is probably the largest bronze sculpture remaining from this period. The temple is noted for its recently reconstructed *chedi* where, according to legend, the famous Emerald Buddha (now in Wat Phra Kaeo in Bangkok) was discovered in 1436 during the reign of the Lanna king Sam Fang Kaen. Lightning is supposed to have damaged the *chedi*, exposing a plaster statue. Some time later the plaster cracked, revealing the true material and the true value of the image.

Wat Ngam Muang, sited on a hill west of Wat Phra Kaeo and reached by a short flight of Naga–flanked stairs, possesses an ancient brick *chedi*

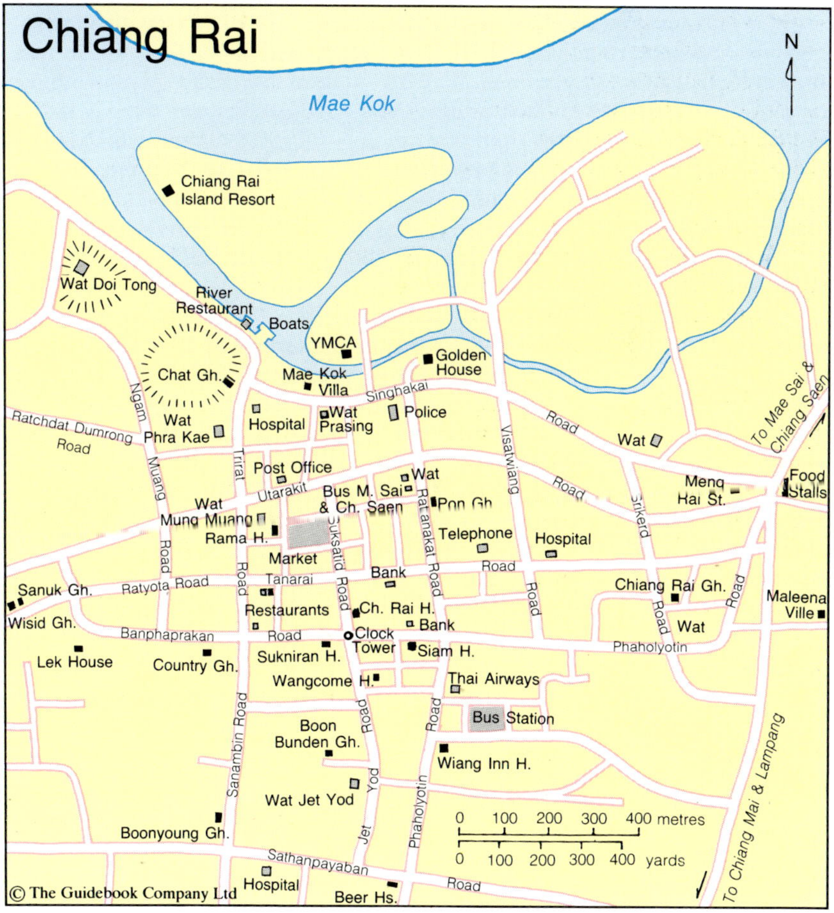

which is the reliquary for the remains of King Mengrai. It was built in 1318 by his son, Chao Khun Kram, but the *chedi* that one sees today was built much later.

Wat Doi Tong, on a hill north of Wat Ngam Muang, comprises a *viharn* and *chedi*. Commanding a fine view of the Kok River and surroundings, tradition has it that this was the vantage point from which King Mengrai first surveyed the site that was to become Chiang Rai. The *chedi* has been restored several times, lastly in 1945 by a Burmese monk, a fact which accounts for its Burmese-style.

Doi Mae Salong, a Kuomintang Village, and Akha Settlements

The excursion to Doi Mae Salong, recommended only to travellers with their own transportation, is one of the most interesting in the area and allows tourists to visit some very conservative and traditional Akha villages within the range of comparatively easy walks. On the way to the peak there is the Hilltribe Resettlement Centre and several other hilltribe villages which are so easily accessible that they have been overrun by tourists, to the point of having completely lost their cultural traditions. The best strategy is to drive straight to the summit and the Kuomintang village of **Santakiri** where there is a modest guesthouse to spend the night and prepare for trekking to the outlying villages.

Santikiri is a fascinating place, being an entirely Chinese community inhabited by former members of the Kuomintang army and their offspring. The houses are built in authentic Chinese style, and the residents would seem to be in direct contact with their ancestral home, at least judging from the abundance of a full range of Chinese products, such as beer and cigarettes, which are not available elsewhere in Thailand. The village affords a beautiful view over vast ranges of mountains, and early in the morning there is a very lively hilltribe market. Surprisingly there are several opulent Chinese mansions and a huge but deserted old peoples' home where there is an excellent Chinese restaurant. These are remainders of a period when Santikiri was an independent enclave ruled by the Kuomintang army. To reach the Akha villages you walk to the end of the village where there is a path that descends into the valley. (It is best to hire a guide able to communicate with the hilltribes.) Two hours walking along a level trail brings you to a cluster of very recent settlements of Loimi Akha who have moved in from Burma only a few years ago; they are still extremely conservative, tenaciously clinging to the old ways.

Mae Sai and Chiang Saen

Mae Sai, 891 km from Bangkok, is Thailand's northernmost town and lies at the end of H110, an extension of H1. Midway to the town from Chiang Rai, **Khunnam Nang Non**, or 'Sleeping Lady Mountain', can be seen off to the left. This sprawling mountain range derives its name from the fact that its shape roughly resembles that of a woman sleeping on her back—the profile of the face being fairly recognizable although the rest of the body is anatomically peculiar. The slopes of this mountain host two interesting caves, **Tham Phum** and **Tham Pla**, located at the base of a limestone formation and set in a Chinese garden with fish ponds and Chinese pavilions. A nearby village, **Ban Tham**, is inhabited by Muslim Chinese Haw who have emigrated from Yunnan.

The town of Mae Sai rests on the banks of the Mae Sai River, which forms the border with Burma. A bridge crosses the river although it is open only to Thais and Burmese (foreigners are not permitted to enter Burma by land), and the one–horse town owes its prosperity to border trade and to the popularity of the village on the Burmese side, Tha Kee Lek**,** where Thais enjoy shopping for souvenirs, herbs, various Chinese products, and other items not readily available in Thailand. On special days and Buddhist holidays, there is a market held right on the bridge which Burmese citizens are allowed to attend; this is an occasion not to be missed, a chance to buy all sorts of strange things. The regular market, on the other hand, is held everyday for tourists and sells mostly products brought from Chiang Mai. It

is nothing more than a smaller version of the night bazaar in Chiang Mai.

There are three small hotels in Mae Sai, but there is little in town to woo the visitor except **Wat Phra That Doi Wao**. The temple is approached by a lane off to the left of Paholyothin Road (the main street and a continuation of H110) a few hundred metres from the river just before the Top North Hotel. A flight of 207 stairs with a Naga balustrade leads to the top of the small hill where the *wat* is located. Dominating the small compound is a white *chedi* with Buddha images in niches on the four sides and green stone scorpions at the corners of the base. Originally built in the reign of King Ong Wao of Chiang Saen to hold a hair of Lord Buddha, it was completely rebuilt in 1953. The location of the temple is rather more remarkable than its contents, affording fine views of the town, the Mae Sai River and mysterious Burma.

Chiang Saen is far more interesting and attractive than Mae Sai. A once powerful fortified city, its former importance is made clear by the Fine Arts Department's list of 75 ruined monuments outside the walls and 66 inside. Much of the old fortifications remain intact and more restoration work is being done, although the remains are not very impressive, being mostly ruined *chedis* scattered around the woods. Nonetheless, there is a pleasant and bucolic atmosphere, enhanced by a dramatic location on the banks of the Mekong River.

It is generally accepted among historians that Chiang Saen was built over the ruins of an earlier settlement in 1328 by Phra Chao Saen Pu, a grandson of King Mengrai. However, recent research stresses the likelihood that the earlier town must have had considerable power and influence long before then. After the ascendancy of Chiang Mai, Chiang Saen became an associate city governed by the Lanna kings. This state of affairs continued until 1558 when the city and surrounding regions were taken over by the Burmese who ruled until 1804 when Rama I seized the city and burnt it to the ground so that it could not be reoccupied. It remained abandoned for 70 years until Chao Inta, a son of the Prince of Lamphun, brought back the descendents of Chiang Saen's former population and rebuilt the town.

H1016 approaches Chiang Saen from the west, passes between grass-covered mounds—the remains of the old city gate—and then swings right to enter the town centre. Just by the old gateway a track off to the left leads to the ruins of **Wat Pa Sak.** Here is Chiang Saen's oldest *chedi*, a magnificent stuccoed structure built in 1295 which combines the ancient formula of a basement adorned by niches covered with a reliquary tower crested by a circular stupa. (This is a southern theme, though in the North it can also be seen at Chedi Chiang Yan of Wat Phra That Haripunchai at Lamphun.) The style of this *chedi* displays various influences, most notably that of the early Haripunchai period. As the temple was built before the founding of the city, its beauty suggests that the valley was already an important centre linked with the rest of the world long before the establishment of the Lanna Kingdom. The site was originally planted with a hundred teak trees (*ton sak*)

thus giving rise to the name, 'The Teak Forest Temple'.

From Wat Pa Sak a track continues north beside the city walls for about 1 km to the northwest corner of the fortifications and a hill on top of which is **Wat Phra That Chom Kitti**. A flight of 350 rough, ancient steps climbs up to the temple although a car can just make it up the narrow 800 m track to the summit, from where there is a fine view of the town and, on the far bank of the Mekong River, Laos. Of principal interest is the 25 m high *chedi*, with a slightly leaning top, constructed on a rectangular base with niches on the four sides containing stucco Buddhas. Just below Wat Phra That Chom Kitti, at the top of the staircase, is the small ruined *chedi* of **Wat Chom Chang.**

Returning back to the city gates, just after the road curves to enter the town there is a **museum** located on the right side. The museum contains some large Chiang Saen bronze images and, more importantly, the finds of the excavations of Wat Chedi Luang and other sites in the city, including marvelous small bronzes, copper fretwork with floral motifs, and stucco heads of whimsical female faces. The museum is open from 8:30 a.m. to 12 noon and from 1 p.m. to 4:30 p.m., Wednesday to Sunday.

Next to the museum is **Wat Chedi Luang**, noted for its 58 m high, octagonal *chedi,* supposedly built in 1331 and rebuilt in 1515. Part of the walls of the old *bot* next to the *chedi* have been roofed over to house a seated Buddha.

From here the road cuts through the centre of the old town before reaching the banks of the Mekong. Along the way are a number of ruined *chedis*, the most notable of which are the fifteenth century **Wat Mung Muang**, **Wat Phra Buat** (restored in the fifteenth century), and, on the opposite side of the road, **Wat Lan Thong**. Nearby is **Wat Phra Chao Lantong**, which was founded during the reign of Tilokaraja.

About 1 km from the museum the road comes to a T–junction by the river. To the left is the village of Ban Sob Ruak (11 km away) and the spot designated as the Golden Triangle; to the right H1129 goes 54 km to Chiang Khong.

To the Golden Triangle After turning left at the T–junction in Chiang Saen where the road meets the Mekong River, the Chiang Saen Guesthouse will be on your left; this is the best place to stay in town, providing basic but comfortable accommodation.

The road, which continues to parallel the Mekong River, shortly deteriorates into a laterite track leading eventually to Mae Sai. Exactly 7.4 km beyond Wat Pha Khao Pan there is a turn to the left which goes 6 km to an Akha village; a few hundred metres past the junction a signpost announces the Golden Triangle. For a panoramic view of this famous juncture, climb up the rough steps on the left just before the sign to **Wat Phra That Pu Khao.** On top of the small hill is an ancient brick image hall housing a large Chiang Saen Buddha. From the temple there is a magnificent view of the river and the 'Golden Triangle.'

The 'Golden Triangle' is the area that produces 50-60% of the world's supply of opium. The name was coined by journalists and repeated usage in the media and sensational fiction has given it an absurd popularity. The 'triangle' is roughly an equilateral one with the base running through Chiang Mai, or just below, into Burma to the west and Laos to the east; the sides take in large chunks of Burmese and Laotian territory, and the apex lies well up in the Shan States of Burma. Although Chiang Rai province is in the very heart of the opium producing area, the spot actually (and erroneously) designated the Golden Triangle is the place near Chiang Saen where Thailand, Burma and Laos meet. This area, far from swarming with fierce opium warlords, is a tranquil and picturesque spot marked by a notice board and a *sala* suitable for a picnic. The opium traffickers obviously conduct their business in more discreet places.

The exact spot often designated as the centre of 'the triangle' is where the Kok River empties into the Mekong thus converging the boundaries of Thailand, Burma and Laos—the west bank is Thailand, the narrow promontory between the Kok and Mekong rivers is Burma, and the east bank is Laos. A small, quiet guesthouse, the Golden Hut, is situated on the banks and offers basic accommodation.

Chiang Khong Should the traveller wish to visit Chiang Khong (and there are one or two good Meo and Yao hilltribe villages in the vicinity) the best route is via H1020, which branches off H1 at Chiang Rai and heads southeast to **Thoeng** before swinging northward to Chiang Khong.

From Chiang Khong it is possible to continue travelling on to Nan. It is also possible to return to Chiang Rai via the recently completed Phayao Mengrai Road.

While the complete journey along H1129 from Chiang Saen to Chiang Khong is not recommended, it is worth travelling the first 4.2 km (the road is surfaced this far) to **Wat Phra That Pha Ngao.** The temple lies off to the right of the road and is approached through a reconstructed brick gateway topped with a *chedi*–like structure. The partially ruined *bot* is currently being restored and contains a fine old Buddha image that was discovered buried in the ground in 1976—a major archaeological find. Behind this image is a large brick-and-plaster bust which is all that remains of the temple's presiding image.

Behind the *bot* is a *chedi* strangely sited atop a naturally rounded rock, and in the compound to the left is a small menagerie of caged black bears and monkeys. Beyond the temple is a steep and rutted but paved track that leads 800 m to the summit of a hill where there is a small ruined *chedi* and a superb view of the Mekong River and Laos.

Another kilometre farther along the main road is **Wat Phra That Song Phi Nong,** a temple that has two identical Buddha statues and two identical *chedis*. According to the chronicles these were built by two brothers (*song phi nong*).

The Weaker Sex

I had another delicate subject to broach. The natives who had been instructed to furnish me with elephants for my journey had provided six of these animals, all of which, however, with the exception of one, were females; and this one was too young to be of much use as a beast of burden, and was quite useless for hunting purposes. Now to offer any one, especially a stranger, a female elephant to ride, is regarded among both Siamese and Laosians as a great insult, and I felt that the object was to expose me to ridicule and contempt, should I unsuspectingly employ these animals, and, above all, ride one of them. Dr. Cheek had informed me that the Laosians delighted thus to insult foreigners, and that even the Siamese representative had once been subjected to the indignity of being offered a she-elephant to ride when visiting Chengmai. So I mentioned the fact to the chief, and reminding him that I had come with the authority of the king of Siam, inquired whether it was done by his direction or with his knowledge. He coolly replied that he knew nothing of it, that the elephants had been drafted in the villages, and that possibly no others were available. Dr. Cheek smiled, and whispered to me something about the "ready tongue" of the Laosians, but finding that no offer of reparation was made, and fearing futher detention, I preferred not to insist on the point, and left the Chow Operat with an expression of thanks for his services, determining to make the best of a bad bargain. My subsequent experience, however, showed that I was unwise in coming to this conclusion.

The natives, in many out of the way places especially, offered me insults, and placed impediments in my way, which they would never have dared to do if I had ridden a "tusker." A she-elephant, indeed, holds much the same place in the estimation of the Siamese and Laosians as a donkey does in England, and a gentleman riding down Rotten Row mounted on the humble ass would hardly be exposed to greater ridicule, certainly not to so much unsuspected "obstruction," as a foreigner in Lao riding a female elephant.

Carl Bock, Temples and Elephants *(1883)*

Phrae, Nan and the Nan River Basin

From Lampang to Phrae

Public transport from Chiang Mai to Nan is convenient and plentiful. Two buses a day (see bus schedule in back) leave the northern capital for Nan via Phrae, taking four hours to cover the distance. By air there are four flights a week from Chiang Mai to Nan, *via* Phrae and Phitsanulok. Flying time to Nan is 45 minutes.

By car the first leg of the journey from Chiang Mai is to Lampang. From Highway 1 take H11 which runs through a landscape of forested, low–lying hills to join H101 and, 16 km later, Den Chai, a small town on the northern railway line from where taxis ply the route to Phrae and Nan. Beyond Den Chai, H101 swings northwards to follow the fertile valley of the Yom River. One of the principal crops here is tobacco, and distinctively shaped brick curing houses dot the landscape.

Wat Phra Luang Just beyond Den Chai, the road passes the village of Dung Men, and after a further 1.9 km Wat Phra Luang lies 800 m down a turn on the left. Lining this side road are some charming old wooden houses which give a good idea of what Chiang Mai and other northern towns must have looked like fifty years ago.

The modern *viharn* of the temple is of little interest, apart from a fine wooden *thammas* inside, but (to the right) there is a curious old manuscript repository with a two–tiered roof and two porticoed entrances on one wall. Behind the *viharn* is a brick *chedi* in Lanna style. Niches in the four sides house standing Buddha images, and the top of the *chedi* leans slightly, giving rise to the temple's local name, That Nuang or 'Leaning Relic'. The exact date of the *chedi* is unknown although it certainly pre-dates the other buildings and was probably part of a previous temple, now long disappeared. Also of interest is the nearby bell tower, a wooden roofed structure raised on sturdy stone pillars.

Phrae

Phrae is quite prosperous from coal mining and, until recently, logging. Local industries include the making of heavy wooden furniture, rattan furniture, and homespun textiles of a distinctive pattern. The furniture is displayed in several shops that line the roads leading into the city, while the textiles are sold in the market downtown. Reasonable accommodation can be found at the Nakorn Phrae Hotel, while several garden restaurants on the outskirts of town offer some of the best food to be found in the North. The downtown area is quite modern, though a drive around the old moats of the city will reveal several quaint wooden mansions which display a triangular gable very similar to the houses of Lampang. Like Lampang, Phrae hosted a large number of Burmese involved in the teak trade, and, even earlier, there was a Burmese enclave left behind from the times of the Burmese occupation of the Lanna kingdom.

Burmese influence is evident in nearly all of the temples of Phrae. Of the Burmese-style temples, **Wat Chom Sawan** is the best example and Wat Luang has a good Burmese *chedi*. Wat Sra Bo Keo is a less notable example but its *chedi* is of some interest. Laotian influences are seen at Wat Si Chum, Wat Pong Sunan, Wat Phra Non and Wat Phra Bat Ming Muang Vora Viharn.

Phrae's most famous temple, **Wat Phra That Cho Hae**, is on a hill outside of town 8 km to the east. H1022 goes from the town centre, crosses H101, and passes through a broad fertile plain to reach the village of Padang from where it is less than a kilometre to the temple compound. Five separate flights of stairs lead up the teak–clad hill; the stairs on the right have two Burmese lions at the base, while the older stairway on the left is flanked by Nagas. Beside the Naga steps is a *sala* containing a reclining Buddha image. At the top of the right–hand stairway is a small shrine housing the famous and revered Buddha image of **Phra Chao Tan Chai,** which is widely believed to have the power to grant wishes. Inside the temple's tiny cloister is a 33 m high *chedi* sheathed with gilded copper plates. The *chedi* is squashed up against the walls of the modern *viharn*, interesting because of its cruciform pattern but spoiled by garish decoration and excessive use of inlaid coloured glass.

Phae Muang Phi Continuing along H101 from Phrae, a side road on the right just before KM 143 goes to Phae Muang Pi or 'Ghost City'. The first 1.5 km of the road is laterite, after which it is surfaced for the 1.7 km before it reaches a dirt track on the right which covers the remaining 2.7 km to Phae Muang Pi. This 'ghost city' is a shallow depression in the ground where soil erosion has produced weird chimney–like rock formations that give the impression of dwellings on an asteroid.

From the Phae Muang Phi turnoff on H101 it is 21 km to the hamlet of Rong Kwang. Beyond Rong Kwang the highway heads northeast towards Nan and winds its way through gently rolling hills extensively replanted with teak trees which in many places overhang the road, producing a beautiful and shady arbour.

A sidetrip to **Sa District** can be made before reaching Nan from Lampang. About 65 km from Rong Kwang, H101 descends into the Nan valley and, after entering the district of Sa, swings left to parallel but not border the river for the remaining 23 km to the town of Nan. At a curve near kilometre marker 117, H1026 leads to the small settlement of Sa.

This sleepy place has one temple worth visiting, **Wat Bun Yeun**, found to the left at the crossroads at the end of the main street. The old *bot*, recently restored, has a three–tiered roof and a fine, ornate portico with a Garuda carved on the pediment. Laotian influence is quite evident in the squat design of the building and the front portico. The beautiful doors are decorated with two superbly carved guardian figures. Behind the *bot* is a small northern-style *chedi* with statues of a lion, a tiger, a deer and a mythical lion at the four corners of the base.

After retracing one's steps back through Sa to H101, the remainder of the journey to Nan passes through flat countryside with the Nan River unseen off to the right. One kilometre before the town a road, signposted 'Khao Noi', branches left from H101 and 200 m along this side road is **Wat Phayawat.** The modern *viharn* contains a Laotian-style *khong phra* that enshrines a seated Buddha. There is also an interesting old *chedi* in the form of a stepped pyramid with niches containing Buddha images.

After the temple, the road rises steeply up a hill on top of which is **Wat Phra That Khao Noi**. The *viharn* contains little of interest, but behind the small white Chiang Saen *chedi*, which is topped with a gold umbrella, is a *sala* housing two fine Buddha statues in the late Chiang Saen style. The larger one is in a meditation posture while the smaller is in the pose of subduing Mara. These two statues—and a fine view of Nan—justify a trip to the hilltop.

Nan

Spread out on the west bank of the river of the same name, **Nan** is a prosperous town, at least judging from the inordinate number of shops selling luxury items. Good accommodation is available in the city at the modern Dhevaraj Hotel and two smaller hostelries.

Until as late as the first decade of the twentieth century, Nan was the capital of a semi-autonomous principality. The city of Nan was founded in 1368, and the history of the principality falls into distinct phases. From the mid-1300s to 1450 there was a close relationship with Sukhothai, after which indirect control passed to the Lanna kingdom. In 1558 Nan fell under Burmese sovereignty and after these invaders were expelled in 1786, allegiance was pledged to Bangkok in 1788. The ruling dynasty retained much autonomy until the area came under the full control of the central government in 1931.

A British surveyor working in the North at the end of the last century described Nan thus: "The walls of the city are in an excellent state of preservation, and are about two miles round. The ricefields are cultivated to their full extent, there being an excellent system of irrigation, which is not allowed to fall into decay. Advantage was taken of a large swamp and, by piling earth in a circle, a reservoir was formed, which supplies hundreds of acres of ricefields, the soil being particularly productive. By a simple calculation the number of men and women who annually contribute rice to the common store in the city is sixty thousand, of which fifty thousand are in that portion of Nan beyond the Me Kawng [Mekong River]... There are thousands of emigrants from Sip Sawng Panna, and Khamus from Luang

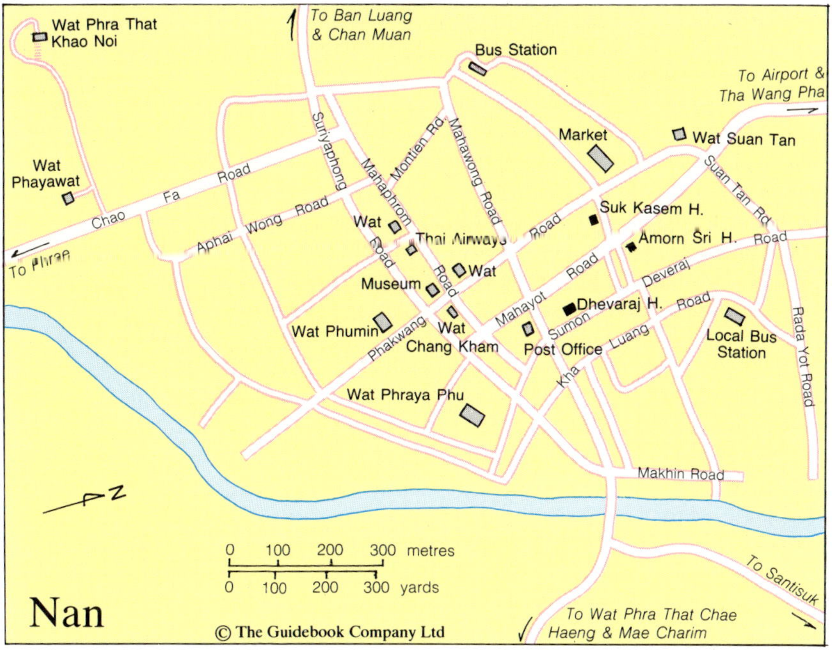

Phrabang, and a growing population of Meo and Yao, for Nan is popular, and their government has been just."

The best starting point for an exploration of Nan is the **National Museum,** which is centrally located in what was formerly a palace. Built in 1903 by the ruler Phra Chao Suriyapong Phalitdej, the ex–palace has few exhibits of interest besides a famous black elephant tusk measuring 94 cm long and weighing 18 kg; it was supposedly brought to Nan from Chiang Tung by a ruler of the city some 300 years ago. What the museum lacks in actual art objects is made up for by well–presented displays of pictures, photographs, and text (in both English and Thai) which give detailed accounts of the city's history, art, and major monuments.

Wat Chang Kham Vora Viharn, directly opposite the museum, gets its name from the *chedi*, which was first built in 1406 but restored several times. On the second tier of the base there are several elephant (*chang*) buttresses on each side.

The two *viharns* in the temple compound are unexceptional; one formerly housed a walking Buddha and a standing Buddha, but in 1981 thieves broke in and stole the head from one and a hand from the other. (The mutilated statues have subsequently been moved to the museum for safekeeping.) These two images were part of a group of five statues commissioned in 1426 by a ruler of Nan, Ngua Ran Pha Sum. Two of the five are now in nearby Wat Phaya Phu, while the fifth image is kept in the monks' residence here. This 145 cm-high walking Buddha is made of pure gold, as was discovered by Alexander Griswold and Kraisri Nimmanhaeminda in 1955 when the plaster then disguising the statue was broken.

Wat Phumin is on the opposite side of the road about 100 m past the traffic lights at Wat Chang Kham Vora Viharn. The foremost landmark of the province, this temple was established in 1596 by a ruler of Nan, Phra Chao Chetabutra Phromin, and extensively renovated in 1867.

The *viharn* follows a cruciform shape with steps leading up to exquisitely carved entrance doors on each of the four sides. The stairways of two opposite entrances are flanked by Nagas with the tail at one doorway and the head at the other. The interior is dominated by a giant centrepiece of four large Buddha statues facing the cardinal points of the compass. The walls are decorated with murals depicting mainly the Khatta Kumara Jataka. The western wall shows the Nimi Jataka, and murals above the door illustrate episodes in the life of the Buddha.

The murals were done during the reign of Rama V, probably at the turn of the century, by Tai Lüe artists. The paintings are remarkable for their freshness and their naïvité, besides documenting valuable information about the dress, fashions, tattoos and hairstyles of the era. It is easy to get lost in time looking at the amazing details, which possess a lively sense of humour rarely seen in Thai art. Also of note is the architecture and the fine workmanship of the pillars, rafters, and the coffered ceiling. All the doors are carved to depict a figure, called Thai Wetsuwan, surrounded by animals and floral motifs.

Wat Phraya Phu has buildings of little intrinsic interest, but the temple does enshrine two of the five Buddha statues cast by Ngua Ran Phan Sum in 1426. Both are made of bronze in the Sukhothai style, and both display superb artistry in the poise of the body and the serenity of the face. They flank an enormous seated Buddha, although the larger statue in no way detracts from their aesthetic impact.

Wat Suan Tan, on the western side of town, is distinguished by its 40 m high *prang* (rounded spire of Khmer design) instead of the more usual *chedi.* The *viharn* was built in the fifteenth century but has been embellished and renovated to such an extent that little remains of the original. It enshrines an important Buddha image, **Phra Chao Thong Tip.** This 4.1 m–high bronze statue is an excellent example of the Sukhothai style. It was commissioned by King Tilokaraja of Chiang Mai in 1449, and according to legend, Tilokaraja, who had just conquered Nan, gave the people just seven days to collect sufficient metal for the statue and set a 100–day time limit for émigré artists from Sukhothai to cast it.

Wat Phra That Chae Haeng is located southeast of the town on the opposite bank of the Nan River. The main features of the temple are the enormous Naga Makara that lead to the entrance and dominate the landscape from far away. In the grounds outside the compound are three old chapels and three *chedis.* The courtyard is dominated by a 55 m-high golden *chedi* with four smaller *chedis* and decorative gilded umbrellas at the corners of the base; it is surrounded by a terrace and low, crenellated walls with ornate doorways. The *viharn* is a marvellous structure showing Laotian influence with a three–tiered, five-level roof. Inside, on a fine altar made of stucco, is a large seated Buddha with two statues of monks facing it and a row of five other Buddha images in front.

Wat Satharos, on the northern outskirts of town, is also worth visiting. The *viharn* is modern yet its carved door and window shutters are of good craftsmanship, although the main attraction is the unusual *chedi* mounted on an abnormally high square base and tapering to an Ayutthaya-style, bell–shaped top. The small, old *bot* is open–sided with pillars supporting a wooden ceiling and tiled roof. The interior is bare except for two old wooden statues, one seated, one standing.

Nan's other great attractions are the **annual boat races** held to celebrate the end of Buddhist Lent (October/November). Staged along the stretch of river near the Governor's residence, the races are an exceptionally colourful affair with about forty highly decorated, Naga–prowed boats—each with up to 50 oarsmen. Each village in the surrounding area sends its own team and its own crowd of enthusiastic supporters who generate wild excitement as the contests get underway. The colour and high spirits make this one of Thailand's most thrilling events.

Wat Phumin in Nan contains some of the most beautiful mural paintings in all of Thailand. Compare the detail in the frieze pictured at top to the unposed photograph on the bottom of page 26. The more things change, the more they stay the same!

(following page) Usually held in October, the annual Lanna Boat Races take place on the Nan river near the town of Nan. Featuring exquisitely decorated and designed long-boats, the regatta is part of the annual kathin season, a time when people present robes to the monks as part of merit-making ceremonies.

Tak and Mae Sot

Tak is hardly worth a trip on its own, but it can be conveniently visited by travelers en route to Kampaeng Phet or Mae Sot. Tak is a clean town with good accommodations and good food, and after a trip to the hilltribe villages along the Burmese border, these simple virtues are more than enough to justify a visit.

Tak is located on the east bank of the Ping River, which at this point is very wide. The town, a provincial capital, is laid out in a rather grand manner, with various government buildings set on huge lawns. The first impression is that there is absolutely nobody living here, but after driving down large and deserted roads one finally reaches the downtown market and the Viengtak Hotel—which is all one wants to see of the city.

Today Meuang Tak ('The City of Tak') owes its prosperity to logging, both legal and illegal. In the old days it owed its importance to being equidistant between Bangkok, Chiang Mai and Moulmein (in Burma). Tak was once under the rule of Lanna, but at some point it was bestowed as a dowry to a subordinate prince, from whom it passed to the direct control of the Siamese capital. The town was never densely populated, and in 1890 there were only 20,000 souls living in the whole district. Its only claim to fame derives from having been the hometown of a young, dynamic governor named Sin, who, under the name of Taksin, was to become King of Siam—in fact, the very last king before the present Chakri dynasty. He is commemorated by a statue at the northern end of town, housed in an orange-roofed pavilion with walls decorated with murals depicting scenes from his life.

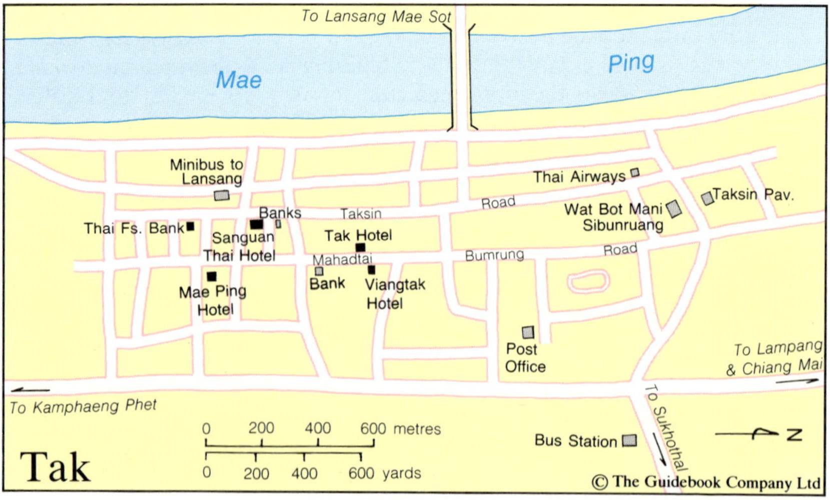

On the opposite side of the road from the Taksin pavilion is Tak's only other major monument, **Wat Bot Mani Sibunruang.** Most noteworthy here is the *chedi,* with a gilded top, and the old *viharn* built in northern style. A modern *bot* houses the Buddha image called Luang Phor Buddhamon, an excellent example of the Sukhothai style.

Excursion to Ban Tak and Bhumipol Dam

There are two roads to the small village of **Ban Tak**, one on each side of the river, each running for approximately 20 km; the road on the right bank (heading north) is H1. There are actually two parts to the village on opposite banks of the river. Once connected by a rickety wooden bridge 600 metres long, today there is a modern bridge which has somehow tainted the charm of the spot. Ban Tak is, however, still a simple and picturesque spot with old wooden houses built on stilts at the water's edge, children playing joyfully in the river, and women washing clothes by the banks—epitomizing the riverine life that has changed hardly at all over the years. Ban Tak was once renown for its traditional wooden houses in the northern style (typically out–leaning walls and dark teak panels), but most of the old farmhouses have now been destroyed or dismantled and moved elsewhere. (The northern houses preserved at the 'Ancient City'—Muang Boran—in Bangkok come from Ban Tak.) However there are still a number of old-style shophouses as well as charming Western-influenced buildings dating from the turn of the century.

Wat Phra Boromathat After crossing the bridge into Ban Tak Tok turn right and follow the river bank for 50 m and then take the first left and then the first right onto H1107 that passes between paddy fields. Turn left after 2.6 km onto a dirt road and 400 m later a short track off to the left leads directly to a flight of Naga-flanked steps that go up to Wat Phra Boromathat. The history of the temple is obscure although it is believed that a sanctuary was built here in very ancient times. The buildings in the compound now are all modern. The *chedi* is the most interesting, entirely covered in gold leaf and surrounded by smaller *chedis* and tiny spired 'houses' with Buddha images inside. The present structure was built about 60 years ago over the site of an earlier *chedi* which was said to have enshrined four hairs and part of the right hand of the Buddha.

Just 1.4 km farther along H1175 a track on the right leads shortly to a Sukhothai-style *stupa* with a square base and rounded top. This *stupa* marks the spot where, in 1262, the 19 year old Prince Ramkhamhaeng, later to become King Ramkhamhaeng of Sukhothai, saved the life of his father, King Sri Intratit during the course of a combat on elephant back.

To visit **Bhumipol Dam** continue on H1 north of Tak to the turnoff at Sam Ngao. The dam area, which lies 2.6 km beyond Sam Ngao, is virtually a small town in its own right, comprising a colony of bungalows, most of which are for workers of the Electricity Generating Authority of Thailand

(EGAT) although some are available for rent to the public. The main hotel is the 26–room 'Guesthouse 100' which is attractively sited on the river bank not far downstream from the dam wall. There is an 18–hole golf course nearby.

Bhumipol Dam, named after Thailand's present king, is also referred to as Yanhee Dam. It is Thailand's largest concrete dam having a 486 m-wide curved crest, a maximum height of 154 m, and a maximum thickness of 52 m. (The first two turbines came into operation in 1964 and another five have subsequently been brought into service.) In addition to generating 553,000 kilowatts of electricity, the dam also provides irrigation in the dry season to Tak and Kamphaeng Phet provinces as well as the Chao Phraya River plain. During the rainy season the dam reduces flood hazards in those areas. Behind the dam the Mae Ping lake stretches 207 km north as far as the town of Hot.

There are floating bungalows and restaurants on the lake, including a floating hotel which makes overnight excursions around the lake; these attractions can be reached by hiring small longtail boats on the shore. Arrangements can be made at the guesthouse for hiring small boats taking up to 15 persons. Larger vessels for touring the entire length of the lake up to Doi Tao can be chartered from the Chiang Mai Lake Tour Company which has offices in both Chiang Mai and Bangkok.

Tak to Mae Sot

The road to Mae Sot and the Burmese border (H105) turns right off of H1 just 3.1 km past the bridge over the Ping River, just south of Tak. Along the way one encounters **Lansang National Park**, a picturesque spot featuring a series of waterfalls. The first waterfall, 200 m beyond the entrance, is small but 2 km further along the narrow track, which parallels a small stream and passes through a bamboo grove, the falls are far more impressive.

The park has several bungalows where it is possible to stay overnight. Small shops near the waterfalls sell drinks and snacks, but campers are advised to bring their own food. Lansang National Park is a mountainous area covered by dipterocarp and mixed deciduous forests. There are also small patches of evergreen and pine trees. The park supports a small population of barking deer, sambar, serow, and bears; even leopards have been reported within the park boundaries. Primates include langurs, macaques, and white-handed gibbons. Hilltribes used to roam here, but since the establishment of the park they have been resettled to a centre on the west side of the mountain.

Doi Musoe Beyond the turnoff to Lansang, H105 begins to climb and curve as the hills start to close in, producing some extremely beautiful scenery. Just before KM 26 a dirt road on the left climbs to Doi Musoe. The track passes a Lisu village after 1.5 km and then, almost next door, a Meo settlement. A little farther along is the entrance to an experimental agricultural station developing the cultivation of coffee and avocado pears.

At the entrance to the agricultural station the track makes a hairpin bend to the left and after 700 m comes to a fork. To the left lies the Hilltribe Centre run by the Ministry of the Interior; to the right a very rough track goes 1.1 km to the sizeable Muser village of **Um Yom.** This sprawling settlement of houses raised up on stilts is nearly overrun by dogs, pigs, chickens, and small sturdy horses, thus providing an authentic insight into hilltribe life. From the hilltribe centre there are several trails which offer good birdwatching. A guide should be hired.

There are a number of other hilltribe villages in the area, the easiest of which to reach is the Muser settlement of **Sompuey**, 1 km left of H105 and 3 km past the Doi Musoe turnoff. A little farther along on the right of the highway is a string of stalls where the tribespeople sell their produce.

Back on H105 it is another 50 km beyond the park before one reaches the town of **Mae Sot**. Something of a boomtown because of the Burmese jade trade, Mae Sot has a couple of large Chinese hotels which provide reasonable accommodation. These are often full, however, because of the large influx of traders and smugglers; travellers arriving late in the evening should be prepared to experience difficulties in finding a room.

There are several restaurants, both in the market and also garden-type restaurants on the outskirts of town. Some serve 'wild food' specialities, supposedly from the jungle, such as boar, deer, and snake.

There are no special landmarks to visit in town, and a trip to the border is the highlight of a visit. There is a busy market here selling Burmese curios, and one can walk to the river (the Maenam Mae, a tributary of the Salween) and watch the Burmese and Thais crossing the river. There is always a potpourri of nationalities and tribes in Mae Sot, and people-watching is invariably amusing.

The 'Death Highway'

From Mae Sot there is a road leading south that runs parallel to the Burmese border and ultimately reaches the district of **Umphang**, the theatre of many infamous episodes in the recent history of Thailand. Umphang used to be accessible only by twice crossing the Burmese border. Due to its isolated position, in the 1960s it became a stronghold of communist insurgents and when construction of a new road started, the communists vowed to stop it at any cost, staging a series of cruel attacks that delayed the completion of the 135 km road for nearly ten years. KM 43 was the site of two massacres, and more than thirty workers were mercilessly gunned down by Meo, Karen, and Thai terrorists.

The area is now under control, and there are frequent army checkpoints. Hilltribe refugees from Laos, previously involved in fighting the communists, have been resettled here in large villages that comprise more than one ethnic group. Such villages are administered by ex–officers of the Kuomintang forces.

Although the full trip along 'the Death Highway' is not recommended, it is safe to drive the first stretch of road through the flat valley of the Maenam Mae which flows from south to north. The valley holds several Shan hamlets and some large Meo resettlement camps.

The area has been in the headlines of Bangkok newspapers as the site of the discovery of a large cache of ancient ceramics, possibly from a burial site, which the Fine Arts Department failed to protect; Bangkok's antique market was flooded with unprecedented quantities of very high quality Burmese and Sukhothai pottery. The local Meo tribesmen have all become 'antique dealers, regularly replenishing their shops with fakes purchased in Chiang Mai.

Sukhothai, Sri Satchanalai, and Phitsanulok

Sukhothai

The old city of **Sukhothai** is located twenty minutes drive from the modern town of Sukhothai, where several hotels provide accommodations for the night. (During the Loy Krathong festival, however, lodgings become extremely scarce.) Sukhothai is a rather unattractive collection of concrete shophouses and though it is certainly not as bad as Reginald Cambell's description of the 1920s ("For of all the desolate, miserable, God–forsaken place on this earth, Sukhothai must surely be one of the worst."), many travellers prefer to stay at Phitsanulok or Tak. Both of these towns are about one hour drive from the ancient city, and both are quite pleasant and attractive towns.

To visit the ruins it is preferable to have your own transportation, although the recent erection of fencing to prevent cars from entering some areas makes visits rather exhausting in any case. Be prepared for long walks in the sun, and make sure that you know the way back so as to return safely from the more isolated ruins.

Sukhothai is often referred to either as the 'first Thai capital' or as the 'cradle of Thai culture', two rather simplistic—even misleading—appellations, since, as has been noted before, the Tais filtered gradually southwards into what is now Thailand and by the time of Sukhothai they had already established several townships over a wide area, integrating with the already existing peoples. Still, it is undeniable that Sukhothai (the name literally means 'The Dawn of Happiness') was the first large Tai kingdom to develop in central Siam, probably in the twelfth century, nearly contemporaneously with the establishment of the Lanna kingdom in northern Thailand. According to local chronicles, the greatest sovereign of Sukhothai, King Ramkhamhaeng, was an ally and a personal friend of Mengrai, the founder of Lanna; and the presence of a firm friend on the northern frontier became a liberating factor in the expansion of Sukhothai.

The central plains of Thailand had been inhabited since the beginning of the first millennium by Mons and Khmers organized into a framework of city–states, nearly all of which ultimately fell under the influence of their more powerful and more organized neighbour, the Khmer empire of Angkor. By the end of the eleventh century Sukhothai was already a fortified city—and the northernmost citadel of the Khmer empire. Tai immigrants had been accepted into the existing population and lived alongside the Khmers, though under the immediate leadership of their own chieftains. (A column of Tai troops acting as allies of the Khmers is depicted in a bas–relief at Angkor; the soldiers are unmistakably 'Thai' in their unrepentant individualism, chatting to each other and marching out of step while the Khmer army marches in perfect military order.)

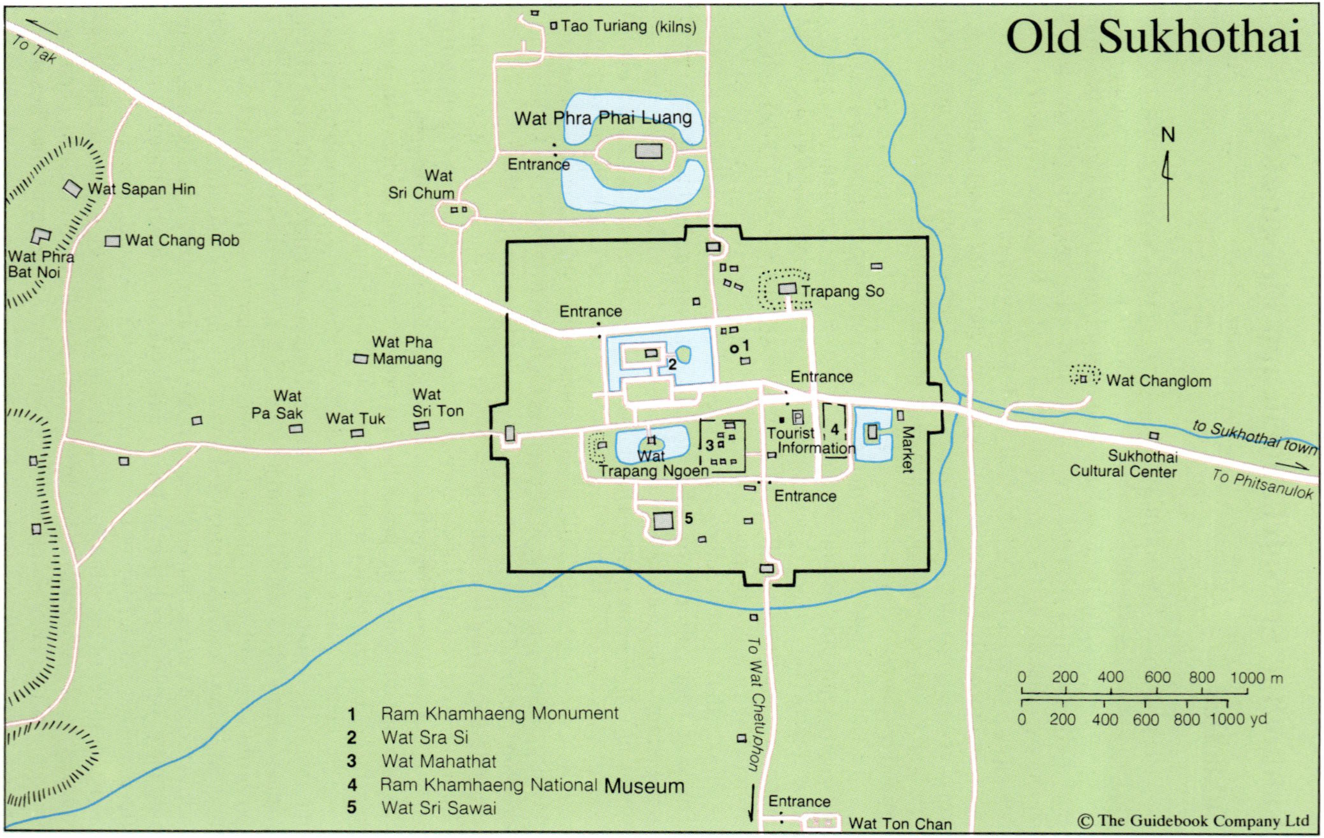
Old Sukhothai
To Tak
Tao Turiang (kilns)
Wat Phra Phai Luang
Entrance
Wat Sri Chum
Wat Sapan Hin
Wat Chang Rob
Wat Phra Bat Noi
Entrance
Trapang So
Wat Pha Mamuang
Wat Pa Sak
Wat Tuk
Wat Sri Ton
Entrance
Wat Trapang Ngoen
Tourist Information
Market
Entrance
Wat Changlom
to Sukhothai town
Sukhothai Cultural Center
To Phitsanulok
To Wat Chetuphon
Entrance
Wat Ton Chan
N
0 200 400 600 800 1000 m
0 200 400 600 800 1000 yd
1 Ram Khamhaeng Monument
2 Wat Sra Si
3 Wat Mahathat
4 Ram Khamhaeng National Museum
5 Wat Sri Sawai
© The Guidebook Company Ltd

The Tai chieftains were nonetheless vassals to the Khmers and certainly chafed under Khmer rule. As soon as the rigid hierarchical structure of the Khmers collapsed for internal reasons at the death of Indravarman II in 1243, the Tais seized the opportunity to seek independence. One chieftain, Sri Intaratit, became the first Tai king of Sukhothai. Under the third king, Ramkhamhaeng (*r.* 1279-1298), this little kingdom expanded to include most of the Tai people living in lower Siam, extending its influence even over the Mons of lower Burma (Ramanadesa) and part of the Malayan Peninsula. A son of Ramkhamhaeng, Lo Tai, managed to lose most of these territories, but the core of the kingdom, the two cities of Sukhothai and Sri Satchanalai, continued to prosper for some time; in 1438 they were absorbed into the realm of influence of a newly emergent Tai kingdom, Ayutthaya, which had sprung up further south.

Sukhothai was a cosmopolitan city, hosting a variety of races and encouraging cultural and commercial exchanges with places as far away as Ceylon, China, and Borneo. Thai monks travelled to Ceylon, returning with much valued knowledge, while communities of Ceylonese monks lived just outside Sukhothai; such exchanges were certainly instrumental in stimulating the creation of many of the monuments which are today regarded as the

Chedi Styles of Sukhotai

The bell-shaped *chedi*, of Sri Lankan origin

Corner tower of Wat Chedi Chet Thaew, Sri Satchanalai, incorporating a bell-shaped finial

Lotus bud *chedi*, as at Wat Trapang Muang, Sukhothai

Bell-shaped *chedi* on a two-storied base, as at Wat Chang Lom, Sri Satchanalai

(pages 200-201) An aerial view of old Sukhothai. Wat Mahathat is in the near-center left, and Wat Sra Si is in the pond in the upper right

earliest masterpieces of Thai art. This eclectic little kingdom is in fact responsible for the genesis of the first distinctively Thai architectural idiom, an idiom which inventively combined elements borrowed from various cultures: Khmer, Mon, and Ceylonese. The same impulse generated the production of large bronze Buddha images remarkable not just for their aesthetic qualities but also for their technical perfection. Pottery workshops produced a massive output of flawless celadon ware (of a kind very similar to the celebrated Chinese celadon) which for two centuries was exported throughout Southeast Asia. Amazingly, some of this pottery is still found in use today among the Dayaks of Borneo.

Sukhothai is undoubtedly an important chapter in the history of Thai art —as well as of Asian art in general— but the present Historical Park may well disappoint visitors who are not deeply immersed in the study of either subject. The ruins, to start with, are by no means impressive in size. Further, most of what one sees are reconstructions or cement copies of originals kept somewhere else in a museum—if they have not been stolen by plunderers. None of the works of art *in situ* remain in the same condition one would expect from looking at books published just a few years ago. Contrary to the Buddhist tenet that a disfigured image of Buddha is a disgrace, everything not removed has been retouched, reconstructed, and finished in cement.

As a general rule, abandoned ruins are more appealing than restorations or reconstructions, the ruins conjuring up romantic visions of forgotten kingdoms or lost Shangri–las while neat and tidy reconstructions lock the viewer in the present. Blandness is certainly evident at Sukhothai, but what makes a visit really disappointing is the total lack of anything to help visualize the everyday life of its bygone inhabitants: their costumes, their tools, their dwellings, their habits and tastes.

What should be credited to the restorers is not so much the salvaging of the collapsed structures, but rather the fact that they have revealed the original layout of the city, an achievement which unfortunately can be appreciated only from the air (see photo on pages 200-201). A bird's–eye view shows that the city which the Tai acquired from Khmers had been planned and developed according to sophisticated concepts which had evolved over ten centuries of civilization. Subsequent Thai embellishments, such as the construction of Wat Mahathat and several other temples, were to reflect the inherited cosmological vision although the additions conspicuously lacked the inherently utilitarian and technical elements of Khmer city planning.

In the words of Thai architect-historian Sumet Jumsai, "A Khmer city had to be in total harmony with the elements, and to achieve this it had to be a reverberation of the rhythm and order of the ultimate macrocosm itself." Practically, such harmony was achieved by designing a well–protected city capable of storing and regulating the water supply of the whole agricultural area; metaphysically, the city was designed to reflect the cosmology of the

The Kings of Sukhothai

King	Reigned	Significant Events
Sri Intaratit	1240s-1270s	Revolt of Thai people against Khmer rule. Sukhothai becomes an independent kingdom.
Ban Muang	1270s-1279	
Ramkhamhaeng	1279-1298	Expansion of the Sukhothai kingdom to cover all of the Central Plains, with suzerainty over parts of the Malay Peninsula, Laos, and lower Burma. The bell-shaped *chedi* is introduced into the kingdom. Construction of Wat Chang Lom at Sri Satchanalai.
Lo Thai	1298-1346(7?)	Most of the empire is lost. Direct contact with Sri Lanka. Restoration of Wat Mahathat at Sukhothai. Creation of the style known as a 'lotus bud' *chedi*. Construction of Wat Chedi Chet Thaew at Sri Satchanalai. Transition to classic Sukhothai style, including walking Buddha images.
Nam Tom	1346-1347	
Mahadarmaraja I	1346(7)-1368(74?)	Mahadarmaraja I, also known as Luthai, writes the *Trai Bhum*. In 1351 another Thai kingdom is born at Ayutthaya. The classical period of Sukhothai sculpture and architecture.
Mahadarmaraja II	1368(74?)-1398	Sukhothai becomes a vassal of Ayutthaya.
Mahadarmaraja III	1398-1419	Last period of Sukhothai independence. Post classic period. Five large Buddha images are cast at Nan, including Buddha Chinarat.
Mahadarmaraja IV	1419-1438	In 1438 Sukhothai is forcibly incorporated into the Ayutthaya kingdom.

universe, with the main temple symbolising Mount Meru, Abode of the Gods in Hindu mythology, and the water reservoirs representing the Primordial Ocean. Pragmatism and mysticism were merged in order to ensure the well-being of the township.

The whole area of Sukhothai encompasses a rectangle of 1,400 m by 1,600m protected by three concentric ramparts and by concentric double moats representing the ocean. A huge basin was created to the east of the city at Wat Phra Pai Luang in order to simultaneously provide both water storage and a symbolic sea for the temple. (The relationship between Sukhothai and Wat Phra Pai Luang is strikingly parallel to that between the ancient Khmer ruins of Angkor Thom and Angkor Wat.) The water was gained by diverting a small stream, Klong Mae Ramphan, and channelling it to the city, to the basin, and to the network of canals irrigating the fields. Once having gained control of the city, the Tais gradually lost control of this complicated hydraulic system: the canals silted, the land became arid, and finally the whole city had to be abandoned.

The site remained derelict and deserted for several centuries until thick vegetation covered most of the ruins. King Rama I rediscovered the city in the early nineteenth century, bringing back to Bangkok a number of statues found lying in the jungles. Rama IV and Rama V both made archaeological expeditions to Sukhothai but neither of them attempted to restore the city. Rama IV, before his accession, reputedly discovered a stone column bearing inscriptions purported to have been written by King Ramkhamhaeng; this graven text has long been regarded as the first document in the Thai language and has been widely used by historians to demonstrate that Ramkhamhaeng had by himself invented the Thai alphabet. The words of this stele have also been frequently quoted to attest to the contentment of the Tais under the righteous leadership of Ramkhamhaeng. The inscription became a sort of manifesto of the whole Thai nation and its love for freedom; at the time of the official anniversary of the 'Invention of the Thai Alphabet', the stone was publicly displayed in Bangkok in a solemn ceremony, with students from every school lining up to pay homage to the ancient work.

It is all the more understandable, therefore, that the authorities and the public conscience were greatly embarrassed by the recent discovery that the stele is most probably a fake, forged as late as the middle of the nineteenth century. The substance of the new theory, proposed by the eminent Thai historian Piriya Krairish, had actually been suspected (and gently suggested) by several scholars, Thais and foreigners alike, at the end of the century—but until quite recently the spurious origin had never been publicly expressed.

The ruins of Sukhothai remained obscured in the jungles until 1953, when they were cleared by the Fine Arts Department as part of a project to instill pride among the Thai citizenry, in line with the principles of the prime minister and military strongman, Pibul Songram. From 1979 to 1988 a massive restoration was conducted with the assistance of UNESCO, contributions from several countries (particularly Japan), and help from various private institutions. Some 60 monuments have been restored, 85 archaeological sites have been excavated, and many city moats and reservoirs have been cleared. Major undertakings included the relocation of over one hundred families living on the site and the re–routing of the highway that used to slice through the old city. Presently, the Sukhothai Historical Park covers 70 square kilometres (26 sq miles), and includes over 790 acres of fenced–in land, many footpaths and appropriate comfort facilities.

Wat Mahathat is the largest and most important temple of the old city of Sukhothai. Located just in front of the Museum, it is the logical starting point of a visit. (Wat Mahathat is situated next to the Royal Palace, of which today only a single *sala* remains, though a speculative model built by the Fine Arts Department gives some idea of how the secular buildings may have looked.) The temple, which contains some two hundred–odd structures, was probably founded in the middle of the thirteenth century by King Sri Intaratit, although it owes its final form to the extensive embellishments carried out by Lo Tai in 1340 to house holy relics; some hairs and a neckbone of the Buddha brought back from Ceylon by a Tai monk named Sisatta. Encircled by moats and flanked by several ponds, the imposing structure of the main sanctuary (once covered in gold) was intended to symbolize Mount Meru, being thus simultaneously the centre of the Universe as well as the centre of the earthly kingdom.

The main sanctuary is a *chedi* raised on a high plinth terminating in a lotus bud finial, a typical Sukhothai form which is an entirely Thai creation developed during the reign of Lo Tai. The *chedi* is surrounded by eight satellite towers, four of which have the distinctive shape of a Khmer *prang*. This pattern is a magical diagram symbolizing the beneficent power of the king, protected by his allies at the eight cardinal points. The *chedi* once had marvellous stucco decorations, most of which are today in unsatisfactory condition; around the base there is a frieze which depicts walking monks and this, in particular, has been entirely redone in a most gross and insensitive manner, destroying whatever was left of its original grace. The less manipulated sections still show strong Ceylonese influence, particularly in the *kala makara* arches that frame scenes of the Buddha.

The compound of Wat Mahathat comprises also several *viharns*, *bots*, and *mondops* (whose large Buddha images are all modern reconstructions), and a number of smaller *chedis*, many of which were built to house the ashes of royalty. Worthy of attention is an unusual stepped *chedi* which bears some relationship to Wat Chamadevi in Lamphun and testifies to the strongcultural links between Sukhothai and Lanna.

Wat Chanasongram, near Wat Mahathat, is identified by a large bell–shaped *chedi*. It is partially encircled by water, and the ordination hall lies on a small islet in a pond.

Wat Trapang Ngoen, just behind Wat Mahathat to the west, is

The central lotus-bud chedi of Wat Mahathat in old Sukhothai (left). Above is the temple's presiding Buddha image. Both pictures were taken during the annual 'light and sound' festival which has become one of Thailand's most popular tourist events.

comprised of several buildings placed around a large lake, with the *bot* and a lotus bud *chedi* placed in the middle; during the rainy season this temple seems to float on the swollen waters.

Similarly, **Wat Sra Si**, dominated by a slender bell–shaped *chedi*, carries to great extreme the concept of the bond between water and temple. It is built on an island which contains a pond within itself, while the *bot* is built on a smaller islet reached by a bridge. Obviously, a profound symbolism motivated this complicated layout. Generally, in Thai monasteries either the *bot* or the *viharn* must face water, so as to remind believers that the Buddha attained enlightenment sitting under a Bodhi tree which faced a river. (When there is no water, the buildings must face east.) When the *bot* is entirely encircled by water it becomes a *bot nam* or 'water chapel', and in such cases there is no need to place the *bai sema* to demarcate the consecrated area; the *bot nam* becomes the 'Boat of Salvation', a symbol of the achieved Nirvana. Such concepts are derived from the Mahayana lineage of Buddhism as practiced by the Khmers.

San Da Pa Daeng is the oldest building of Sukhothai, a Khmer edifice built of laterite in the middle of the twelfth century. It is comprised of a square cell and an antechamber; the *prang* topping the cell has collapsed, giving the structure a rather distorted and uncharacteristic shape.

Wat Sri Sawai lies southwest of Wat Mahathat. Distinguished by three imposing Khmer *prangs*, the temple was begun in the twelfth century by Indravarman II but was left unfinished. The Tai converted the Hindu sanctuary into a Buddhist temple, completing the laterite *prangs* with a finish of bricks and stucco. In the fifteenth century a *viharn* was added to the front.

Wat Chetuphon, located outside the city walls to the south, dates from the fourtheenth century. Encircled by a double moat, it is characterized by the use of large slabs of schist instead of the normal wooden panels. These imposing megaliths lend the site a rather primitive appearance. In fact, such usage is a Ceylonese tradition, as can be seen in some stone cloisters at Polonnaruwa, Sir Lanka. At the centre of the temple complex there is a ruined brick edifice, originally sheltered by a wooden superstructure, featuring large representations of Buddha in his four principal postures.

Wat Trapang Tong Lang is a large *mondop* that featured four particularly beautiful stucco scenes on each side. Sadly, these scenes have either deteriorated or been defaced and they are now better appreciated by looking at old photographs rather than the actual objects.

Wat Phra Phai Luang is located about 1 km beyond the northern gate and is enclosed in a complex of moats that delimit an area half the size of the city. It lies next to the large reservoir controlling the water supply of the township. Built during the reign of the Khmer king Jayavarman VII(*r.* 1181-1219), it originally contained three laterite *prangs* (of which only one remains) and was a Hindu temple. In the late fourteenth century it was completely remodelled by a Thai king, Mahadarmaraja II, who added several

Buddhist buildings and a stepped-pyramid chedi, now completely in ruins.

Not far from Wat Phra Phai Luang is the site of the **kilns** of Sukhothai. A few have now been restored, and it is possible to gain some appreciation of the design of the kilns of those times. These kilns were established early in the fourteenth century—some historians say with the assistance of Chinese potters—and produced mostly architectural elements in a light gray monochrome: mythical animals, figurines, and other cult objects. (The industry responsible for the large ceramic output which was exported all over Southeast Asia was not located here but rather at Sri Satchanalai).

Wat Sri Chum lies southeast of Wat Phra Phai Luang and features a massive square *mondop* which enshrines one of Thailand's largest seated Buddhas in the posture of subduing Mara. This image is 15 metres high and 11.3 metres wide at the lap. The walls of the *mondop*, 3 metres thick, contain a passage leading to the top; the ceilings of the passage are decorated with engraved slabs which are one of the few remaining examples of Sukhothai draughtsmanship. The slabs closely resemble the paintings of Polonnaruva and were possibly even executed by Ceylonese artisans.

Wat Sapan Hin is located about 2 km west of the city atop a small hill off to the left of H12 in the direction of Tak. This 'Temple of the Stone Bridge' gets its name from the slate slab pathway leading up the hill. Among the ruins of the *viharn* stands a huge Buddha image with its right hand raised in the attitude of giving protection.

Sri Satchanalai

Sri Satchanalai was the second city of the Sukhothai kingdom, and holds an important place in the history or Southeast Asian art not only because of its monuments, but also because it was once a production center of celadon (and other kinds of stoneware) that was exported all over the region for more than three hundred years. Celadon has been a very popular — and expensive —collector's item for many years.

Sri Satchanalai is located on the west bank of the river Yom, halfway between Sukhothai and Uttaradit, and it is a rather pleasant place because of its picturesque location and its serene atmosphere. Until quite recently, the site was rarely visited since it was accessible only by ferry or over a small wooden bridge. The construction of a proper bridge and the establishment of an official archaeological park have now put it on the tourist map; the farmers living in a cluster of villages surrounding the ruins have become tourist-minded and they all have their little shop of souvenirs and 'antiques'. Tour buses are a common sight, but by and large the atmosphere has remained very pleasant, especially in the early morning, and nearly every visitor seems to remember it as more pleasant than Sukhothai. Besides the atmosphere, many visitors prefer the compactness of Sri Satchanalai compared to sprawling Sukhothai.

The old walled city and the major monuments lie along a track leading off to the right after the bridge. The first ruins to appear are those of **Wat Khok Singha Ram**, which was built in the fourteenth century; only some laterite columns and three bell-shaped *chedis* remain. A kilometre further one reaches the heart of the city.

Wat Chang Lom, the 'Temple Surrounded by Elephants', is an imposing structure constructed by Ramkhamhaeng in 1290. Behind the ruins of the *viharn*, a large bell–shaped *chedi* stands on a two-storey basement decorated with 39 elephant buttresses of which many remain, although somewhat disfigured. This is a typical Ceylonese architectural element that will be often found in Thai architecture, as also is the bell–shaped *chedi*. The earliest bell–shaped *chedi* in Thailand appears at Wat Chang Lom. On the shaft of the umbrella spire of the *chedi* there is a depiction of walking Buddhas, a treatment unique to this monument.

Stairs lead to the platform between the two storeys; it was designed to symbolize the ascent to salvation and to allow devotees to circumambulate the relic tower. It is still usable today, and affords the visitor a nice view over the adjacent Wat Chedi Chet Thaew and the surrounding ruins.

Wat Chedi Chet Thaew was built in the reign of King Lo Tai in the middle of the fourteenth century and is comprised of several *chedis* of various shapes and sizes, the tallest begin decorated with a typical lotus bud finial. Other *chedis* display a Srivijayan influence, witnessing the fact that Ramkhamhaeng had consolidated his sovereignty over the southern part of Thailand and had invited a revered monk from Nakorn Sri Thammarat (in the south) to come and reside in Sukhothai. Among the stucco reliefs that decorate the *chedi* there is a large Buddha sheltered by Naga; this image was in pristine condition until recently, when it was decapitated by vandals.

Wat Khao Phanom Pleung and **Wat Khao Suwan Kiri**, located atop a small hill in the middle of the city, are accessible along a laterite flight of steps, and the pair will reward climbers with a worthwhile view of the surrounding landscape. Also of some interest are **Wat Suan Kaew Utayan Noi**, with a louts bud *chedi* and a well-preserved *viharn* and the fourteenth-fifteenth century **Lak Muang** ('City Pillar'), housed in a chapel next to a stepped-pyramid *chedi*. At **Wat Nang Phya** there are some surviving details of the original stucco decorations of the walls.

South of Sri Satchanalai on a small peninsula formed by a bend in the river Yom, lay the city of **Chalieng**, once a small Khmer outpost and probably the oldest settlement in the area. Today Chalieng is a small and tidy village, worthy of a visit because of **Wat Sri Mahathat Chalieng**, possibly the most impressive monument in the area. The temple appears to have been built by King Ramkhamhaeng in 1285-1288 on top of a Khmer edifice. The very fine *prang* that dominates the temple is, however, not the original Khmer structure but rather a construction dating from the fifteenth century; by that time the area had become a province of the kingdom of Ayutthaya, and

the Ayutthaya kings had adopted the Khmer style again. Of the original edifice built by Ramkhamhaeng there remains a *viharn* which houses a large laterite-and-stucco image of Buddha subduing Mara and also a stele with a walking Buddha, also in laterite and stucco. Both images rank amongst the masterpieces of Sukhothai art. Still visible are the remains of a wall which originally encircled the *chedi*, built of enormous blocks of stone; the walls display a clear Khmer influence but were probably part of Ramkhamhaeng's construction.

The **kilns of Ban Ko Noi**, located a few kilometres north of the walled city, lie by the river Yom, the source of the precious clay that made the fortune of this little kingdom. Sri Satchanalai was also called Sawankhalok, and it is this earlier name which is most often given to the lustrous ceramics the city produced. To reach the village, return to the bridge and then follow the track that runs parallel to the river. Recent archaeological excavations have shed new light on this chapter of art, and every collector of ceramics should make it a point to visit the site. Since 1980 a Thai-Australian project headed by Don Hein has uncovered over 200 kilns and enough evidence to suggest the existence of 800 more. According to paleo–magnetic tests, some of the kilns date back to the tenth century, a discovery which has confounded the old theory that ceramics were introduced into Sukhothai by Chinese potters in the thirteenth century.

The presence of Don Hein in this little village has had great significance on local society as well. The archaeologist seems to have succeeded in educating the local population to cease looting, and has instilled in them a sense of pride for their history and their past. The resultant sense of identity has been boosted by soliciting active participation by villagers in the excavations, and by the creation of a little museum. Further, Hein has helped to re–establish kilns that now produce stoneware items to sell to tourists.

Phitsanulok

About 58 km east of new Sukhothai, along H12, lies the important communications and commercial centre of Phitsanulok. The journey passes through flat countryside which lies between the valleys of the Yom and Nan rivers.

The town lies on the borderline of the central and northern regions and has therefore always held strategic and political importance, but never more so than during the Ayutthayan period when it was a recruiting station and rallying ground for armies on expeditions into the Burmese-occupied North. Phitsanulok is also famous as the birthplace of King Naresuan.

Evidence of the town's long and rich past, however, was largely destroyed by a great fire some years ago and today the modern buildings are tasteless in design and monotonous in their concrete uniformity. Nevertheless, Phitsanulok is saved from unremitting ugliness by the Nan

River, a busy communications link. The river banks are pleasantly tree–lined and a string of houseboats and rafts moored on both sides of the river add the colour and flavour of traditional riverine life. These riverboats host some excellent restaurants. One specialty not to miss while in Phitsanulok (but not served in the boat restaurants) is *Pak Boong Roi Fah*, a green spinach-like vegetable that is served by tossing it from the wok it's prepared in, through the air, and across the street where a waiter catches it on your plate in a show of great dexterity.

Phitsanulok has good airconditioned hotels, making it a convenient overnight stop and there is one temple worth visiting, which contains a highly revered Buddha image.

Pitsanulok's most famous landmark, **Wat Phra Sri Mahathat**, faces the river on the left of the bridge coming into town. Fortunately, the temple was unscathed by the recent fire and its gilded Khmer-style *prang* dominates Phitsanulok's skyline. The temple's primary claim to fame is the Buddha image of Phra Buddha Chinaraj which is enshrined in the main chapel and attracts hundreds of devotees daily. This veneration has had the unfortunate side–effect of stimulating a lively trade in religious objects and other souvenirs, although even this commercial bustle cannot destroy the stunning beauty of the central image. Dating from the early fifteenth century, the highly polished bronze statue of the seated Buddha is an excellent example of late Sukhothai art, the characteristics of which are noticeable in the fingers of equal length, the exaggerated curve of the overlapped legs, and the somewhat rounded, serious face. The image, of which many copies exist (the best known is in Bangkok's Marble Temple), has a halo (*ketumal*) surrounding the head and shoulders and the whole statue is stunningly set off by a black backdrop decorated with gilded angels and flowers. The impact of the central image is further heightened by the architecture of the *bot,* which is a fine example of the traditional three–tiered roof with low–sweeping eaves; from the inside this style has the effect of diminishing the side walls, resulting in an accentuation of the nave and focussing the attention on the statue at the end.

There are other fine Buddha images flanking the main statue and, in front, are two very beautiful wooden *thammas*. The doors of the chapel, which was constructed in 1756, are elaborately decorated with inlaid mother-of-pearl against a black background. On the inside walls on both sides of the doorway there are restored mural paintings depicting, on the left, the Buddhist story of Phra Vessandon Chadok (a Jataka tale), and, on the right, episodes in the Buddha's life. In the cloisters and chapels surrounding the principal shrine are collections of Buddha statues, ceramics and other artifacts—some of which are of great value, although they are exhibited in such a cluttered fashion as to hinder full appreciation. At the back of the temple compound is an open area which offers a fine view of the central *prang*. Here also are the remains of ten laterite columns, all that survives of an earlier *viharn*, and a tall standing Buddha.

The Songkran Festival is the ancient Thai New Year. Held nationwide every April 13th, it is Thailand's most popular festival and attracts hundreds of thousands of Thais to flock to Chiang Mai to partake in the festivities, the major activity of which would seem to be getting soaked. Songkran is, in fact, a religious holiday during which Buddha images are brought out of the temples for a ritual bath (above) and sometimes borne on a procession around the town.

Festivals of Northern Thailand

All religious occasions are celebrated in the North with particular zest. A look at a Buddhist calendar will always tell when holidays occur. Two festivals are especially important throughout the region: Songkran (the Thai New Year), celebrated on April 13th, and Yi Peng, celebrated on the full moon of November. Both have now become major tourist attractions (for Thais as well as foreigners) but the vast majority of Lanna people still celebrate them according to tradition.

In addition to the traditional festivals, recent years have seen a plethora of tourist festivals springing up, some organized by local administrations and some sponsored by the Tourism Authority of Thailand. Of this second group, only the Flower Festival of Chiang Mai has developed into a genuinely cheerful carnival, while the others (the Umbrella Festival, the Lamyai Fair, the Banana Festival in Kamphaeng Phet, etc.) are nothing more than country fairs where a large crowd of locals gather to raise dust and drink the local rot-gut against a background of attractive local maids in hybrid costumes. The much publicized Loy Krathong Festival of Sukhothai is a prime example of such synthetic, though often fun, festivals.

With a few exceptions, the dates of religious festivals vary according to the lunar calendar, and thus are known centuries in advance, while the dates set for festivals organized by local authorities are often determined at the very last minute. It is therefore impossible to give exact dates for many 'theme' festivals, and one should check with T.A.T. (the Tourism Authority of Thailand) or well-informed people well in advance—and then double check the date with a phone call to a local hotel. The following is a nearly comprehensive list of annual festivals held in northern Thailand.

January

Chiang Mai Winter Fair (Begining of month)

During the first days of the year the Chiang Mai municipality organizes a 'Winter Fair' featuring a carnival, a large night market, various exhibitions and performances, (sometimes fights between bulls), sport competitions and, especially, the most prestigious beauty pageant of the North; the selection of Miss Chiang Mai. Most of the activities take place in the evening at the municipal stadium and may be of some interest to Western tourists.

Borsan Umbrella Festival (Late January or early February)

This is a rather modest show, climaxing dramatically in the parade of a dozen maidens riding bicycles (with umbrellas, of course) along the two hundred metre stretch of road in Borsan, a village just to the east of Chiang Mai. The purpose would seem to be to sell umbrellas. The largest paper umbrella in the world, a very useful item, is usually on display.

February

Makha Bucha (February lunar date, nationwide)

Wat Prathat on Doi Suthep is one place where this Buddhist holiday is celebrated in a very grand way, with thousands of worshippers walking up the hill to the temple near the peak of Doi Suthep.

Chinese New Year (Lunar date, usually in February)

Chinese New Year is celebrated all over the country, but in Chiang Mai the shops do not close since few shopkeepers here are Chinese (unlike the case in the rest of the country).

Most of the hilltribe people celebrate their new year according to the Chinese calendar, though their reckoning of the proper date may differ by a few days. This is without a doubt the best time to visit mountain villages, as everybody is dressed in their finery, and the dances and hullabaloo go on for days. Also, traveling in the mountains is much safer during this period, as robberies are usually suspended for the festivities.

The Chiang Mai Flower Festival (Normally around Chinese New Year)

If one can find accommodation, this festival features a lovely floral parade, with local beauties sitting on large floats made of riotously coloured blooms. The public gardens in town are decorated with special displays of plants and flowers. The parade usually starts at the railway station, moves up Tapae Road and ends at Suan Prung Gate on Boonruangburi Road.

Luang Wieng Lakon (Held in Lampang sometime in February)

This is a parade with a historical theme organized in grand style by the Society for the Preservation of Lanna Culture. It is one of the most beautiful events in the north, a stunning display of traditional costumes, antiques, elephants, horses, soldiers, and—as always—beautiful girls.

April

Poi Sang Long (April 4-6 in Mae Hong Son)

Held in one of Thailand's most scenic areas, this event celebrates the ordination of novices belonging to the Shan (Tai Yai) group. Offerings to monks are carried through town in a gala procession, including a *Chong Phrara* (a gaudily decorated wooden castle). There are also dances by performers in animal costumes.

Songkran (April 13, nationwide)

The Thai New Year is an ancient religious festival celebrated all over the country by paying respect to elders and by reverencing Buddha images by pouring lustral water over the shoulders and the hands of the image. Over the

centuries this water blessing has also evolved into a sort of water fight. The rules of warfare are quite simple: anybody can throw water at anybody else at any time. Chiang Mai is the most famous and popular venue where the water battles are fought, but it is also a very wet occasion most everywhere in the countryside—though in the villages the religious aspects are better preserved without sacrificing any of the fun.

A number of merit-making activities take place at Songkran, most of them at the temple. Freeing birds and turtles is supposed to bring happiness to the liberator, and the animals' release obviously symbolizes the cleansing of the accumulated evils of the old year before entering the new one. The bathing of Buddha images has a similar significance. The statues are often carried in a procession around town, and many images normally kept under lock and key deep inside a *bot,* are at this time displayed in front of the temples. Songkran is thus the ideal week for art lovers to appreciate images that are otherwise difficult to see.

Another Songkran tradition is making small sand pagodas. To express their intent to help the monks in the renovation and rebuilding of monasteries, laypeople bring to the temple quantities of sand which are then shaped into little *chedis* and festooned with colourful paper flags. Chiang Mai and Chiang Rai are the best places to observe this particular tradition.

Throughout the North, the Songkran holiday can last up to a full week, with most shops and offices closed and crowds of people crammed into the hotels and restaurants. It is nearly impossible to find accommodation, even in the smallest town, unless one has booked well in advance—so be certain you have a firm reservation.

Chiang Mai is the largest venue, hosting two large parades: a religious procession on April 13th and a larger secular parade to pay respect to the Governor, on the 15th. Nearly every local community also has some kind of celebration. In Lampang in recent years the Society for the Preservation of Lampang Culture has organized a rather spectacular ceremony the day before Songkran, reviving an old tradition of carrying the blessed water to the grounds where an especially revered Buddha image, the *Phra Kew Don Tau,* is displayed (the image is usually housed at Wat Prathat Lampang Luang).

May

Visakha Puja (May lunar date, nationwide)

This is the holiest of all Buddhist holidays during the year, marking the birth, enlightenment and death of the Lord Buddha, which all happened on this date. As on Makha Bucha, temples throughout the country are packed with people who listen to sermons by revered monks, and in the evening there are solemn candle-lit processions circumambulating around the main monastery of the temples.

Lychee Fair (May 22-29 in Chiang Rai)

Chiang Rai, Thailand's northernmost province, is known for the high quality of the lychees that grow in its orchards, and this fair celebrates the harvest season. In addition to sales of the fruit, there are displays of other agricultural products and local handicrafts as well as a beauty contest to select the juiciest Miss Lychee.

June

June is a month when several animist ceremonies are performed, such as the ceremonial killing of the buffalo and the spirit dances in Chiang Mai. Dates and locations vary and should be obtained from well-informed people. Also in this month there are merit-making ceremonies at Tapae Gate in Chiang Mai to commemorate the anniversary of the founding of the city.

August

Longan Fair (Early August in Lamphun)

The longan, known in Thai as *lamyai,* is one of the prize fruits grown in northern Thailand, and the peak of the harvest season comes in August. This fair, held in the provincial capital of Lamphun, about half an hour south of Chiang Mai, features one contest to judge the choisest fruit and another to select the year's Miss Lamyai.

H.M. The Queen's Birthday (August 12, nationwide)

Throughout Thailand, public buildings are decorated to honour Her Majesty Queen Sirikit on the occasion of her birthday. The most splendid creations are to be seen in Bangkok, particularly along Ratchadamnoen Avenue and in the area around the Grand Palace, where government offices, trees, streets and even private businesses are garlanded with coloured lights.

October

Lanna Boat Races (Sometime in October, held in Nan)

This well-known regatta is part of the festival that accompanies the annual *kathin* season, the time when devout laymen present robes to the monks of local temples in merit-making ceremonies. The beauty of the races are enhanced by the distinctive Nan boats, long hollowed-out logs painted with bright colours and adorned with fanciful designs.

November

Yi Peng and **Loy Kratong** (Full moon of November in Chiang Mai and nationwide)

People who have witnessed the Loy Kratong festival in Bangkok and have listened to the special music played all over the country on this day, may be surprised to discover that in northern Thailand Yi Peng (literally the 'second moon', according to the Lanna calendar) is a religious holiday. Throughout Lanna the temples are full of villagers praying and making all sorts of unusual offerings to the monastery. The monks give special sermons and recite Buddhist texts. Traditionally, scrolls with Buddhist stories were hung outside the temple to illustrate the monk's readings; in some small villages in Lampang province this custom is still followed. Candles are lit in front of every house, and in Chiang Mai ceremonial gates are made from palm leaves and hung with paper lanterns.

A peculiar tradition of Yi Peng is that of launching hot air balloons which are believed to whisk away bad luck and to carry one's wishes to the heavens. These balloons are cleverly made of paper and then filled with hot, sooty gas produced by a primitive oil lamp. The Siamese *kratong*, the floral float carrying candles and joss sticks over water, has a similar intent, but the *kratong* appears to have been introduced in the North only in relatively recent times. Nowadays, however, Loy Kratong and Yi Peng have come to be celebrated at the same time (on the full moon of November). The Ping river is literally covered with kratongs, not all of them the traditional floats made of biodegradable banana leaf but some of indestructable styrofoam which unfortunately pollutes the waters of the North for several weeks after the festival. Chiang Mai also hosts a grand parade, as well as several other activities. The huge crowds and the excessive use of firecrackers can make the event a rather frightening experience.

The Festival of Sukhothai (Full moon of November, held nationwide)

The tradition of Loy Krathong, the launching of floral floats (*kratong*) in ponds and rivers to carry away wishes, supposedly originated in the old capital of Sukhothai. In reality, it appears to be an old animistic ritual revived for fun by the Bangkok court in the middle of the last century, but a legend of Sukhothai origin has helped to justify the historical credibility of the biggest tourist festival of the year in Thailand; the Loy Krathong Festival of Sukhothai. This big event is given so much publicity that it is often believed to be a longstanding tradition when in reality it was initiated just a few years ago. The Historical Park is the venue of a spectacular 'son et lumieres' (sound and light) show and a grand parade, as well as theatrical performances and dances. Royal personages often grace the occasion, and incredible crowds gather for three days among the ruins, transformed for the occasion into a fairground. It would be a wonderful event but for the stamina required to make it through the entire program—and the crowds—from morning to late night.

December

H.M. The King's Birthday (December 5, nationwide)

The deep reverence felt by all Thais for their King is perhaps unique in the modern world, and His Majesty's birthday provides an annual occasion for public expression of this love. Government buildings, businesses, and homes all over the country are elaborately decorated; and the area around the Grand Palace is spectacularly illuminated.

Further Reading

Ecology and Wildlife

Thailand Development Resource Institute. *Thailand; Natural Resources Profile*. 1987

The bleak ecological future of this once bountiful country is clearly delineated in this detailed and painstakingly researched report compiled by Thai and international experts. This document is a model of the type of research that should be undertaken by all nations of the world.

Dobias, Robert. *The Shell Guide to [Thailand's] National Parks.* The Shell Company of Thailand, Bangkok. 1982

Now somewhat outdated and unfortunately out of print, this valuable book can still be found in the corners of used bookstores, the Weekend Market in Bangkok, or bookstores in Hong Kong. It remains the best source of information on the major national parks of Thailand. There should be a new edition of this book, but Bangkok publishers seem to believe that foreign tourists aren't interested in the country's national parks and wildlife. If you disagree, please ask for the title in Bangkok's bookstores.

Lekagul, Bonsong and Jeffrey McNeely. *Mammals of Thailand.* LACW, Bangkok

Although bulky and expensive, this scholarly tome on the mammals of Thailand is equally useful for either biologists or laymen wishing to understand what is happening to Thailand's vanishing fauna.

Lekagul, Bonsong, and Edward W. Cronin. *Bird Guide of Thailand.* ACW, Bangkok 2nd ed.,1974

The classic handbook for birdwatching in Thailand. Out of print and very rare on bookstore shelves, a new edition with all new paintings of superb quality should be published in 1990.

Winkler, Manfred. *A Casual Stroll through Siam's Orchid World.* 2nd ed., Thai Wattana Panich Press, 1988

An almost complete description of Thailand's wild orchids by a graphic artist who has spent much time walking and stalking these elusive plants in the forests. Beautifully illustrated and produced, this book should be a great pleasure even for readers who are not orchid aficionados.

Opium and Drugs

Boucaud, Andre and Louis Boucaud. *Burma's Golden Triangle: On the Trail of the Opium Warlords.* Asia Books, Bangkok; Asia 2000, Hong Kong. 1989

Although largely about Burma, much of Burma's drug story is relevant to Thailand, which is a major conduit. The two French authors, twin brothers, spent years rubbing shoulders with their subjects. This book sheds light on the byzantine complexity of the drug trade in what the world knows as the 'Golden Triangle'.

McCoy, Alfred W. *The Politics of Heroin in Southeast Asia*. Harper and Row, New York. 1972

Although badly outdated, this is the classic work on a still timely subject: the secrets of the narcotics trade. It is a book that every trekker should read before walking into a trekking agency. A more recent book, *The Underground Empire* by James Mills, devotes large sections to drugs in northern Thailand, focusing on the murder of the wife of an American D.E.A. agent stationed in Chiang Mai some years ago. Lots of interesting and detailed material on the complicity of the Thai police in Chiang Mai.

Ethnology and Hilltribes

Freeman, Michael. *Hilltribes of Thailand*. Asia Books, Bangkok. 1989

An excellent photographic portrayal of the northern hilltribes and their lifestyles—probably the finest in the genre of 'souvenir' books. Freeman is undoubtedly the most accomplished and the most frequently published photographer of Thailand's hilltribes.

Grunfeld, Frederic. *Wayfarers of the Thai Forest*. Time-Life Books, London. 1982

The photographs in this book (by Michael Freeman) are some of the most exclusive and evocative ever made of a primitive culture, the Akha. The text, however, is somewhat stodgy and mirrors the essentially stultifying views of the anthropological fraternity, but it is nonetheless useful and accurate.

Jumsai, Sumet. *Naga: Cultural Origins in Siam and the West Pacific*. Oxford Univ. Press, Singapore. 1988

Although culminating in a highly debatable and controversial theory (the author proposes that the cultural origins of the Siamese originated in the western Pacific), this book offers excellent background and many useful insights into the religious significance of some Thai customs and architectural features, including those of the North. If read with a discerning eye, this is one of the most illuminating cultural surveys to examine Thailand.

Lewis, Paul and Elaine Lewis. *Peoples of the Golden Triangle*. Thames and Hudson, London. 1982

A classic. By far the most comprehensive work ever published on the hilltribes collectively, this beautiful book is illustrated with a wealth of photographs on every aspect of hilltribe culture: religion, costumes, and daily life. Information on handicrafts will help to identify what you see and what you may want to buy. The bibliography is exhaustive. If you were to have only one book about the hilltribes, this is the one.

Seidenfaden, Erik. *The Thai Peoples.* Siam Society, Bangkok. 1967
A book researched in the first decade of this century by a Dane in the service of the Thai government, this work is still invaluable as a source for basic facts, in spite of its rather old-fashioned style and point of view. Siedenfaden always lets you know, in a most academic manner, whether the women of whatever ethnic group he is discussing are attractive or not.

History

A definitive book on the history of Thailand, much less northern Thailand, has yet to be written. Rather than reading through the stereotyped and misleading generalizations—not to mention blatant inaccuracies—offered by the standard works which largely ignore the distinctive history of Lanna Thai, it is probably better to gain some insight by reading the adventures of the past century's travellers, who, though often opinionated, at least provide a glimpse of what life was like in northern Thailand not so long ago. Below are a few of the classics in this genre.

Anon. *An Englishman's Siamese Journals, 1890-1893.* Siam Media (reprint)

Hallett, Holt. *A Thousand Miles on an Elephant in the Shan States.* London 1890, reprint by White Lotus, 1988

Bock, Carl. *Temples and Elephants.* London 1883, reprint by Oxford Univ. Press, 1986

Le May, Reginald. *An Asian Arcady.* Cambridge. 1926 Reprint by White Lotus, 1986.
This title is by far the best historical and geographical account of the North at the turn of the century.

Wyatt, David K. *Thailand: A Short History.* Yale University Press, New Haven and London. 1982
This is the best general history published to date about Thailand. Wyatt even bothers to include, albeit in brief, numerous references to Lanna history.

Art

There has yet to be published a comprehensive book devoted solely to the arts of Lanna Thai. Below is a selected list of texts which deal with Thai art in general or with more specialized aspects of northern Thai art. Readers wanting to know more should look into the scholarly articles occasionally printed in *The Journal of the Siam Society* or in *Muang Boran*, a bilingual (Thai-English) journal.

Boisselier, Jean. *The Heritage of Thai Sculpture*. Reprinted by Asia Books, Bangkok. 1987 (Originally published in French by Office du Livre, 1974)
This is the classic text on Thai sculpture, although the author's views on Chiang Saen and Lanna sculpture are somewhat outdated.

Cheeseman, Patricia, and Songsak Prangwatthanakun. *Lanna Textiles*. Suriwong Book Center, Chiang Mai. 1987

Krairiksh, Piriya. *The Sacred Image: Sculptures from Thailand*. Cologne. 1979
Actually a catalogue for an exhibition of Thai art in Cologne, Germany, this book presents its author's revolutionary theories in a clear and accessible form. All in all it is an excellent book.

Stratton, Carol and Miriam McNair Scott. *The Art of Sukhothai: Thailand's Golden Age*. Oxford Univ. Press, 1981
The classic work on Sukhothai, this book is nicely illustrated in addition to a fine text.

Van Beek, Steve and Luca Invernizzi Tettoni. *The Arts of Thailand*. Travel Publishing Asia, Hong Kong. 1985
A basic introduction to the subject for the layman, beautifully illustrated. Certaintly the most visually attractive book published concerning art in Thailand.

General Reading

Glauberman, Stu. *Chiang Mai*. Times Editions. Singapore. 1986
A small format, hardbound book designed for the traveller who either doesn't want to—or can't spend too much time in the North. Beautifully photographed by none other than Luca Invernizzi Tettoni (who else?) and designed with flair.

Suwannarangsi, Duangdao. *Back to the Mountains* (In Thai language only)
Ms. Duangdao is Thailand's leading landscape photographer, and this book is a stunning collection of what she does best. A journalist for T.A.T., she spent years wandering the hills and forests of northern Thailand, and with her lens captured views of the North that few people have ever seen. If you liked her photo on page 120 of this guide, you'll love her book.

Useful Phone Numbers

Telephone directory assistance	Tel. 13
Emergency number for police or ambulance	191
Fire	236193
Tourist Authority of Thailand (T.A.T)	235334
Tourist Police (Open 0600-2400)	232508, 222977
Immigration (next to airport)	213510
Chiang Mai International Airport	222022
Thai International Airways (incl. domestic flights)	211044-7
Railway Station (same day booking) 244795, (advance booking)	242094
Bus Station (Arcade)	242664
Places of worship:	
Bahai Center, 77/24 Ramingnivet Tippanetr Rd.	235221
Services: Thursdays 7:30 p.m.	
Chiang Mai Community Church, opposite McCormick Hospital	242661
Services: Sundays 5:00 p.m.	
Chiang Mai First Church, 10 Charoen Rat Rd.	243072
Services: Sundays 10 a.m.	
Seven Fountains Catholic Chapel, 97 Huay Kaeo Rd.	221247
Services: Sundays 9:30 a.m.	
Alliance Francaise, 138 Charoen Prathet Rd.	235277
British Council, 198 Bamrung Rat Rd.	242103
Chiang Mai Motorbike Touring Club, (ask for David Unkovich)	210518
USIS/AUA, 24 Ratchadamnoen Rd, USIS and Library, AUA211377,	211973
Y.M.C.A., 2/4 Mengrairasmi Rd.	221819
Y.W.C.A., Superhighway	252284
Main Post Office, Charoen Muang Rd.	241070
Consulates:	
India, 113 Bamrung Rat Rd., near Prince Royal intersection	243066
Japan, 12/1 Boonreungrit Rd., near Sri Tokyo Hotel	221451
U.S.A., 387 Wichayanon Rd., across from Municipal Bldg.	252629-31
Chiang Mai Museum, Superhighway, near Wat Chet Yod	
(Open 9:00-16:00, closed Mons. & Tues.)	221308
Chiang Mai University,	
entrances located on Huay Kaeo and Suthep Rds	221699
Lanna Hospital, Suthep Rd.	215020-22
Chiang Mai Bowl, Chiang Inn, Chang Klan Rd.	236005
Lanna Golf Course, Chotana Rd. (one km north of Superhighway)	221911
Auto Rental	
Avis Rent-a-car, 14/14 Huay Kaeo Rd.	(053)221316
(Offices in the Chiang Inn and Dusit Inn Hotels)	
Hertz Car Rent, 12/3 Loi Krao Rd.	(053)235496
(Offices in the Chiang Mai, Phucome and Chiang Mai Plaza Hotels)	

Map Key for Chiang Mai Hotels, Restaurants, and Nightspots

The following is a list of Chiang Mai's hotels, restaurants and nightspots recommended in the following practical information section. The numbers before each place are the key numbers for locating the establishments on the map of Chiang Mai on the following two pages. The prices listed for the hotels and public transport are, of course, subject to change. The reader should use them for comparison sake only; they were valid as of the summer of 1989.

The spelling of Thai place names is a difficult task since there is no generally accepted transliteration of Thai into English. We have tried to be consistent throughout the book in the spellings of places mentioned, however, the reader should be aware that they will find many different spellings of these places on road signs, tourist brochures, etc.

Restaurants

1. The Hill
2. Times Square Roof Garden
3. Boat Restaurant
4. Daret's
5. J.J. Bakery and Cafe
6. Fuang Fah
7. White Orchid
8. Kaiwan
9. Suki Coca
10. The Chalet
11. Galae Restaurant
12. Babylon
13. Ban Suan
14. Pensione La Villa
15. Papillon
16. Whole Earth
17. Al-Shiraz
18. Kaithong
19. Nang Nual Seafood
20. Rummit Pochana
21. Bain Garden Restaurant
22. Sorn Jarn
23. Bier Stube
24. Mabuhay Restaurant
25. Aroon Rai
26. Ta-Krite Restaurant #1
27. Ta-Krite Restaurant #2
28. Kao Soi Faham
29. Anusarn Market
30. Chiang Mai Gate Market
31. Chang Puak Gate Market
32. Thor Loong Market
33. Ratchawong Road
34. Inthawarorot Road

Hotels and Guest Houses

35. Chiang Inn
36. Chiang Mai Hills Hotel
37. Chiang Mai President Hotel
38. Chiang Mai Plaza Hotel
39. Chiang Mai Orchid Hotel
40. Diamond Hotel
41. Porn Ping Hotel
42. Poy Luang Hotel
43. Prince Hotel
44. Rincome Hotel
45. Dusit Inn
46. Mae Ping Hotel
47. Montri Hotel
48. Suriwongse Hotel
49. Chiang Mai Guest House
50. Galare Guest House
51. Isra Guest House
52. Je T'Aime Guest House
53. Paocome Guest House
54. Rimping Guest House
55. River View Lodge
56. Saitam Guest House
57. Times Square Guest House
58. Top North Guest House

Nightclubs, Bars, Discos and Cinemas

59. The Riverside Cafe
60. Marble Pub
61. The Gambler
62. The West Side Bar
63. Hennesy Nightclub
64. Chiang Mai Teahouse
65. Blue Moon Nightclub
66. Honey Chiang Mai Nightclub
67. Sangtawan Cinema
68. Nakorn Chiang Mai Cinema
69. Thipanet Cinema

Chiang Mai Hotels, Restaurants, Nightclubs, Bars, Discos and Cinemas

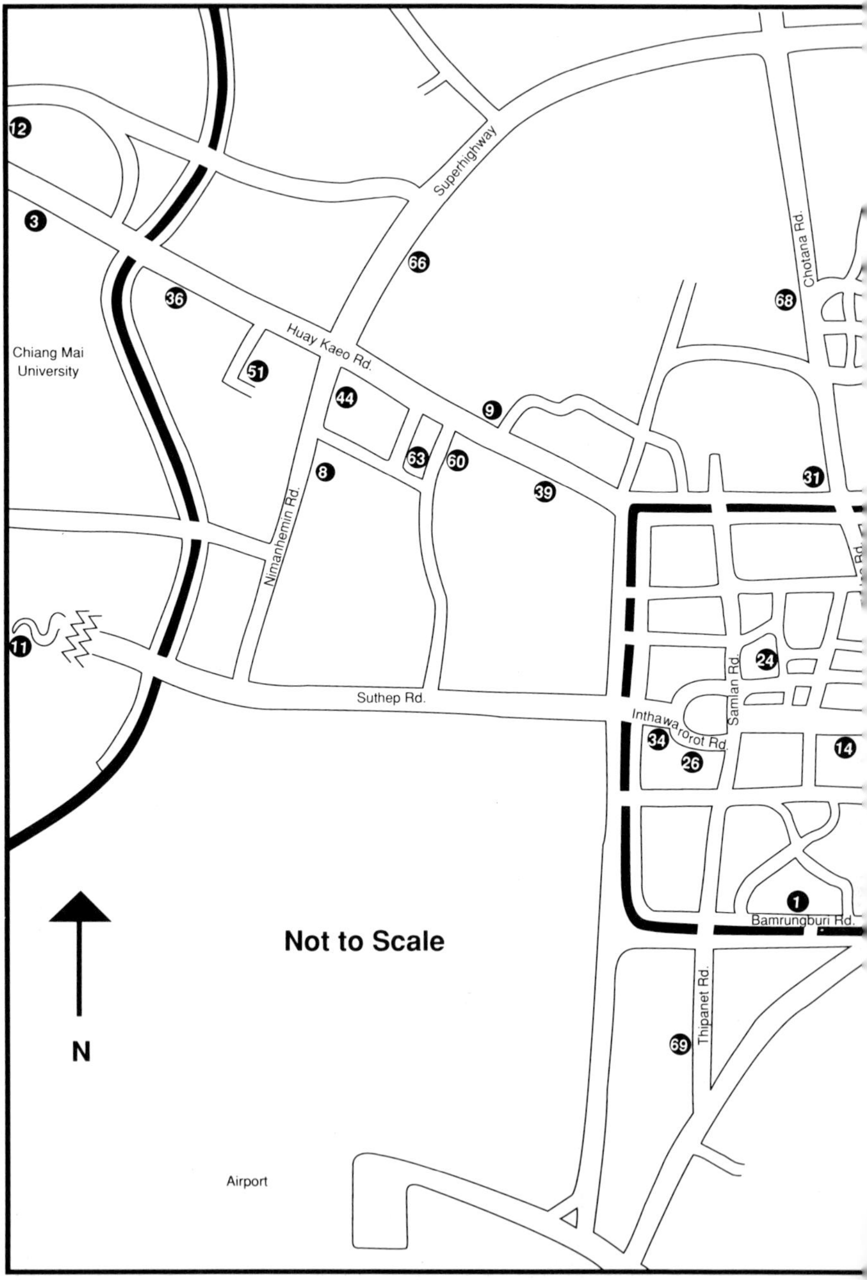

(Key to map on previous page)

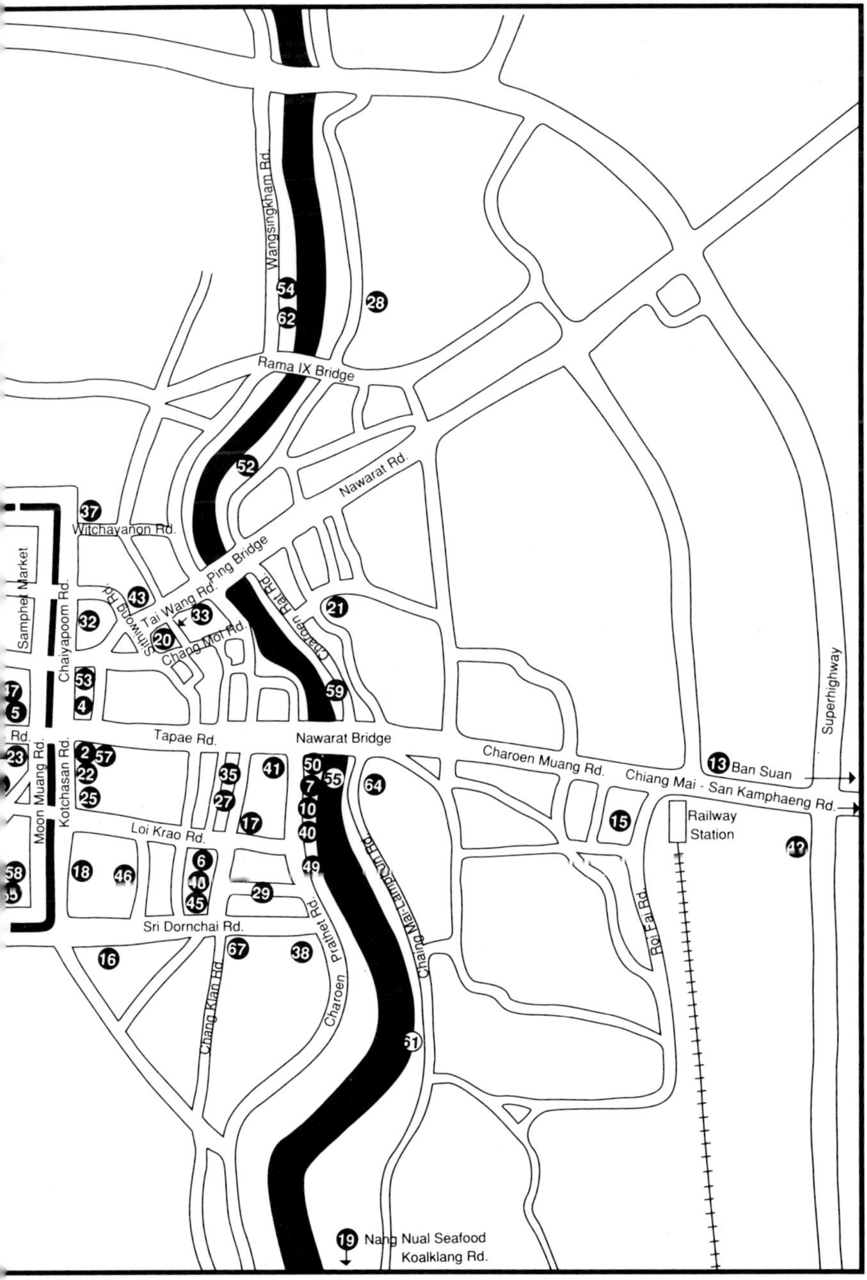

Restaurants of Chiang Mai

1) The Hill Restaurant
122 Suan San Sai
Bamrungburi Road

This restaurant is reminiscent of the Tom Sawyer House at Disneyland being a giant multi-level wooden treehouse meandering through a minature forest. Well worth a visit to experience its unique atmosphere and live music. The food is only average but inexpensive.

2) Times Square Roof Garden
2/10 Soi 6 Tapae Road, Tapae Gate

French and Thai food. A centrally located eatery opposite Tapae Gate, 50 metres off of Tapae Road; it's very hard to find the entrance which is through the Times Square Guest House and up four floors. Small and cosy, it has a nice view of Doi Suthep and is apparently the only outdoor rooftop cafe in town. Very popular with French travellers.

3) Boat Restaurant
15/87-90 Huay Kaeo Road (near Chiang Mai University)

Specializing in home made ice-cream and baked goods, this is one of four branches in Thailand and very popular with people of all ages but especially students from Chiang Mai University. Kind of funky in a Thai way and extremely cheap, the Boat Restaurant features a small menu of Thai and European food as well as cakes, cookies etc.

4) Daret Restaurant
Chaiyapoom Road (near Tapae Gate, opposite the Montri Hotel across the canal).

Thai and European food. Probably the first traveller's restaurant *cum* hang-out in Chiang Mai, it dates back about fifteen years and is still very popular with the budget-minded, especially for its delicious fruit shakes and juices. Now in new premises (close to the old ones) offering casual outside seating. The food is not of high quality but very inexpensive, and Daret's is a great place to meet fellow travellers and swap stories.

5) J.J. Bakery and Fast Food
Tapae Gate, (in the Montri Hotel), Tel. 211070

A Western-style coffee shop serving Thai and European food, J.J.'s is new, clean, airconditioned and features cheap, but good food. Opens early (6 a.m.) and offers a wide variety of breakfast dishes including coffees, brown breads and croissants made in the shop's bakery. Also offers Thai curries for lunch, displayed to make selection easy, ice-cream and fruit drinks. Probably the best breakfast place in town.

6) Fuang Fah Restaurant
110 Chang Klan Road, (in the Novotel Suriwongse Hotel)

An airconditioned and expensive international-type hotel coffeeshop, this is a good example of an upmarket restaurant where the traveller can have a splurge. Music at night from a Western-style band.

7) White Orchid
33/10 Charoen Prathet Road. (Behind the Orchid Hotel on the Ping river)

Chinese. Very central and easy to find, it is said to be the best Chinese restaurant in town, so do expect the prices to be above average. High standard of service and impressive surroundings—especially good location for Loy Kratong Festival.

8) Kaiwan Restaurant
181 Nimanhemin Road (near Rincome Hotel), Tel. 222147, 221687

Generally Thai dishes, but with other Asian specialities also. Features a pleasant veranda garden.and enjoys a long established reputation. One dish worth mentioning is the *kratong-tong* (little folded, crispy, pastry shells filled with creamed chicken and peas).

9) Chiang Mai Suki Coca
32/7 Huay Kaeo Road, Tel. 221706 (opposite Orchid Hotel)

Specializing in Thai-style 'Japanese' Sukiyaki. A fun way of eating with friends, you cook the dishes yourself over a gas cooker set in the middle of each table. Prices about 80 baht per person.

10) The Chalet
71 Charoen Prathet Road, Tel. 236810 (very close to the Diamond Hotel)

French food. European owned and managed. Housed in a very appealing old, Northern style house it is centrally located but fairly quiet. Prices tend to be on the high side so this is not a busy restaurant and it is thus ideal for those who like quiet.

11) Galae Restaurant
Near the Northern Agricultural Development Centre on the far end of Suthep Road on the lower slope of Suthep mountain.

Generally Thai food, though some European and Chinese. Known more for its romantic setting than its food, tnis is a great place to pass a couple of hours, day or night, under trees overlooking a reservoir and the lights of Chiang Mai. Service can be slow and money is easy to spend here, but still worth a visit.

12) Babylon
100/63 Huay Kaeo Road (opposite university gates).

Italian food. An old, reliable, and well-known establishment favoured by European expatriates. Recently renovated, the prices are not especially cheap but most dishes are of high quality.

13) Ban Suan
51/3 Chiang Mai - San Kamphaeng Road, Tel. 242116

Northern Thai, though offering Vietnamese and Burmese food as well. Out of town and difficult to find by oneself , it lies about one kilometre towards San Kamphaeng from the Superhighway and then a hundred yards off to the right of the main road on a small lane. This is one of the most relaxing and beautiful restaurants in Chiang Mai, consisting of a mixture of Northern-style buildings among trees and landscaped gardens. Prices are considerable, but still a very good value, especially the simple northern dishes. With drinks the bill shouldn't be much more than 100-150 baht per person.

14) Pensione La Villa
145 Ratchadamnoen Road

Italian food. Outdoor, pleasant setting and said by some to have the best pizza and salads in town. Run by 'Lele' from Italy. Large wood-fired oven opens into the restaurant.

15) Papillon Restaurant
12/1 Rot Fai Road (West side of railway station)

French. Run by two Frenchmen, Daniel and Remy. This place is convenient for travellers arriving or leaving by train and hankering for French food, be it baked goods or full meals and breakfasts at 50 baht; set meal at 100 baht, most dishes average around 60 baht.

16) Whole Earth
88 Sri Dornchai Road, Tel. 232463

Indian and Thai vegetarian dishes. Over the years seating has been expanded in its large and well-kept compound. It's easy to find and well worth trying for its comfortable atmosphere and unbelievably cheap prices.

17) Al-Shiraz
123-123/1 Chang Klan Road (opposite the Night Bazzar) Tel. 234338

Indian, Pakistani, and Arabic food. Good central location. Best of its kind in Chiang Mai selling Tandoori chicken, mutton, chicken and prawn biriyani; mutton and chicken tikka; kebab etc. Set meals priced between 60-120 baht.

18) Kaithong
67 Kotchasan Road, Tel. 232735

'Jungle food', and Northern Thai. For a taste of the bizarre, you can attempt snake soup, cobra steaks, crocodile meat (if available), roasted grubs, and other insectiform delicacies, while sitting alongside their very-much-alive next of kin. Right on Kotchasarn Road, it's unpretentious in appearance but beware of the prices.

19) Nang Nual Seafood
27/2 Koalklang Road, Tel. 241771, 241274

Seafood and Chinese. Said to have been built for 30 million baht, this restaurant, located beside the Ping River, gives the traveller a chance to splurge on surprisingly fresh seafood for an amazingly small cost. Exotic varieties of live birds and animals are kept in a clean garden environment to enhance the atmosphere. It is located well outside of town (two kilometers from the Nawapat Bridge) off the Lamphun-Chiang Mai Highway. This establishment is one of a chain in Thailand well-known for quality seafood.

20) Rummit Pochana
22 Sithiwong Road (close to New Asia Hotel), Tel. 234059

Chinese, Yunnanese cuisine. Typical of many Chinese restaurants, this place serves exquisite Yunnanese food in a shophouse interior. Opium warlords are said to favor this establishment, and two rivals once entertained with a gun-fight here years ago.

21) Bain Garden Restaurant
2/2 Wat Gate, Soi 1 off Charoen Rat Road, Tel. 244392

Quiet garden restaurant with a Europen and Thai menu. Located in the large garden property of a long established European family, it may take a while to find but is well worth the effort since the peaceful atmosphere is as pleasing as the food. Very inexpensive considering the quality decor and ambience. Across the street is a fortress-like mansion rumoured to be Opium King Khun Sa's Chiang Mai residence.

22) Sorn Jarn Restaurant
23 Kotchasan Road

Northern Thai. Open for twenty years, this tiny establishment is quite famous among the locals but also easy to miss (it's just a few metres north of the well-posted Aroon Rai Restaurant). One problem is that the menu is only in Thai and no one speaks a word of English! But the food is displayed in front of the shophouse so all you have to do is point at what you want. Not expensive.

23) Bier Stube Restaurant
33/6A Moon Muang Road, Tel. 210869

German food in a garden. Amiable atmosphere with excellent 'man-sized' meals. As reliable as any restaurant can be with the friendly owners present all the time. Central location and good food make this a good place to go if you have a hankering for wiener-schnitzel. Menu samples: Smoked loin pork and sauerkraut, 60 baht; pepper steak with french fries, 75 baht; full breakfast, 30 baht. Large variety of European food with a menu listing 54 dishes.

24) Mabuhay Restaurant
1 Inthawarorot Road, Soi 1 Tel. 211989

Filipino food. Great little family restaurant run by Anny from the Philippines and her Thai husband. Beautiful old teak house and garden. Anny suggests her fried boneless sea fish. Also excellent chocolate cake and pastries. Inexpensive.

25) Aroon Rai Restaurant
45 Kotchasan Road, Tel. 236947

Northern Thai and Chinese food. Central and easy to find with inside and outside seating, this is an old favourite of Chiang Mai. A large variety of food is on display and there is an English menu. Easy atmosphere and not expensive. Many exotic northern specialties you probably won't dare to try are also available!

26) Ta-krite Restaurant
17-19 Samlan Road Soi 1 (beside Wat Phra Sing)
27) Ta-krite Restaurant (another branch)
3rd Floor CM Bldg. (beside Night Bazaar)

Thai food. Having successfully established their first restaurant on Soi 1 Wat Phra Sing, the owner recently opened Takrite 2 with exactly the same menu in an airconditioned, third floor premises beside the Night Bazaar. Nice contrast between the two places as Takrai 1 is in a lovely garden setting. The food is highly recommended, perhaps some of the best available in Chiang Mai, and inexpensive with a simple menu in English.

28) Kao Soi Faham
352/22 Charoen Rat Road, (near the Rama IX Bridge) in Faham

Serving almost exclusively a curried noodle soup dish called *khao soi* with chicken, beef or pork, this speciality of Chiang Mai (and only available in northern Thailand) is absolutely delicious and not to be missed. Unfortunately the original site where the Lumduan family sold their famous *khao soi* for nearly fifty years has been closed. The new location is slightly further down the road (coming from town) about 200 yards, just north of the Rama IX Bridge on your right. A good lunch may be had for only 20 baht!

Chiang Mai Food Markets

Good, inexpensive food can be had at Chiang Mai's open air food markets which are usually open until the wee hours of the night. Consisting of a dozen or so stalls, each preparing their own speciality, you point at what you want and it is brought to a fold-out table with stools. Pay directly to each stall for what you order. The principal markets are;

29) Anusarn Market along a lane connecting Chang Klan Rd. and Charoen Prathet Rd. near the Night Market.

30) Chiang Mai Gate Market around the middle of the southern wall and moat of the old city.

31) Chang Puak Gate Market in the middle of the northern part of the old wall and moat.

32) Thor Loong Market opposite Samphet Market just north of where Chang Moi Rd. meets the moat. This is the best place for fresh fruits in town.

A couple of streets should be mentioned which have rows of good and inexpensive Chinese-Thai restaurants favoured by the locals. These are

33) Ratchawong Road between Chang Moi and Kaeo Nawarat Roads near the Prince Hotel, and

34) Inthawarorot Road in the middle of the old city not far from Wat Phra Sing.

Chiang Mai Nightlife

Clubs, bars, and music

59) The Riverside, 9-11 Charoen Rat Rd., Tel. 243239

Overlooking the Ping River with outdoor and indoor sitting, The Riverside Cafe is a superb place to spend an evening. Live music begins around 7 p.m. and continues until closing at 2 a.m. Food is also served, but it's the convivial atmosphere and riverside setting that make this establishment special.

60) Marble Pub, 100/3-4 Huay Kaeo Rd. (just past the Chiang Mai Orchid Hotel)

Open evenings until 1 a.m., the Marble has a nice decor and a comfortable ambience. A local jazz band led by a Chiang Mai personality, "Daeng Fantastic", boogies until late most evenings. This bar is popular with Chiang Mai University students.

61) The Gambler, Opposite Kawila Camp on the Chiang Mai-Lamphun Rd.

Another popular riverside cafe *cum* restaurant open until 1 a.m. and featuring live music nightly.

62) The West Side Wat Sing Kham Rd. on the river bank

Candlelight and live folk music create a pleasant atmosphere for evening drinks.

63) Hennesy Nightclub, Muangmai Hotel, Huay Kaeo Rd.

The Hennesy Nightclub is a large, old-fashioned 'taxi' dance hall patronized almost exclusively by Thai males who dance with taxi girls dressed in what look like orange cheerleader outfits and white tennis shoes. One pays the girls by the dance. A fascinating 'slice-of-life' that any visitor should experience at least once.

64) Chiang Mai Teahouse, 27 Chiang Mai-Lamphun Rd. 100 metres south of the Nawarat Bridge on the left

Open until 3 a.m., the Chiang Mai Teahouse is something of an institution in Chiang Mai, featuring a wide selection of teas, coffees, and baked goods. Once a popular spot for the Thai hippy crowd, the Teahouse has now been discovered by foreign travellers as well. Live music every night; open for lunch, too.

65) Blue Moon, Moon Muang Rd.

A large Thai-style nightclub featuring attractive hostesses who are available for dancing and conversation. Once considered 'naughty', the Blue Moon is tame by today's standards and sometimes features *'ramwong'* dancing, the Thai equivalent of big-band ballroom dancing. Fun for old and young alike of both sexes.

66) Honey Chiang Mai, Superhighway, Tel. 222498

This is an enormous 'entertainment complex' featuring a night club, massage parlour, and restaurants. Located off the Superhighway not far from the Rincome Hotel, the entertainment is male-oriented but one also often sees families at the restaurant and nightclub, which sometimes features comic performances.

Cinemas (English sound track or special sound room)

67) Sangtawan Cinema, corner of Chang Klan and Sri Dornchai Rd., Tel. 234486

68) Nakorn Chiang Mai Cinema, (Also known as the *Hin On*) 181/12 Chotana Rd., Tel. 221254

69) Thipanet Cinema, Thipanet Rd. (near the Chiang Mai Cultural Center), Tel. 235682

Discos

The Plaza, Chiang Mai Plaza Hotel, Tel. 252050
This is Chiang Mai's largest and most popular discotheque.
(50-90 baht per person including one drink).

Club 77, Chiang Mai Orchard Hotel, Huey Kaeo Rd., Tel. 221625, 222091
(70 baht per person including one drink)

The Wall, Chiang Inn Hotel, Tel. 235655, 236220
(90 baht per person including one drink)

Chiang Mai Hotels

*	less than 100 baht	**	100–500 baht
***	500–1,000 baht	****	1,000+ baht

35) Chiang Inn, 100 Chang Klan Road. Tel. (053) 235655, 236220.
170 rooms, airconditioned. ***

36) Chiang Mai Hills Hotel, 18 Huay Kaeo Road. Tel. (053) 210030-5, 221066
116 rooms, airconditioned. ***

37) Chiang Mai President Hotel, 226 Witchayanon Road. Tel. 252050, 251030
242 rooms, airconditioned. ****

38) Chiang Mai Plaza Hotel, 92 Sri Dornchai Road. Tel. 252050
242 rooms, airconditioned. ****

39) Chiang Mai Orchid Hotel, 100–102 Huay Kaeo Road. Tel. 221625, 222091
265 rooms, airconditioned. ****

40) Diamond Hotel, 33/10 Charoen Prathet Road. Tel. 234153, 234155
145 rooms, airconditioned. ***

41) Porn Ping Hotel, 46–48 Charoen Prathet. Tel. 235405, 235643
180 rooms, airconditioned. ***

42) Poy Luang Hotel, 146 Superhighway. Tel. 242633, 252490
224 rooms, airconditioned. ****

43) Prince Hotel, 3 Tai Wang Road. Tel. 236396, 236744
112 rooms, airconditioned. ****

44) Rincome Hotel, 301 Huay Kaeo Road. Tel. 221044, 221123
158 rooms, airconditioned. ****

45) Dusit Inn Hotel, 112 Chang Klan Road. Tel. 251034, 236835
200 rooms, airconditioned. ****

46) Mae Ping Hotel, Sri Dornchai Road. Tel. 251060
374 rooms, airconditioned. ****

47) Montri Hotel, 2–6 Ratchadamnoen Road. Tel. 211069, 211070
80 rooms, airconditioned. **

48) Suriwongse Hotel, 110 Chang Klan Road. Tel. 236981, 236789
170 rooms, airconditioned. ****

CHIANG MAI GUEST HOUSES

49) Chiang Mai Guest House, 91 Charoen Prathet Road. Tel. 236501
29 rooms, fan and airconditioned. **

50) Galare Guest House, Charoen Prathet Road. Tel. 233885
30 rooms, fan and airconditioned. **

51) Isra Guest House, 109/24 Huay Kaeo Road. Tel. 214924
9 rooms, fan only. *

52) Je T'aime Guest House, 247–9 Charoen Rat Road. Tel. 241912
24 rooms, fan only. *

53) Paocome Guest House, 9 Chang Moi Soi 3 Road. Tel. 252377
12 rooms, fan only. *

54) Rimping Guest House, 8 Wangsingkham Road. Tel. 232664
13 rooms, fan only. *

55) River View Lodge, 25 Charoen Prathet Road. Tel. 251109-10
36 rooms, airconditioned. ***

56) Saitam Guest House, 21 Moon Muang Soi 2 Road. Tel. 211575
17 rooms, fan only. *

57) Times Square Guest House, 2/10 Tapae Soi 6. Tel. 232448
10 rooms, fan and airconditioned. **

58) Top North Guest House, 15 Moon Muang Soi 2. Tel. 213900
43 rooms, fan and airconditioned. **

CHIANG MAI RESORTS

Chiang Dao Hill Resort, 28 Moo 6 Tambol Ping Kong. Tel. 236995, 232434.
****

Erawan Resort, Mae Rim-Samerng Road. Tel. 232450. ****

Krisada Doi Resort, KM 14 Hangdong-Samerng Road. Tel. 248419. ***

Hotels of Northern Thailand (outside of Chiang Mai)

Chiang Rai Hotels

Areepracharat Hotel, 541 Phaholyothin Road. Tel. 711166
15 rooms, non-airconditioned. *

Chiang Rai Hotel, 519 Suksatid Road. Tel. 711266, 712118
68 rooms, non-airconditioned. **

Chiang Rai Island Resort, 1129 Singhakai Road. Tel. 711865, 711591
8 bungalows, 13 rooms, airconditioned. ***

Krung Thong Hotel, 412 Sanambin Road. Tel. 711033, 711212
110 rooms, fan and airconditioned. **

Phaowattana Hotel, 150 Tanaraj Road. Tel. 711722
50 rooms, non-airconditioned. *

Rama Hotel, 331/4 Trirat Road. Tel. 711344, 711739
43 rooms, fan and airconditioned. **

Ruang Nakorn Hotel, 25 Ruangnakoen Road. Tel. 711566, 711567
61 rooms, fan and airconditioned. **

Siam Hotel, 531/6–8 Banphaprakan Road. Tel. 711077
52 rooms, non-airconditioned. **

Siriwattana Hotel, 485 Utarakit Road. Tel. 711055, 712036
36 rooms, non-airconditioned. *

Sukniran Hotel, 424/1 Banphaprakan Road. Tel. 711955, 712036
105 rooms, fan and airconditioned. **

Wangcome Hotel, 868/90 Premawaphat Road. Tel. 711800, 711811
221 rooms, airconditioned. **

Wiang Inn Hotel, 893 Phaholyotin Road. Tel. 711533, 711543
260 rooms, airconditioned. **

Lampang Hotels

Asia Lampang Hotel, 229 Boonyawat Road. Tel. 217844, 217690
72 rooms, fan and airconditioned. **

Aroonsuk Hotel, 90/9 Boonyawat Road. Tel. 217344, 217532
50 rooms, fan and airconditioned. *

Chatchai Hotel, 380 Chatchai Road. Tel. 217500
24 rooms, non-airconditioned. *

Khelang Nakorn Hotel, 720 Suan Dork Roak. Tel. 217137
47 rooms, fan and airconditioned. **

Lampang Hotel, 696 Suan Dork Road. Tel. 217311, 217312
52 rooms, fan and airconditioned. *

Lucky Hotel, Kao Mithuan Road. Tel. 217042
28 rooms, fan and airconditioned. *

Ruang Sak Hotel, 271 Tipchang Road. Tel. 217841
17 rooms, non-airconditioned. *

Rattana Khelang Hotel, Prasanmaitree Road. Tel. 217197
30 rooms, non-airconditioned. *

Sri Sa-Nga Hotel, 213–215/1–2 Boonyawat Road. Tel. 217070, 217811
34 rooms, non-airconditioned. *

Thip Chang Lampang Hotel, 54/22 Thakrownoi Road. Tel. 218222, 218822
120 rooms, airconditioned. **

Thap Thim Thong Hotel, Kao Mithuna Road. Tel. 217142
23 rooms, non-airconditioned. *

Lamphun Hotels

Chamchan Hotel, Tambon Viangthong
17 rooms, non-airconditioned. *

Notanon Hotel, 51/2 Inthayongyot Road. Tel. 511176
18 rooms, non-airconditioned. *

Mae Hong Son Hotels

Galare Guest House, 23 Pang Lo Nikitum Soi 2. Tel. 611150
10 rooms, non-airconditioned. *

Mae Hong Son Resort, 24 Ban Huay Dua. Tel. 611406
40 rooms, fan and airconditioned. ***

Mae Tee Hotel, 55 Khunlum Phra Athit Road. Tel. 611121
38 rooms, fan and airconditioned. **

Myitniyom Hotel, 90/1 Khunlum Phra Athit Road. Tel. 611139
40 rooms, fan and airconditioned. **

Siam Hotel, 23 Khunlum Phra Athit Road. Tel. 611148
26 rooms, fan and airconditioned. **

Sa Nguan Sin Hotel, 35 Singha Nat Road. Tel. 611241
20 rooms, non-airconditioned. *

Mae Sariang Hotels

Mit Aree Hotel, 158 Mae Sariang Road.
49 rooms, fan and airconditioned. *

Mittra Khunyuam Hotel, Mae Sariang-Mae Hong Sorn Road.
18 rooms, non-airconditioned. *

Wiang Pai Hotel, Mae Hong Son-Mae Malai Road.
15 rooms, non-airconditioned. *

Nan Hotels

Dhevaraj Hotel, 466 Sumon Deveraj Road. Tel. 710094, 710212
154 rooms, fan and airconditioned. **

Nanfha Hotel, 438–40 Sumon Deveraj Road. Tel. 710284
23 rooms, non-airconditioned. *

Suk Kasem Hotel, 29–31 Ananthavoraritdej Road. Tel. 710141
42 rooms, fan and airconditioned. **

Phayao Hotels

Chalermsak Hotel, 915 Phaholyothin Road. Tel. 431063, 431772
40 rooms, non-airconditioned. *

Than Thong Hotel, 55–57 Phaholyothin Road. Tel. 431342, 431302
96 rooms, fan and airconditioned. **

Wattana Hotel, 69 Donsanam Road. Tel. 431203
34 rooms, fan and airconditioned. *

Phrae Hotels

Kanchana Hotel, 102 Charoenmuang Road. Tel. 511504
12 rooms, non-airconditioned. *

Nakorn Phrae Hotel, 29 Rathadamnoen Road. Tel. 511177, 511969
250 rooms, fan and airconditioned. **

Chiang Saen Hotels

Chiang Saen Guesthouse, 45 Mekong Riverside
10 rooms. *

Poon Suk
5 rooms. *

Fang Hotels

Aung Kam
10 bungalows. **

Sri Chukji
30 rooms. *

Wiang Kaew
8 bungalows. **

Y.M.C.A.
Dormitory with 12 beds. *

Mae Sai Hotels

Mae Sai Hotel, 125/5 Phaholyothin Road
25 rooms. **

Top North, 521/7–8 Phaholyothin Road
20 rooms. **

Sinwatana (Siwhong), 24 Phaholyothin Road
22 rooms. *

Phitsanulok Hotels

Amarintr Nakorn, 3/1 Chaophaya Road. Tel. 258588, 258331
130 rooms, airconditioned. **

The Rajapruk, Visutkasat Road. Tel. 258477, 258788-9
101 rooms, airconditioned. ***

Sukhothai Hotels

Although Phitsanulok and Tae further away from the ruins than the town of Sukhothai is, we recommend staying in Phitsanulok or Tak.

Tak Hotels

Mae Ping Hotel, Mahadtai Buamrung Road. Tel. 511807, 511819
45 rooms, fan and airconditioned. *

Sanguan Thai Hotel, Taksin Road. Tel. 511265
42 rooms, fan and airconditioned. **

Viangtak Hotel, 25/3 Mahadtai Bumrung Road. Tel. 511910, 511950
182 rooms, airconditioned. Bangkok reservations; 233-2690. **

Uttaradit Hotels

Thanothai, 149/53 Kasemraj Road. Tel. 411669
23 rooms, fan and airconditioned. **

Vivat Hotel, 159 Borroma-art (outside town on Highway 102). Tel. 411778
80 rooms, fan and airconditioned. **

Northern Thailand Air Services:

FLIGHT NUMBER	TG	146	160	142	170	174	100	104	106	112	102	108	110	130	180	184	186	134	190	194	196	235
DAYS OF OPERATION		DAILY	1 3 5	DAILY	DAILY	2 4 6 7	DAILY	DAILY	DAILY	DAILY	1 2 5 6 7	DAILY	DAILY	DAILY	DAILY	1 2 4 6 7	DAILY	2.4	13567	2.5.7	234567	DAILY
AIRCRAFT		143	SH3	143	SH3	SH3	310	310	310	AB4	AB6	AB3	AB4	141	AT7	SH3	AT7	143	AT7	AT4	AT7	SH3
BANGKOK	d	1550	------	0715	------	------	0730	1200	1545	1630	1800	1900	2045	1115				0830				
PHITSANULOK	a	1640	------	0800	------	------																
	d	------	0845	0830	0835	0845																
LOEI	a	------	0935																			
TAK	a	------	------			0920																
	d	------	------			0935																
MAE SOT	a	------	------			1005																
	d	------	------			1020																
PHRAE	a	------	------		1005																	
	d	------	------		0935																	
NAN	a	------	------		1005																	
	d	------	------		1020																	
LAMPANG	a	------	------	0905																		
	d		------	------																		
CHIANG MAI	a	------	------	------	1110	1120	0835	1305	1650	1735	1905	2005	2150					0940				
	d	------	------	------	------	------	------	------	------	------	------	------	------		0915	1130	1355	1010	1135	1155	1615	0700
CHAING RAI	a	------	------	------	------	------	------	------	------	------	------	------	------	1240	0955	1220	1435					
MAE HONG SON	a	------	------	------	------	------	------	------	------	------	------	------	------	------	------	------	------	1040	1215	1240	1655	
KHON KAEN	a	------	------	------	------	------	------	------	------	------	------	------	------	------	------	------	------	------	------	------	------	0845
	d	------	------	------	------	------	------	------	------	------	------	------	------	------	------	------	------	------	------	------	------	0905
SAKON NAKHON	a	------	------	------	------	------	------	------	------	------	------	------	------	------	------	------	------	------	------	------	------	0950

FLIGHT NUMBER	TG	146	160	142	170	174	100	104	106	112	102	108	110	130	180	184	186	134	190	194	196	235
DAYS OF OPERATION		DAILY	1 3 5	DAILY	DAILY	2 4 6 7	DAILY	DAILY	DAILY	DAILY	1 2 5 6 7	DAILY	DAILY	1 3 5 7	DAILY	1 2 4 6 7	DAILY	2 4 6	DAILY	2 3 4 5 7	DAILY	DAILY
AIRCRAFT		143	SH3	143	SH3	SH3	310	310	310	AB4	AB6	AB3	AB4	143	SH6	SH3	SH6	143	SH6	SH3	SH6	SH3
SAKON NAKHON	d	------	------	------	------	------	------	------	------	------	------	------	------	------	------	------	------	------	------	------	------	1640
KHON KAEN	a	------	------	------	------	------	------	------	------	------	------	------	------	------	------	------	------	------	------	------	------	1725
	d	------	------	------	------	------	------	------	------	------	------	------	------	------	------	------	------	------	------	------	------	1745
MAE HONG SON	d	------	------	------	------	------	------	------	------	------	------	------	------	------	------	------	------	1325	240	1255	1705	
CHIANG RAI	d	------	------	------	------	------	------	------	------	------	------	------	------	1405	1025	1240	1450					
CHIANG MAI	a	------	------	------	------	------	------	------	------	------	------	------	------		1115	1330	1540		320	1335	1745	1930
	d	------	------	------	1350	1355	0745	0920	1405	1735	1815	1945	2045									
LAMPANG	a	------	------	------																		
	d	------	------	0935																		
NAN	a	------	------			1445																
	d	------	------			1500																
PHARE	a	------	------			1530																
	d	------	------			1545																
MAE SOT	a	------	------		1450																	
	d	------	------		1505																	
TAK	a	------	------		1535																	
	d	------	------		1550																	
LOEI	d	------	1535																			
PHITSANULOK	a	------	1625	1010	1825	1630												1415				
	d	1705	------	1640	------	------												1445				
BANGKOK	a	1750	------	1125	------	------	0850	1025	1510	1840	1920	2050	2150	1525				1530				

Valid Summer 1990

Airfares: (one-way)*

Bangkok-Chiang Mai	**1,335** Bht.
Bangkok-Phitsanulok	**765** Bht.
Bangkok-Mae Hong Son	**1,495** Bht.
Bangkok-Chiang Rai	**1,570** Bht.
Bangkok-Lampang	945 Bht.
Chiang mai-Mae Hong Son	310 Bht.
Chiang Mai-Khon Kaen	1.780 Bht.
Chiang Mai-Sakon Nakhon	1.065 Bht.
Chiang Mai-Chiang Rai	300 Bht.
Phitsanulok-Loei	340 Bht.
Phitsanulok-Lampang	430 Bht.
Phitsanulok-Phrae	290 Bht.
Phitsanulok-Chiang Mai	505 Bht.
Phitsanulok-Tak	215 Bht.
Phitsanulok-Mae Sot	370 Bht.
Phitsanulok-Nan	480 Bht.

Call 211044-7 in Chiang Mai or 5236121 in Bangkok for the latest schedules and airfares

* roundtrip double o/w fare

RAILWAY SCHEDULE AND FARES

NORTHERN LINE......						BANGKOK - CHIANG MAI			
STATIONS		RAP. 59	ORD. 101	ORD. 91	RAP. 37	EXP. 7	EXP. 5 SP	RAP. 57	RAP. 35
		2-3	2-3	2-3	2-3	1-2-3	2	2-3	2-3
Bangkok	d.	06.40	07.06	08.30	15.00	18.00	19.40	20.00	22.00
Don Muang	a.	07.21	07.48	09.10	15.39	18.40	20.20	20.40	22.43
Bang Pa-in	d.	ll	08.22	09.50	ll	ll	ll	ll	ll
Ayutthaya	d.	08.03	08.34	10.05	16.20	19.23	21.02	21.21	23.24
Ban Phachi	d.	08.23	08.56	10.32	16.41	ll	ll	ll	ll
Lop Buri	d.	09.07	09.49	11.34	17.27	20.20	ll	22.17	00.22
Ban Takhli	d.	10.01	10.57	12.59	18.21	21.18	ll	23.07	01.12
Nakhon Sawan	d.	10.46	11.57	14.01	19.05	22.03	23.34	23.55	02.06
Taphan Hin	d.	11.53	13.24	15.59	20.15	23.06	ll	01.23	03.31
Phichit	d.	12.18	13.57	16.31	20.39	23.31	ll	01.48	03.56
Phitsanulok	a.	12.56	14.45	17.25	21.17	00.07	01.27	02.28	04.37
	d.	12.58	14.55		21.19	00.12	01.32	02.30	04.39
Uttaradit	d.	14.29	16.47		22.56	01.42	ll	03.59	06.11
Sila At	d.	14.42	17.00		23.13	01.56	03.03	04.04	06.24
Den Chai	a.	15.33	18.00		00.20	02.47	03.55	04.55	07.15
	d.	15.36			00.25	02.51	03.58		07.18
Mae Mo	a.	17.06			02.09	04.24	ll		08.50
Nakhon Lampang	a.	17.42			02.45	05.00	05.59		09.37
Khun Tan	a.	18.33			03.44	06.00	06.52		10.39
Lamphun	a.	19.27			04.28	06.45	ll		11.24
Chiang Mai	a.	19.50			04.50	07.05	07.55		11.45

FARES				NORTHERN LINE
FROM BANGKOK TO		SINGLE (B)		
Stations	Kms.	1st	2nd	3rd
Don Muang	22	18	10	5
Bang Pa-In	58	49	26	12
Ayutthaya	71	60	31	15
Lop Buri	133	111	57	28
Ban Takhli	193	157	80	39
Nakhon Sawan	246	197	99	48
Taphan Hin	319	245	122	58
Phichit	347	266	131	63
Phitsanulok	389	292	143	69
Uttaradit	485	356	172	82
Sila At	488	359	174	83
Den Chai	534	389	188	90
Mae Mo	609	440	211	100
Nakhon Lampang	642	463	221	106
Khun Tan	683	490	233	111
Lamphun	729	520	247	118
Chiang Mai	751	537	255	121

VALID SUMMER 1990 ALL TRAINS RUN DAILY

CHIANG MAI - BANGKOK									
STATIONS		RAP. 58	RAP. 38	EXP. 8	EXP. 6 SP	RAP. 60	ORD. 92	ORD. 102	RAP. 36
		2-3	2-3	1-2-3	2	2-3	2-3	2-3	2-3
Chiang Mai	d.		16.05	17.25	19.10	20.45			06.30
Lamphun	d.		16.27	17.48	‖	21.06			07.01
Khun Tan	d.		17.18	18.39	20.18	21.58			07.57
Nakhon Lampang	d.		18.20	19.37	21.08	22.52			08.48
Mae Mo	d.		18.57	20.15	‖	23.28			09.26
Den Chai	a.		20.29	21.47	23.10	01.00			10.58
	d.	18.55	20.34	21.51	23.13	01.05		06.05	11.01
Sila At	d.	19.46	21.33	22.50	00.12	02.02		07.21	12.00
Uttaradit	d.	19.51	21.38	22.55	‖	02.06		07.25	12.04
Phitsanulok	a.	21.31	23.05	00.09	‖	03.51		09.21	13.45
	d.	21.33	23.07	00.11	‖	03.54	06.05	09.24	13.50
Phichit	d.	22.15	23.48	00.54	‖	04.45	06.57	10.07	14.33
Taphan Hin	d.	22.41	00.13	01.21	‖	05.12	07.35	10.36	15.00
Nakhon Sawan	d.	00.14	01.24	02.24	03.32	06.22	09.56	12.16	16.14
Ban Takhli	d.	00.59	02.07	03.09	‖	07.05	10.02	13.14	16.57
Lop Buri	d.	01.58	02.59	04.03	‖	08.00	11.32	14.32	17.55
Ban Phachi	d.	02.43	03.43	‖	‖	08.56	12.49	15.39	18.47
Ayutthaya	a.	03.02	04.03	05.00	06.03	09.16	13.18	15.56	19.07
Bang Pa-In	a.	‖	‖	‖	‖	‖	13.43	16.09	‖
Don Muang	a.	03.43	04.46	05.44	06.53	09.59	14.22	16.14	19.49
Bangkok	a.	04.25	05.25	06.25	07.35	10.40	15.05	17.25	20.30

SUPPLEMENTARY CHARGES

Express train charge		Baht	30.00	per person,
Rapid train charge		Baht	20.00	per person.
Special express train charge		Baht	50.00	per person.
Air-conditioned 2nd, 3rd, coach charge		Baht	50.00	per person.
Sleeping berth charges				
Air-conditioned 1st class berth	single cabin	Baht	350.00	per person.
	double cabin	Baht	250.00	per person.
Air-conditioned 2nd class berth	upper	Baht	170.00	per person.
	lower	Baht	200.00	per person.
2nd class berth	upper	Baht	70.00	per person.
	lower	Baht	100.00	per person.
2nd class berth (Only special express)	upper	Baht	200.00	per person.
	lower	Baht	250.00	per person.

Bus Schedules

Chiang Mai Bus Departures

Buses leave from Chiang Mai Arcade Bus Station, Tel. (053) 242664. All buses listed are airconditioned. For buses to Chiang Saen and Chiang Khong see the Chiang Rai bus departure information where you must change buses if coming from Chiang Mai.

Destination	Departure time (Duration)	Fare (Baht)
Bangkok *Via* Nakon Sawan (Platform No. 14)	0930/1000/1915/1930 2000/2030/2100 (10 hours)	180-220 baht
Chiang Rai *Via* the new road (Platform No. 27)	0700/0830/0930/1130/1200 1300/1400/1530/1645 (3 hours)	83 baht
Mae Hong Son *Via* Mae Sarieng (Platform No. 11)	2100 (8 hours)	175 baht
Mae Sai *Via* Chiang Rai	0700/0830/1300/1400 (4 hours)	83 baht
Phayao *Via* the new road (Platform No. 28)	0800/1200/1630 (3 hours)	57 baht
Phitsanulok *Via* Tak, Sukhothai (Platform No. 13)	0800/1000/1200/1810 (4 hours)	100 baht
Khon Kaen *Via* Tak, Sukhothai, and Phitsanulok (Platform No. 13)	0800/1810/1830 (12 hours)	275 baht
N. Ratchasima (Korat) (Platform No. 7)	0800/1700/1900/2000/2030 (11 hours)	300 baht
Udon Thani *Via* Loei (Platform No. 28)	2030 (9 hours)	242 baht
Nan *Via* Phrae (Platform No. 26)	1000/2200 (4 hours)	99 baht

Chiang Mai Bus Departures for local nearby destinations

These buses leave from the Chang Puak Bus Station (Chotana Rd.) and are not airconditioned. Tel. (053) 211586.

Doi Suthep	0600-1530 (every 30 min) (departs from Chang Puak Gate)	(going) 30 baht (return) 20 baht
Borsan, **San Kamphaeng**	0600-1800 (every 15 min.) (fifteen minute journey)	3 baht
Hot	0600-1800 (every 30 min.) (two to three hour journey)	22 baht
Via Hang Dong	(thirty minute journey)	5 baht
Via Chom Thong	(one hour journey)	11 baht
Lamphun	0600-1800 (every 15 min.) (30-45 minute journey)	6 baht
Fang (aircon. bus)	0800-1600 (every hour) (3 hour journey)	60 baht
Tha Ton	0600/0720/0900/1130 (4 hour journey)	37 baht

(A boat departs for Chiang Rai at 1230, it's a three hour journey and costs 160 baht)

Chiang Rai Bus Departures

(All buses listed are airconditioned)

Bangkok *Via* Sukhothai	1800/1830/1900 (10 hours)	283 baht
Chiang Mai	0700/0800/0830/1100 1200/1430/1530/1645 (3 hours)	83 baht

(A boat departs for Tha Ton at 1000. It is a five hour journey and costs 160 baht, then a further four hours by bus to Chiang Mai for 37 baht.)

Mae Sai *Via* Mae Chan	0600-1800 (every 15 min.) (one and a half hour journey)	14 baht
Chiang Saen *Via* Mae Chan	0600-1800 (every 20 min.) (one and a half hour journey)	14 baht
Chiang Khong	0600-1800 (every 20 min.) (two and a half hour jouney)	31 baht
Nan	0930 (4 hours)	60 baht
Khon Kaen	1345/1800 (11 hours)	173 baht

Glossary

amphoe	A secondary administrative district; equivalent to 'county'
ban	Village of —' as a prefix to a town; *mu baan* means 'a village'
bot or ***ubosoth***	The main shrine of a temple; where monks are ordained
Bo or **Bodhi** ***tree***	The tree beneath which the Buddha meditated and attained enlightenment
changwat	A primary administrative district; equivalent to a province; pronounced *jangwat*
chedi	A stupa; a solid monument, usually with a pointed spire, which enshrines relics of the Buddha or his disciples, or contains the ashes of important persons (pronounced *jedii*)
chofa	A slender, curved decoration, shaped rather like a swan's neck, adorning each end of the ridge of the roof of a *bot* or a *viharn*
Deva	A celestial being
doi	A large mountain; means 'Mount' when used as a prefix in proper names
finial	A usually ornamented upper extremity of a structure
galae	A V-shaped decoration on the peak of the roof of houses found in Chiang Mai valley
Jataka	Stories of the previous lives of the Buddha, consisting of about 570 stories of which the last ten are the most important
klong	Canal
khao	Hill; hills
maenam	River; literally, 'mother of the waters'
mondop	Square building housing a Buddha image or other sacred object

Naga	Mythical king of snakes; most commonly found as a sculpted balustrade to stairs leading to a temple building; a half-brother of the Garuda, its sworn enemy. (From Sanskrit, *naak* in Thai)
Nirvana	The state of extinction of suffering which is reached after enlightenment has been attained and one is released from the cycle of death and rebirth
prang	A Buddhist monument in Thailand in imitation of a Khmer tower (*prasat*) with a finger-like spire
prasat or ***prasart***	A tower sanctuary in Khmer architecture. In Thai architecture it is a royal religious edifice, usually of a cruciform pattern and topped by a *prang*.
ramakian	The Thai version of the 2,500 year old Indian epic, the Ramayana; it recounts the story of Rama and the rescue of his wife, Sita, from the clutches of Totsakan, King of the Demons
sala	A small open-sided pavilion used as meeting or resting place, whether secular or religious. Often found in temple compounds and frequently built over or by a body of water
sema or ***bai sema***	The stone slabs, often carved, placed at the eight cardinal directions to demarcate the boundaries of a *bot*
Singha	A mythical lion and popular symbol of strength and power
soi	A lane or alley
stupa or ***stupika***	An English-language synomym of the Thai word *chedi*
tham	A cave
thammas	Pulpit or preaching chair
thanon	Road or street
that	A northern and northeastern (originally Lao) form of reliquary tower with a square base and a decorative spire
viharn	Main hall of a temple used for day to day purposes
wat	Temple; refers to the whole temple compound including shrines and, normally, a monastery

Index

CHIANG MAI